OXFORD MEDICAL PUBLICATIONS

The Evaluation of National Health Systems

The Evaluation of National Health Systems

George E. Cumper

Oxford   New York   Tokyo
OXFORD UNIVERSITY PRESS
1991

Oxford University Press, Walton Street, Oxford OX2 6DP
Oxford New York Toronto
Delhi Bombay Calcutta Madras Karachi
Petaling Jaya Singapore Hong Kong Tokyo
Nairobi Dar es Salaam Cape Town
Melbourne Auckland
and associated companies in
Berlin Ibadan

Oxford is a trade mark of Oxford University Press

Published in the United States
by Oxford University Press, New York

British Library Cataloguing in Publication Data
Cumper, G. E. (George Edward) 1924–
The evaluation of national health systems.
1. National health services. Assessment
I. Title
362.1
ISBN 0-19-261803-2

Library of Congress Cataloging in Publication Data
Cumper, George E. (George Edward), 1924–
The evaluation of national health systems / George E. Cumper.
1. Medical care–Evaluation. 2. Medical policy–Evaluation.
I. Title.
RA399.A1C86 1991   362.1–dc20   90-7666
ISBN 0-19-261803-2

Typeset by Downdell Limited, Oxford
Printed in Great Britain by
Bookcraft Ltd, Midsomer Norton, Avon

Preface

The peculiarities of this book—some would say oddities—spring from the nature of its subject and from the experience it reflects. The writer's experience of evaluation work has come mainly from his service with the World Health Organization's Regional Office in the South-East Asia region and partly from teaching and research with the Evaluation and Planning Centre at the London School of Hygiene and Tropical Medicine. In each case an indebtedness should be acknowledged which includes both the colleagues with whom one has worked on specific investigations and the much wider circle of those whose influence has been of a more general kind. In South-East Asia, without prejudice, one should name Bill Towle and Steve Sapirie, without forgetting the many colleagues, national and international, with whom one has sat in dusty offices and on verandas solving, to our own satisfaction, the health planning problems of the world. Among general influences one should name, again without prejudice, Mali Thaineua, who was old enough to have practised community health care before it became fashionable and could still beat all comers at table tennis. In London there is a specific obligation to Carol McCormack, Godfrey Walker, Affette McCaw, and others who worked, often in amicable discordance, on the Jamaica Health Service Evaluation Project, with others named in the Appendix. There is a more general obligation to Patrick Vaughan, Gill Walt, David Bradley, Anne Mills, and to all the students who made teaching a bracing intellectual obstacle course.

Another kind of experience should be mentioned. The writer has received health care, public and private, at many points between Kingston, Jamaica and Djakarta, Indonesia, and has learned to regard health professionals with a mixture of exasperation and abject gratitude. Hopefully this will be allowed to offset, in what follows, the fact that he is neither physician, nurse, nor even epidemiologist.

Two subsections of this book—5.2.2 on establishing standards of health care for Jamaica 1987, and 5.4.3 on the legal framework of Jamaica's health service—are substantially the agreed contributions of colleagues. The first is largely the work of Dr G.J.A. Walker, and the second of Mrs Gloria Cumper.

This book argues that many disciplines must be brought to bear on the evaluation of a health system. It is impossible, and would be futile, to attempt to provide full references in all of these disciplines. References to

basic authorities are provided mainly where the argument concerns fundamentals, as in health planning. Otherwise, the writer has cited articles which
make interesting specific points (or points he finds interesting), in the confidence that the reader will be able to trace from them any more basic references
he requires. It is hoped in this way to avoid the danger that, for the practitioner, a list of references defeats its object by its own abundance.

G.E.C.

Kingston, Jamaica
January 1990

Contents

1 Introduction

In this sceptical world, few things are universally accepted as good. Salvation is judged irrelevant by a secular society; motherhood is an indulgence to be controlled through family planning; even apple pie may contain harmful additives. Only health commands universal respect, as an aim for ourselves and a benefit to be conferred on others. Socialist governments routinely allot health services a generous share of the state budget; revolutionary regimes give a high priority to health campaigns; conservative countries complain about the increasing costs of health care, without questioning the need for its expansion by conventional or 'alternative' means.

The pursuit of health is not self-evidently the highest human activity. Even if one accepts the messianic concept incorporated in the constitution of the World Health Organization—health as the highest degree of physical, mental, and social well-being—and rejects the frivolous proposal, said to have been current at one World Health Assembly, that the sexual should be added to the list; still there may be spiritual values it does not encompass. Should we preach to St Simeon on his pillar the benefits of exercise, or the dangers of exposure to ultraviolet A? The more limited physiological concept of health which most of us work with, and which is used in this book, gives health a lower place on the ladder of human ambitions. But it is still important enough to justify strenuous efforts to improve the social provision of health care and the efficiency of the other activities (such as water supply and sanitation) which contribute to health.

Health care is generally regarded as a plannable activity, even by governments usually averse to planning, and is being increasingly classified as one which poses unique and serious problems of management. It therefore requires evaluation of the existing health system, as a basis from which to initiate plans and maintain their effectiveness. There is now an abundant literature on planning, in general and for the health sector in particular (for a widely used book on planning in general see Waterston 1965, and for some revisions of view Waterston 1971; and for health sector planning Gish 1975, 1977 and Schofield 1984), and on the evaluation of individual health projects and programmes (e.g. Drummond *et al.* 1987). But there is little guidance for governments or individual administrators who wish to assess complete national systems of health care. It is true that in WHO's outline of a global strategy for 'health for all' (WHO 1981a) a chapter is devoted to national evaluation and monitoring, but in terms designed to meet the needs of the organization's Executive Board rather than those of the countries themselves. The need for such guidance is particularly acute in developing countries. This book is aimed at helping health administrators in these countries—not by purporting to supply a universally valid procedure, but by identifying the essential issues and tasks involved and showing how fellow workers have tackled them in a selection of cases.

The following sections in this introduction deal in more detail with the pressures for health system evaluation at national level, and its relation to project and programme evaluation, and to district and national planning; and with the specific country evaluations from which examples (hortatory or horrid) will be drawn. Chapter 2 deals with the state of the art in the well-developed field of economic evaluation of health projects, and argues that such evaluations differ in kind from the kind of system-wide exercise discussed here. Chapter 3 sets out a logical basis for evaluation in terms of the comparison of actual health system performance with standards of various kinds. Chapter 4 provides guidance on the information needed to assemble a comprehensive picture of a national system in a form useful for evaluation, including the resource distribution and pattern of management. Chapter 5 deals with the identification of standards against which performance may be measured, and Chapter 6 with the approaches and techniques through which these standards can be applied. Chapter 7 discusses what the evaluator can do to ensure that the results of his work are converted into effective action. Chapter 8 suggests something of the future of evaluation as a contribution to better health care.

1.1   The need for national health system evaluation

In principle, the need for evaluation follows directly from the concept of management as a cyclical process. Plans are formulated on the basis of policy, translated into programmes and budgets, and implemented through operations. The results of these operations are assessed to detect departures from policy, plan, programme, and budget objectives. This assessment generates a new cycle of replanning at the appropriate level of the organization. A particular formulation of this approach to management, developed by WHO since the 1970s and known as the Managerial Process for National Health Development (see, for example WHO 1981a, 1981b, 1984), is widely accepted by developing and even developed countries. There is of course a great distinction between acceptance of the logic of the approach, and its useful and consistent application. There are furthermore genuine difficulties in the way of introducing such formal management concepts into existing health care systems. Some of these difficulties will be referred to in later chapters. Nevertheless, this book is based on acceptance of evaluation as an essential component of the management process in the health sector.

There are a number of immediate reasons why the capacity to evaluate one's national health system is important today, particularly in developing countries. The most easily identified of these is the fact that external aid agencies have come increasingly to demand such evaluation—for example, in the form of the World Bank's country sector reports—as a means of generating health projects and a condition for funding them. Often such reports have been prepared by the staff of the agency involved, with nationals participating only as providers of data.

This is not entirely satisfactory, even from the agency's point of view. Limitations of time, and ignorance of local particularities, make for a rather superficial kind of evaluation. From the national point of view, to hand over evaluation to outsiders gives them an undesirable degree of control over the national management process, already liable to be distorted by the financial leverage available to, and sometimes exploited by, the potential funding agency (which may, for example, prefer a new hospital to the repair of the old because the former is easier to document and to supervise). It is better if evaluation can be a national exercise directed to national goals and contributing to the efficiency of the national management system.

The increasing role of national sector reports and other comprehensive evaluations reflects broader changes in the attitudes of both aid agencies and national governments. One such change is the shift toward a more positive concept of health service management. On the agency side, this manifests itself particularly in the trend away from assistance to individual projects and toward aid for broader programmes and for the central functions of ministries of health, such as planning and statistics. On the national side, governments have moved away from a merely reactive pattern of behaviour under which the main aim of management was to keep an existing health service system in being, expanding here and there according to the pressures exerted by medical professionals and by politically powerful pressure groups. They have become conscious of the possibility of managing the health sector so as to respond to some broader concept of social need (see, for example WHO 1979, 1980)—a reorientation which is only possible on the basis of some comprehensive evaluation of the system as it has been. This shift of viewpoint has been most conspicious when it has followed from a massive political event such as the Nicaraguan revolution or the creation of an independent Zimbabwe. But it has also involved countries with no obvious political discontinuities, such as the territories of the Commonwealth Caribbean. Moreover, it goes deeper than the rhetoric of Health for All by the Year 2000 to which virtually all governments are nominally committed. This rhetoric is the articulation of social and technical changes which have increased the political power of the health professionals in all countries, and within health have made the epidemiologists, economists, planners, administrators, and community health managers serious competitors for power with the traditional clinical specialists. When Bangladesh was trying to reshape its health services after independence, a senior health administrator asked a visiting WHO group 'Why should I sit here to be harassed for $200 a month when I could earn $2000 as a consultant?'. He and they knew what the answer was; the money might still be with the clinicians, but in terms of social obligation and power it was on the other side that the action lay.

The need for comprehensive evaluation has been given an extra edge by the economic stringency which has gripped most of the developing world since the mid-1970s (see, for example Musgrove 1987). The period of slow, but real, economic expansion in the 1960s had encouraged an attitude to planning which saw it largely in terms of new developments—hospitals, health centres, immunization campaigns—to be plugged into a basic health care system which was itself expanding; and evaluation, therefore, as the search for such developments and for their justification. There was seldom a question of contraction, or of new components to be financed by the transfer of money and resources from elsewhere in the system. For many developing countries (and also for some international agencies) the period of unquestioned plenty ended in the mid-1970s. From that point, the national incomes of many poor countries began to fall, in per capita and even in aggregate terms. Jamaica, for example, underwent a 20 per cent contraction in national income between 1974 and 1980—starting, admittedly, from a level which put it at that time among the more prosperous of the then developing countries, and therefore better able to resist adversity than some of the much poorer countries of sub-Saharan Africa which experienced similar contractions. Such large falls in national income inevitably implied falls in the national resources available for health and other social services. But many countries reacted to the situation with disbelief, assuming the hard times would soon end and therefore borrowing to maintain social expenditure. The costs of this borrowing shortly became an additional charge on government budgets, limiting further the resources available for health. The course of events can be traced, for example, in the successive annual reports of the World Bank. It is only recently that it has become fully accepted that the rational response to recession may be a shift of national health resources between uses to preserve the position of the most vulnerable social groups (see, for example UNICEF 1987), and it is still not clear how, concretely, this can be done. All this implies a kind of re-evaluation of the national health system much more unforgiving than would be acceptable in prosperous times.

There are thus fundamental factors underlying the increasing recognition of the need for comprehensive evaluation of national health systems. They have been presented above in terms of the situation of developing countries, since these are the main concern of the present book. But in slightly different terms they manifest themselves also in the developed countries. There too the implications of the growing commitment to community health have come into conflict with the limitations on public resources, and this has led, if not to overall re-evaluation, at least to fairly invasive studies of particular issues and problems—in the UK, for example, the 'Black' report on inequalities in health (DHSS 1980), the Korner reports on health statistics (see, for example Knox 1987) and the re-examination of questions of health service management and resource allocation which has resulted in the current changes (conveniently, if irreverently, summarized in the Economist magazine, at least up to 1989; see Economist, 1989*a*, 1989*b*). In both the US and the UK it has led to intensive discussion of the relative roles of public and private financing of health care, with results whose inconclusiveness has not prevented their being vigorously projected into the developing world by international and bilateral agencies. In what follows, we sometimes reverse this process; conclusions drawn from the experience of developing countries will sometimes be found to apply in unexpected ways to the health sector in the developed world.

1.2   Is programme and project evaluation enough?

The years since World War II have seen the development, mainly by economists, of a range of quantitative techniques for the evaluation of public and private projects (see Mills and Thomas 1984; also Barnum 1987; Elzinga 1981 for critical reviews) and these have been increasingly applied to health services and health-related activities. The present state of development of these techniques is reviewed in Chapter 2. They enable us to assess, for a particular project or programme, its cost in relation to the achievement of a single concrete objective (for example, a death averted) or in relation to its overall yield of benefits, and to select for implementation those activities which have the most favourable ratio of cost to effectiveness (CE) or cost to benefit (CB). Can we not, then, evaluate a national health system simply by combining the results of these micro-evaluations? Is there a need for separate techniques of macro-evaluation?

For a variety of reasons, the answer to the last question is 'yes'. At the practical level, CE and CB analyses are expensive in terms of money and management time; and the more complete and rigorous the analysis, the more expensive. It is inconceivable that all activities of the health sector in a poor country should be covered by micro-evaluations. Yet unless the coverage is complete, not only for existing activities but for their possible alternatives, there is no guarantee that the final selection of activities will be the most desirable.

Furthermore, the standard techniques have certain basic limitations. They depend on assumptions about how policy choices can be translated into individual economic terms which are open to question, and they are least effective when dealing with projects which generate benefits of different kinds and for different groups of people. This is a common situation in the health field, and particularly for the kind of activity favoured by policies of Primary Health Care—for example, health centres providing a range of services whose costs are difficult to separate, or rural water supply schemes whose benefits are not only a matter of health.

Hence micro-evaluation techniques are particularly suited to free-standing projects intended to deal with problems already identified through broad national planning and evaluation. These have been the kind of project preferred in the past by international agencies, and it is these agencies which in developing countries have often been the sponsors of CE and CB analysis. Yet they too have become increasingly aware that the real difficulties lie at the stage of project identification rather than later justification, and that this identification must be based on a broad sectoral evaluation. This is particularly true of countries committed to a substantial shift in approach to health development such as that represented by the endorsement of Health for All or reorientation toward Primary Health Care.

This does not mean that micro-evaluations have nothing to contribute to national health system evaluation. They can be important components in such an evaluation, but they may need to be seen in a broader context than that for which they were originally intended (see Section 6.3.1 below).

1.3   National evaluation and national and district planning

It is the received wisdom that evaluation is an integral part of the cycle which also includes planning and implementation, and that plans are necessarily based on ongoing evaluations at all levels. Is there a justification for setting up national health system evaluation as an activity in its own right?

There is no simple answer to this question, since the status of a national evaluation will vary according to the situation. There is no doubt that much early planning in the health field was based on a rather casual assessment of the initial state of affairs. Part of the explanation may have been that, particularly in an atmosphere of optimism, general expansion, and honourable high-mindedness, planning is more fun than evaluation, and if done with a broad brush requires less intellectual investment. But it is also true that when purposeful health development begins, it is part of the problem that the data for proper evaluation are often not available. Further, in the poorest countries, the gap between what existed and what was acceptable was so great that the initial steps could be decided on a basis of common knowledge. Unfortunately this knowledge tended to be that common to the medical profession, particularly its members in the government services, and led to an under-estimate of the importance of self-care and of the private sector. But it is arguable that without some such short cuts, health planning in the poorest countries cannot get started.

Once a satisfactory machinery for health planning, mangement, and evaluation has been installed, the situation should in principle be very different. Evaluation in the broad sense—the comparison of planned with actual performance, with a view to corrective action—should take place regularly at all levels of the health service organization. It is true that the content and timing will differ from level to level. At lower levels, where the process is often referred to as monitoring, the comparisons will be so frequent as to be almost continuous, and the standards against which performance is compared will be very specific ones laid down in detailed operational plans. At higher levels evaluation will take place less frequently and the standards applied will be based more on broad programme objectives and less on operational details. But the essence of evaluation will surely be the same at all levels?

This is only true if we take a very mechanistic view of the planning and management process, seeing it as a means by which the intentions of the planner-administrator are automatically translated into action. This view can only be justified on the assumptions that all action to improve health care takes place within a single organization, and that all members of that organization share the values of some philosopher-king at its head. These assumptions have only to be stated to be seen to be wrong in fact, and against the spirit of Primary Health Care as set out in the Alma Ata declaration. But to abandon them has important implications for evaluation, particularly at the national level.

If we accept that health workers have interests, perceptions, and loyalties distinct from those of the organization they serve, we must ask what evaluation means to them as individuals. It involves them as subordinates in the transmission of information about their activities which may be self-condemnatory, and as supervisors in action on the information received which generates unwelcome conflict with subordinates. Hence effective organizational monitoring and evaluation depends partly on the assertion of the interests of the organization over those of the individuals, teams, and units of which it is composed. The ways in which this can be done—training, education, and persuasion generally; negotiation; the provision of financial incentives; the exercise of authority—make up a large part of the task of operational management. Most of these procedures work much better within the organization than outside it, and more easily at lower levels of organization than higher. Hence so far as monitoring and evaluation

8   *Introduction*

depend on organizational imperatives to bring about the accurate provision of information on performance, and appropriate action by supervisors to bring performance into line with objectives, they present more difficult problems the higher the level of the organization at which they operate.

This is all the more true if we accept that the evaluation of a national health system must take into account not only the work of the ministry of health (and of state or provincial health departments where these exist) but also the activities of the private health care sector, commercial or otherwise, and the health care provided by individuals and households for themselves. The relation of the official planner-administrator to these agencies is much more a matter of negotiation and persuasion than of the exercise of authority; he is not well equipped to force them to participate in the evaluation process, either by providing accurate information by which their performance can be evaluated or by taking action to correct any deviations from what is expected of them. In the extreme, there are health-related factors (such as the level of incomes and employment) which the planner can neither influence nor control. All he can hope to do is to predict the behaviour of those variables which lie outside his organizational purview, and incorporate these predictions into his plans and evaluations.

Because of these factors, evaluation of a national health system differs from evaluation at lower levels not merely in degree, but also in kind. It cannot be based solely on conformity to a plan, since the plan itself and even its policy foundations are themselves subject to evaluation. It cannot rely only on the information on performance generated within the organizational structure of the ministry of health, since the activities of other agencies may be equally important to its conclusions. If carried out by senior ministry personnel, it cannot assume their impartiality, since its conclusions will affect the future of programmes to which they are committed. It cannot even assume that the ministry as a whole will conform to some Platonic ideal of detachment, since the evaluation may affect the share of the national budget which goes to organized health care in competition not only with non-health activities, but also with health-related activities outside the ministry's scope, such as water supply and nutrition. At this level, evaluation, like planning, is a political activity, concerned with the quest for power within a country's institutional framework or even outside it, and cannot be wholly contained by any prescriptive formulae. Nevertheless it seems worth attempting to set out in this book some guidelines which will render it more systematic, and domesticate it in the service of health development.

Health system evaluations can be undertaken in the absence of a planning system, through institutional devices such as commissions (the health section of the West India Royal Commission of 1938, HMSO 1945, is an example) or, less satisfactorily, by external agencies. If they aim at fundamental analysis, they cannot be wholly contained within a pre-existing planning framework, since such a framework is itself one of the things to be evaluated. But they are most likely to be useful if they are linked to a working health planning system. How, and how far, this can be done is discussed in Chapter 7.

1.4   Basis for the study

It is a characteristic of the national health system evaluations which have been done so far in developing countries that their results usually disappear into the files of the agencies or governments which commissioned them. Only in a few cases (e.g. Zimbabwe, Ghana) are the results of the evaluations publicly available, in whole or part (Segall 1983; Ghana Health Assessment Project Team 1981). Hence it is not practicable to base this study on a comprehensive literature review of past work or on a professional consensus reached through formal academic conferences. Instead, the study draws on the experience of the author and of his colleagues (especially at WHO and the London School of Hygiene and Tropical Medicine) in evaluating national systems and in using evaluations carried out by others.

The most important single documentary source used is the report of the *Jamaica Health Services Evaluation Project* carried out in 1983–5 by the Ministry of Health, Jamaica, and the Evaluation and Planning Centre, London School of Hygiene and Tropical Medicine, with funding from the UK Overseas Development Administration (Ministry of Health, Jamaica/ LSHTM 1986). This was an interdisciplinary project, with staff representing health planning, epidemiology, community health, anthropology, and economics. Based in the Ministry of Health, it was designed to evaluate public and, so far as data permitted, private health care, in terms of quantity and quality, using medical administrative, economic, and social criteria. The economic field had already been opened up in an earlier study (Cumper 1982, 1986). A fuller account of this project is given in the Appendix.

Participants in this project also assisted with the *World Bank Jamaica Health Sector Review* in 1983. This review was carried out under World Bank auspices by staff of the Ministry of Health, Jamaica, with assistance later from the Hope Foundation. The somewhat chequered history of this review was illuminating as a guide to the difficulties facing attempts at national self-evaluation.

The author took part, as a WHO staff member, in a number of *Country Health Programming* (CHP) exercises in South-East Asia (Nepal 1974; Thailand 1976; Bangladesh 1977, see WHO/Ministry of Health Dacca 1977; Burma 1978; Sri Lanka 1979, see Simeonov 1976). These, but for WHO's taboo on the word, could fairly have been called national health planning exercises, and included a strong element of evaluation—in many cases the first attempt at national health evaluation in the countries concerned. CHP was based on quantitative techniques developed by a research unit at WHO headquarters in the early 1970s. As the procedure was developed in WHO's South-East Asia region, the evaluation and planning work was done substantially by national health professionals with WHO staff as co-ordinators (elsewhere the balance between nationals and outsiders was often different). The Bangladesh CHP was particularly instructive since the author was present throughout and also had the opportunity for some systematic retrospective assessment of the results (Cumper 1979).

Another, though subsidiary, component of the study is the use of international statistical comparisons as an ingredient in national health system evaluation. Work done in this field had been incorporated in a monograph on determinants of health levels in developing countries (Cumper 1984) which is also drawn on in the following chapters.

Any study of this kind which is based largely on the experience of one or a few persons must be somewhat idiosyncratic. What is written below is believed to reflect not only the writer's own experience, but also the evaluative literature which circulates unpublished within international and bilateral agencies, dealing with national health systems or with projects and programmes with national implications. Thus, hopefully, the degree of idiosyncrasy is partly controlled. But the responsibility for what is said below rests more fully with the author than in most books of this kind.

2 Micro-evaluation: who needs it?

People responsible for the allocation of resources to and within the health sector obviously need criteria to guide them in their work. Their professional backgrounds may be various: doctors, professional administrators, accountants, bankers. The extent of their responsibility, too, may vary from management of a single institution to oversight of national and international programmes. In the last two decades a range of techniques has become available to help them evaluate single projects and programmes, referred to broadly as cost–effectiveness analysis (CEA) and cost–benefit analysis (CBA) (see, for example Drummond 1980; Drummond *et al.* 1987; but see also Elzinga 1981). It is argued here that these techniques are not sufficient for evaluation of health care systems at the national level. But to keep the argument in perspective, it is necessary to emphasize that these techniques do meet real needs, even though these are not the needs of the health system evaluator.

Like so many management tools with an economic component, project evaluation through cost–effectiveness and cost–benefit analysis was adopted in the health field long after it had become established elsewhere. CBA, for example, is generally reckoned to have originated with the interwar dam construction programme of the US Corps of Engineers, where costly capital projects had to be justified in terms of (mainly indirect) benefits they brought to state and regional economic activity. Other concepts were developed mainly within the private sector to evaluate very large investment projects—for example, the internal rate of return (IRR) as a concise measure of long run profitability. A particular impetus was given to CBA by the growth in the postwar years of the international financing of investment projects where at least one of the partners concerned was a public rather than a private agency—a national government, an international development agency—and so was obligated to consider the long run social effects of the investment rather than its short run commercial returns. Common features of the situations where this type of evaluation was applied were the size of the project (too large or innovative for its effects to be intuitively obvious, though still small relative to the whole national economy); the fact that the decision involved wider interests than immediate profitability; and a recognition that professional criteria were not adequate as a guide to the 'right' decision. It was not enough that a dam should represent the best engineering practice, or a new model car fulfil the dreams of the advertising manager. Where there was resistance to new patterns of project evaluation, it often sprang from this last factor, since it implied a shift of power and status within the organization concerned—the victory, as it was often seen, of grey and faceless accountancy over the life-affirming disciplines of science and engineering (see, for example Williams 1985).

Health care is, above all others, the industry which has been traditionally managed by its own professionals, and one would expect it to offer the most stubborn resistance to new forms of evaluation. This has been broadly true; the columns of *The Lancet* show that for many practitioners, the introduction of non-medical standards into health service management represents a process of diabolical seduction, with the economist often cast in the role of the tempter.

Imagine a surgeon, old enough to be fully qualified in his craft and to look matrons fearlessly in the eye, but young enough to feel that he still has much to learn. His good angel (whom we recognize by the white coat he wears over his well-cut suit) has guided him through medical school and endowed him with a range of techniques conforming with the best practice of his colleagues. The angel has gone further, teaching his charge to be cautiously critical of this practice and to adopt only those procedures which are of proven effectiveness; and, as between procedures of equal effectiveness, to prefer those which are simplest and least trying to the patient (no radical mastectomist he!). The good angel begins to feel he can relax his vigilance. One day he absents himself to attend a meeting of the hospital ethics committee; the surgeon, his list completed, sits in the cafeteria wishing for new intellectual worlds to conquer.

He expounds his frustration to his neighbour, a person whom he judges, from his sober dress and air of self-confident penury, to belong to the hospital's accounting department. The bad angel (for it is he) shows sympathetic interest. 'Why not' he says, 'try calculating the cost of the procedures you use? Not, of course, that cost should ever deter you from using the procedure which is in the patient's best interests; but it would add an extra dimension to your choice. I can recommend some books to guide you, and even help you myself if you wish it.' The books which the bad angel suggests, here and below, are taken from Drummond (1980, 1987) and other standard sources.

The surgeon consults his good angel, who gives rather grudging permission, and spends his evenings over the next three months wrestling with the mysteries of imputing overheads, separating capital from recurrent costs and annuitizing investments. Presented with the results, the good angel is less than enthusiastic. Gentlemen, he implies, do not read each other's accounts. The bad angel is more receptive.

'Really,' he says, 'these results are most interesting. It is clear that different procedures have very different costs, even when the procedures are directed toward the same end. Do you think you could devise a way of showing the cost of reaching a given level of effectiveness, so that we might at least be sure that we are comparing like with like? Since so much of what you do is directed toward saving lives, perhaps you could give us a measure of the cost of averting a death by one route or another?' The surgeon agrees; he is becoming intrigued, and also dimly aware of the possibility of one, or even several, publishable papers ahead in a field none of his rivals have yet touched.

After some weeks' work—really, he is beginning to wish he did not have to spend so much time in the theatre, let alone seeing his patients afterwards as his good angel insists—the surgeon presents his results. The bad angel is enthusiastic; might he show them to some colleagues in his department who are interested in such things? The surgeon agrees absently, but confesses that he is uneasy. He feels there is still much to be done. What of hip joint replacements and other procedures which are intended not to save lives but to make life more tolerable? Indeed, among procedures which are primarily life-saving, what of the differences in the quality of the life they save (see, for example Barnum 1987)? How does one compare the cost of a successful kidney transplant with that of the procedure which leaves the patient dependent on a dialysis machine?

The bad angel is most helpful. 'These problems are not entirely new,' he says, 'and I can provide you with a further list of books which will be useful. Further, our department considers your work so important that we have arranged for another surgeon to share your lists until it is completed. And you will, of course, have your own micro-computer and, if you wish it, a quiet room in the administration block.'

The quiet room is a great advantage (among other things, it takes the surgeon away from the reproachful glances of his good angel), and after some further months he proudly presents his results. 'Here is a list of the commonest procedures we use in this hospital. For each procedure, we have not only the cost, but also the probabilities of the various outcomes, the average number of years of extra life made possible, and the quality of that life measured according to an accepted scale. Putting all these together, we have our final column: the cost of each procedure per quality adjusted life year!'

'Excellent!' says the bad angel. 'Really excellent! I must take these immediately to our committee, which is about to take some rather important decisions about the future of the hospital. If you will meet me when I have more leisure—say, in a week's time—I can tell you (in strict confidence, of course) the results of our deliberations, in which you will find that you have played a very important part.'

When they meet again, the bad angel appears preternaturally solemn. 'I am afraid,' he says, 'that this has not worked out quite as I had expected. Having considered our budget, our waiting lists, and the information you prepared for us, we have decided that there are some areas where we must—shall we say—lighten our load. Your own specialization is one such area, and I regret that your post will have to go. However, do not be downcast; you are needed for an even more important duty. You must know that others have been working on the same lines in other hospitals, as well as in the community health services and public health generally. It has been decided to establish a permanent research conference at the highest level where we shall all come together to achieve the greatest ambition of us all; a bigger budget for the health services! You will be a member of this permanent conference. I may say that your good angel pleaded that you should be allowed to remain a surgeon, but we had regretfully to overrule him. Your new skills are of much greater importance than your surgical skills. Let me welcome you to the planning team!'

At first the ex-surgeon found his new work most stimulating. It was good to be with colleagues who had faced the same problems as himself in their search for measures of the relation between cost and effectiveness in their own fields of health care, all seeking ways to put their evaluation on a common basis. It was exciting to be set a new and even broader objective; for it was explained that they were now serving not merely the powers who controlled the health services and allocated the health budget where it would do most good, but the even higher powers who determined the size of that budget. These hard-hearted gods cared little about lives saved or even quality adjusted life years. Prayers to them must be in the language of money (cynics said, of votes), and the benefits as well as the costs of health care must therefore be expressed in these terms.

Yet as time went on the ex-surgeon began to feel that things were happening that he did not enjoy and his good angel would not have approved. Nor of course would many doctors (see Williams A 1985; Hoffenberg 1987). He was distressed, but not deeply discouraged by the failure of some of his colleagues to agree with the details of his methods; why, for example, could they not accept his cherished scale of degrees of health? But his disquiet went deeper than this.

For one thing, putting a money value on the benefits of health care turned out to be a more difficult business than he had expected. There was, first, the embarrassing fact that the specialists in preventive and promotive care, and even in clinical medicine, were often vaguer about the benefits their activities provided than, he felt, any surgeon ought to tolerate. (He made an honourable exception for immunization, the self-confidence of whose practitioners warmed his heart.)

Even when the benefits were well defined, how to value them? Easiest to handle was the way in which the prevention of disease reduced the need for curative care later; the costs saved to the health services here were surely calculable, and were all the more important because they would have fallen on the very health authorities who were sponsoring the exercise. But what of the effect of extra years of health and productive life on the country's economy, and what of its value to the patient involved?

Sometimes these difficulties seemed insoluble. Then the bad angel was always at hand with a plausible assumption or a helpful reference. For the productive value of those extra years, why not base it on the average earnings of the employed for the relevant time and place? For their value to the client, why not look at what the person benefited would pay—estimated, perhaps, from what he did pay for the service involved, or by more subtle means? Or, if these assumptions seemed too crude, add more to correct the defect—downgrade average earnings, for example, to what one would expect from the worker at the margin of employment (a trick the ex-surgeon learned to refer to nonchalantly as 'shadow pricing'). He did not feel able to challenge any of these assumptions individually. But he began to feel that he was wandering further and further into a shadow world.

But what disquieted him most was to realize that the calculations of himself and his new colleagues were no longer intellectual playthings, but the bases for decisions whose morality he was not sure he could accept. The good angel was never seen in the precincts of the research conference, but sometimes the ex-surgeon seemed to hear his voice asking awkward questions. 'Do you really want to forbid kidney transplantation to patients over 65, because they will not live as long to enjoy the results as youngsters of 60? Or reduce the budget for cardiac surgery in order to provide more money for nutrition education which will, if your colleagues' latest calculations are correct, reduce coronary heart disease a generation from now? As a surgeon, you may have made arrogant decisions about the priority of individual patients; but it was a simple and venal arrogance, and you bore the responsibility for the outcome. Now you are planning to make life and death decisions, on the basis of devious and disputable calculations, for people whom you will never see. Can you still say 'first do no harm'?'

Yet the ex-surgeon did not often feel like this. Usually he was buoyed up by enjoyment of his own skills, partnership in a common cause and, above all, the expectation of success—the delineation of a health service so logically planned, efficiently organized, and scientifically justified that the higher powers would have no option but to give it the increased resources which it deserved, and which would remove many of the awkward dilemmas of resource allocation. At long last the plan was completed (with many caveats about insufficient information and the need for further research). He and his colleagues awaited with some complacency the verdict of the higher powers.

This, when it came, was shattering. In public, nothing derogatory was said; indeed, the highest tribute was paid to the innovative thinking and devoted public service of the research team. So important was it felt to be that the team was to be given permanent status (with a somewhat reduced budget) as a unit within an ambiguously titled division of the Ministry which already dealt with alternative medicine, parapsychology, and customers' complaints. But in spite of the most determined leaking to the media, nothing of the team's recommendations found its way even into a discussion document. In confidence, the bad angel, with a carefully doleful face, was happy to explain why.

'You must know' he said, 'that when faced with your proposal, the higher powers showed it to their own group of the great and the good. Some of these simply disagreed with your calculations (or with any calculations except their own). Others, however, accepted your figures but translated them into their own terms. The health services, they pointed out, were run through institutions, which would be seriously affected by your plan. Some would be expanded, some contracted, and virtually all changed. Could the management system cope with this—particularly as there would certainly be complaints from the Medical Association, the College of Nurses, and the Union of Miscellaneous Health Workers that their professional status had been violated, complaints which on previous form could only be bought off by a substantial increase in salaries which would bring cries of 'foul' from the rest of the civil service? As for an increase in the overall budget, this would disturb the delicate balance between the ministries which was the only thing which made the annual expenditure negotiations possible without splitting the Cabinet; and this for the benefit of a minister who was, at the moment, very much on the wrong wing of the party! And, as a trusted adviser pointed out, there were not many votes to be gained from health, and these could be got in other, cheaper ways. It was for these unworthy reasons that your proposals were definitively rejected. Perhaps, however, under the next government . . .'

The ex-surgeon was overwhelmed by the consciousness of having spent the best years of his career on something which might be immoral and was certainly unprofitable. 'Bad angel', he said, 'I put you and all your works behind me. I shall return to being a simple surgeon. I shall not forswear my calculations altogether, but I shall confine them within limits which my good angel would approve.'

'As you wish' says the bad angel. 'I am aware that you have some cause to be angry with me, particularly as you may find that the years we have worked together have done some harm to your dexterity and to your place in the surgeons' pecking order. I would suggest an alternative. I have many friends in those international agencies which are in the business of providing advice and loans, often unsought, to poor countries. They are now into health, and have a great need for people with your experience to guarantee to their ruling bodies that they are doing good on sound banking principles. Why not become an international consultant on economic evaluation? Here you will be able to consider the worth of a project on its merits. Those obstructive political complications will be the concern of the grateful national governments, and you need never hear of them.'

And so, with brightening eyes, our hero contemplates his new career. It is to be hoped, for the sake of his future clients, that he correctly understands the lessons of his experience. The most important of these is not that micro-evaluation is technically difficult (which it is), or that the application of its results is often obstructed by self-interest and inertia (which is also true); it is that the multiplication of micro-evaluations does not constitute a macro-evaluation.

The bad angel led his pupil across the line between micro- and macro-evaluation by the offer of temptations nicely adjusted to his professional enthusiasms. Two minor temptations—to make the maximum use of one's professional skills, and to have these recognized by those who hold power—lead to the major temptation; to construct, from the materials of one's own science, a world model which can serve both as a description of the ideal state, and a guide to how this ideal is to be attained. Such constructions contravene the principle, which most people would accept once it is made explicit, that as a guide to human action, science can play only an instrumental role—as a way of analysing the consistency of goals based on values determined from outside science, and of finding the most efficient ways to attain them. The temptation to believe that one's discipline generates its own values is one to which both doctors and economists are prone.

Western economists have devoted a great deal of effort to the construction of world models which purport to show that on certain rather stringent assumptions the interplay of individual choices about economic matters—work, spending, saving, investing, and so on—results in an allocation of resources which is unique. Further, it is optimal at least in the sense that no individual can improve his lot without making someone else worse off. These general equilibrium models can be used for various purposes. In the extreme, they can be treated as direct guides to policy—the best attainable world is one in which individual choice is unfettered, and the way to that world lies through the removal of restrictions on choice. These models can also be treated as a tool for exploring the pure mathematics of resource allocation (in which role they turn out to have important areas of overlap with models based on quite different institutional premises). But working economists tend to use them (often without realizing it) for a different purpose; as a framework within which to solve problems of partial analysis. If, for example, we want to estimate the costs and benefits of a health programme, we need some assurance that the economic data we feed in to the calculation—salaries, prices of supplies, production increases—are not arbitrary numbers but represent values in some socially important sense, and will not change, or will change in predictable ways, when our programme is introduced. This assurance we get from the general equilibrium model of the economy.

But the assurance is only valid if the change we analyse is small in relation to the economic system within which it takes place. If it is large, it may alter the shape of the system at the general equilibrium level. If we are concerned with the introduction of a new surgical procedure in a developed country, it is reasonable to assume that with or without the change, the key economic variables will be much the same. If we are considering a nationwide malaria control programme in a poor country, such an assumption is much less reasonable; the introduction of the programme may have significant effects on population, production, and the prices and interest rates we use to estimate costs and benefits. This applies equally if we are considering simultaneously a number of changes which, while individually small, in aggregate are capable of changing the shape of the economic system. The evaluation of a whole national health system calls for just such considera- tion. Hence, even on strictly economic grounds, it cannot be carried out simply by applying the techniques of micro-evaluation.

It might be thought that these difficulties can be evaded if we stop short of full cost–benefit analysis, confining ourselves to relating the costs of a health programme as they present themselves to the health service manager (which are relatively objective observables) with the outcomes measured in non-economic terms, such as the saving of quality adjusted life years. At the national level, this is objectionable on two grounds. One is that it takes no account of private costs—for example, the work-time lost waiting in a health centre queue—which raise the same problems of valuation as benefits. The other is that the fallacy of composition applies on the epidemiological side as much as on the economic.

Suppose, for example, that we measure the beneficial impact of a life-saving innovation in terms of the average age at death of the relevant popu- lation group in the absence of the innovation, and the average expectation of life for people of that age. We have assumed, in effect, that each person whose life has been saved has henceforward the same chances of survival as the rest of the population at that age. This may not be strictly true (a very low birth-weight child whose life has been saved by intensive care may possibly have worse than average life chances) but it is a plausible assump- tion when we are considering a single problem. But does this mean that if two innovations are introduced simultaneously, their beneficial results are simply additive? Evidently not; the simultaneous introduction of immuniza- tion against measles, and a new antibiotic to treat the respiratory infections which are often its sequelae, would evidently involve an interaction so that the net benefit would be less than the sum for the two programmes separately. In this case a specific model could be set up to deal with the interaction. But if we are to envisage many simultaneous programme variations (as implicitly we must for evaluating a national system), the modelling becomes impossibly complicated. Hence on the epidemiological side too there are limits to the use which can be made of micro-evaluation.

It should be said that even if it were possible to extend the epidemiological and economic techniques used in micro-analysis (perhaps by a massive exercise in number-crunching) so that they were able to deal with many different configurations of a national health system, and out of these select the most efficient, they would still fall short of what is required for national health system evaluation in two basic ways. They would not take account of the fact that such systems are required to meet standards which are neither epidemiological nor economic—for example, social policy, consistency with the national administrative structure, and political feasibility. Nor would they allow for the fact that these standards must be met not only by the ideal health system itself, but by the path by which we are to reach that ideal from the imperfect present. These problems are referred to again in the chapters that follow.

Yet our surgeon-planner was not wrong in his first steps in micro-evaluation. He applied the techniques of CE analysis to a limited range of procedures in order to assist in the making of decisions whose basis and limitations he knew. It was only when he and his colleagues attempted to use CE and CB analysis as a basis for comprehensive health system evaluations which in themselves would be a sufficient guide for planning that they overstepped the bounds of micro-evaluation and were rebuffed—rightly, if for the wrong reasons.

Will his skills be legitimately employed if he joins the ranks of those who, on behalf of international agencies, carry out CE and CB analyses of national health projects for which loans and grants are sought? Here he will be dealing with the costs and benefits of a single activity (though possibly one with variants of method and scope). There may be gaps in the available data, and difficult decisions about technical matters such as the 'shadow pricing' of labour or foreign exchange. But in the nature of the case he will be protected from the hubris of supposing that his evaluation is the only element in the acceptance or rejection of the project. He may be able to testify that one variant or another has lower costs (financial or social) in relation to the specified objective (lives saved, cases averted, or whatever), or that its rate of return is greater than the cost of borrowing or the return on investment in general in the economy concerned. But he will not be concerned with the process by which this project, and not one of the many conceivable alternatives, was selected for appraisal by the agency and the national government.

Yet this process may be more important for health planning than the greater sophistication of techniques of micro-evaluation. Ideally, a project emerges from a well-specified national plan. In the real world of the 1980s, where few countries have managed to hold on to binding long-term plans, the process is likely to be more political or even random. Nevertheless, if it has any rationality, it must depend ultimately on a scanning of the field of existing health care activities and a comparison of the results with some standard—in other words, on a national health system evaluation. In recent years international aid agencies have increasingly recognized the importance of systematic project identification, without which the gains from micro-evaluation are limited.

In the heyday of health planning for (and sometimes by) developing countries, in the 1970s and early 1980s, evaluation was thought of as a component of the planning function, and the responsibility of planning staff. For example, in WHO's Country Health Programming exercises the initial step was a stocktaking of the national health situation. From this point of view, if an agency wishes to improve the quality of macro-evaluation in a developing country its logical recourse is to strengthening the national planning institutions, and many aid projects do include provision for this purpose. This approach has a certain risk attached to it; if the health planning unit or agency does not establish itself successfully, the evaluation function will not be carried out. Experience seems to show that autonomous units intended to carry out a full range of planning functions in medically controlled ministries arouse considerable resistance—much greater than attaches to the function of evaluation. This may be fundamentally because planning lies uneasily on the boundary between staff and line management; the stronger the planning unit, the more power it takes away from senior levels of political and administrative management.

From the point of view of the international agency, this difficulty can be circumvented if it prepares its own national sector reports (as the World Bank, for example, has done for some years, and as the UK Overseas Development Administration does for its priority target countries). But this is unsatisfactory from the national point of view; external evaluations do not meet its internal management needs, including the need for information to equip it to negotiate with potential aid donors.

A possible solution to the problem is for countries (particularly small ones) to recognize that the planning function need not be carried out through specialized planning units of the conventional type. It may actually be more efficient (again, particularly in small countries) for the function to be treated as a normal obligation of senior managers, provided they are furnished with an adequate base of epidemiological, statistical, and economic information organized in a way which enables them to identify the areas where action is needed. After all, the substance of planning has been achieved in the past without formal planning machinery—witness the setting up of the UK National Health Service, or the substantial investment in maternal and child health made in the Commonwealth Caribbean after the Second World War (Colonial Office 1944, 1955) on the basis of the West India Royal Commission of 1938 (HMSO 1945). This approach implies the need not for a separate planning unit, but for a much less controversial programme evaluation unit whose output will provide a framework for the planning function and into whose repertoire of techniques micro-evaluation will naturally fit.

3 Strategy for evaluating a national health system

This chapter examines the logical basis for evaluation, and some of the special issues which arise in the evaluation of national health systems.

3.1 Evaluation: comparing performance with standards

In the health field, the term evaluation covers a wide range of activities, from clinical audit in hospitals through cost–benefit and cost–effectiveness analysis of projects to national sector reviews by international agencies. Broadly, it can be defined as the comparison of the *performance* of an individual or institution with the *standards* appropriate to its function. Seen as part of the process of management, it carries the implication that any divergence is to lead to corrective action. When applied at the national level, this innocent-sounding definition raises certain difficulties which have to be solved before effective evaluation can take place.

First of all, how is performance to be measured? Clearly, performance indicators must be related to standards—it is pointless to construct indicators for aspects of performance for which no standards, explicit or implicit, can be established. (One must also, in practice, take account of the availability of data, which is discussed in later chapters.) Thus our choice of indicators depends on our idea of the relevant standards. But what standards are to be considered relevant? The answer to this question, in turn, depends on the function to be performed by the institution being evaluated, and the possibilities the situation offers for corrective action.

Both of these factors vary from level to level of the health system. If we consider a single institution, such as a health centre, its functions are rather narrowly defined and the possibilities for corrective action within the limits of its own authority and resources are restricted. For evaluation at this level it will be appropriate to choose a few specific standards and hence a small number of indicators of performance. If we consider a national health system as a whole, its functions are much broader and the range of possibilities for corrective action is greater. Hence there is a much greater range of standards which could be applied, and a correspondingly greater range of possible performance indicators. This means that the choice among possible standards becomes of critical importance; and this depends on a clear definition of the level at which the system is being considered.

This proposition is particularly helpful because it can be used to clarify the distinction between variables which are subject to management action (and so are appropriate topics for evaluation) and constraints which management at a particular level must accept as given. Factors which appear as constraints at lower levels become controllable variables at higher levels. For example in the management of a health centre the institution's budget and establishment are constraints, whereas from the point of view of the health ministry the allocation of funds and staff between institutions and programmes is an evaluable management decision. This does not mean that at lower levels a clear specification of constraints is not a useful datum as a background for evaluation, but it does mean that it is a factor for which standards need not be specified at that level.

It would be possible, without too much abuse of words, for an evaluator to define the national health system in at least four different ways. The narrowest definition would relate the evaluation to the *government health services*. This is convenient in countries where data on non-governmental health care activities are scarce. But these are often the very countries where health, however defined, depends heavily on non-governmental activities; these may fall nominally under the responsibility of the ministry of health, but its control over them is tenuous. Hence a concentration on the government health services cannot be the preferred basis for health system evaluation. A broader definition would cover the *health care services*, whether these are provided by government or the private sector, Western or traditional. (Household care may or may not be included on this definition.) All activities would be included here if their primary purpose was the improvement of physical health, following the lines of the definition of health care used in national accounting. A broader definition still would cover all those *health-related activities* which make a substantial contribution to the improvement of physical health, including water supply, sanitation, and education. An even broader definition would take as its point of departure the passage in the constitution of the World Health Organization which identified health with the highest degree of physical, mental, and social well-being—in other words, with *human welfare*—and would include all activities which had a bearing on health in this sense. For the purposes of this book, we shall reject the first definition as too narrow, and the last as too broad to be meaningful. We shall consider the evaluation of a national health system as being the evaluation of all health-related activities, while accepting that for practical reasons we usually have to confine our attention to the health care services.

If we define the national health system in terms of activities which contribute to physical health, there are certain functions related to human welfare which lie outside the scope of our evaluation—for example, defence and the maximization of national production, except where they may contribute to the improvement or otherwise of the physical health of the population. There are also factors which we must take as constraints on planning and management in the health sector, such as social policy commitments to human rights and equity, the size of the national income and the overall system of government and administration. The standards we use must all be related, within these constraints, to the function of the improvement of physical health, and the performance indicators in turn must be related to these standards.

It is necessary to emphasize the limits of health system evaluation because otherwise it may degenerate into a general review of the welfare aspects of the society, becoming too diffuse to be useful. This does not mean, however, that the only acceptable standards and indicators are direct measurements of physical health. At any level, but particularly at the national level, health system evaluation must look much further afield than this.

3.2   Evaluation at national level: opening the black box

At whatever level we analyse the health system, there is a sense in which health impact is the fundamental measure by which performance is to be evaluated. Building on this, we might treat the health system as a 'black box' whose inner workings were of no interest to us, since we could evaluate it solely on the basis of its inputs of clients and health resources and its output of health levels. But there are several reasons why this is neither desirable nor practicable. There are well-known difficulties in assessing the impact even of limited health measures with well-defined goals. Statistical measures of health levels are often neither timely nor reliable, particularly when they concern rare events such as infant deaths from a specific cause. General measures of health are multidimensional; mortality alone, for instance, may need to be combined with morbidity and severity to assess changes in the impact of a programme directed against a particular disease. Causation, too, is multidimensional; there is no one-to-one relation between an input and a change in health levels. Furthermore, we are dealing with a 'lagged' system; changes in health activities do not necessarily manifest themselves immediately, but may have effects spread over many years. The difficulties are compounded when we are dealing at the national level with broad policies and system changes, rather than specific institutions and disease campaigns.

We need to break open the black box to see what are the mechanisms linking inputs to the health care system with health impact as its output. The terms conventionally used to classify the contents of the box vary somewhat from investigator to investigator. Here we shall distinguish the *structure* determining the box's capabilities; the *process* which results when inputs are fed into this structure; and the *outcome* of the process which determines the impact on health levels. This classification comes from studies of individual institutions and programmes, but it still has meaning when applied to the national health system as a whole.

Understanding what is inside the black box—that is, analysing the health system—is a necessary part of evaluation. It releases us from the dilemma about measuring health levels; instead of setting up our standards and performance indicators in terms of impact, we can devise standards for structure, process and outcome which we can equate with impact on the basis of experience and technical knowledge. We can, for example, measure the level of immunization against a specific disease in terms of the numbers of people immunized and the technical specification of the process used. This kind of understanding is also needed for management purposes, enabling us to translate divergences between standard and performance into appropriate corrective action.

But—to push the metaphor a little further—we may find when we open the box that its working depends on the application of standards which have nothing to do with its primary purpose—a cut-out, say, to limit the power it can draw from outside, as a budget limits the resources a health programme can claim. There are many of these external standards in the health system, connected, for example, with personnel practices and financial procedures, and they must be included in the scope of evaluation.

It follows that in evaluating a national health system, we must pay attention to three types of standard and their corresponding performance indicators:

(1) standards arising from the policy–planning–budgeting–implementation cycle;

(2) standards formulated independently of this cycle (mainly concerned with the management of the implementation phase of the cycle), based upon considerations of general social policy, laws and the associated regulations, technical (medical) norms, administrative efficiency and cost, and market equilibrium between the health sector and the rest of the economy;

(3) standards based directly on public preferences and attitudes.

Each of these types of standard is valid for certain purposes, and all must be taken into account in a comprehensive evaluation.

The policy–planning–budgeting–implementation cycle can in principle be used as a powerful instrument of evaluation since each stage in the cycle can be regarded as an attempt to make more concrete and specific what has been developed in the preceding stage, and can therefore be tested against that stage for consistency and probable effectiveness. Each stage can be looked on both as an aspect of performance (e.g. a health plan can be seen as an achievement to be tested against national health policy) and a standard of evaluation (e.g. a plan can be used as a standard to evaluate a particular year's health budget). How effective evaluation on this basis can be depends on the precision with which policies, plans, and budgets are stated. We rarely find the ideal situation in which each level of the policy–planning–budgeting process is embodied in a document appropriate to that level and enjoying full official support; and in many developing countries nominal plans and policies in any case have little influence on what actually happens. Hence they cannot be the sole basis for evaluation.

A second way of evaluating performance is through comparison with management standards formulated independently of the planning cycle. In the literature on health service management in the 1970s these standards were neglected since if one takes planning as the only intellectually respectable way to run a health service they appear as constraints or background influences rather than positive factors in their own right. But they are of great practical importance in situations where planning is inadequate, or formal plans are rendered inoperative by rapid economic or social change. In such circumstances, it is management standards which maintain the cohesion and impetus of health care systems. It is obvious that standards formulated on professional and technical grounds play a crucial role in the field of health care, where inputs and processes can be controlled for management purposes more effectively than outcomes or, especially, impact. It is largely on the basis of such standards that we are justified in assuming that planned changes in inputs will result in the desired impact on health. But administrative and financial standards (as incorporated, for example, in civil service and finance regulations) are also of great importance, and so, over a longer period, are those expressed in the legal structure of the health sector. Standards based on economic efficiency are still not universal in developing countries, though they have become more common in the period of economic stringency since 1975. The standards imposed by the need to keep the health sector in equilibrium with the rest of the economy—for example, to keep nurses' salaries competitive with those of secretaries—though seldom explicitly formulated, are an important concern of health sector management in many developing countries.

A third form of evaluation occurs when we compare performance with public need and demand. These terms have been defined differently by various authors. Here need is used to mean the gap between present health status and that technically attainable, as professionally defined by providers of health care or epidemiologists. Demand, on the other hand, is used to mean the actual or potential expression by the public of their desires in relation to health and to the activities of health care providers. Need and demand are not identical. An activity may be demanded but not needed— for example, a caesarean delivery undertaken for the convenience of the mother or (perish the thought!) of the obstetrician. Alternatively, an activity may be needed but not demanded—for example, immunization against polio in a population which has been free of the disease for many years. At first sight, need appears to be a promising basis for evaluation; it is objective (or at least seems so to health professionals) and can be based on well-tried epidemiological techniques. But the apparent objectivity is deceptive. Most statements of need are based implicitly on some assumption about available resources. If this assumption is made explicit, and we set out to base our standards on a reconciliation of resources with need, we are back with the planning process. Hence, need in our terminology does not provide an independent source of standards for evaluation but is usually implicit in the planning process.

Demand, as expressed, for example, in interviews with consumers, through user pressure groups or by deduction from consumer behaviour, is a less congenial standard than need to medical planners. Consumers' subjective feelings toward the health care system tend to be dismissed as irrational if they do not coincide with need; if they enter into health planning, it is so that, through health education, they may be brought into line with professionally approved behaviour. Patients in distress in whom no ailment can be found, for example, are seen as cluttering up the practitioner's waiting room and may be fobbed off with a bottle of pink peppermint solution, or a chit bearing three letters which the naive nurse-pharmacist does not at first recognize as standing for 'Any Damn Thing'. But this is a blinkered point of view. The consumer has a scale of values to which the health professional has only limited access, and his preferences about health care have value in their own right. Though partly subjective in nature, they can be objectively observed, and they provide an independent standard which must be taken into account in a comprehensive evaluation.

3.3   Choosing standards: trace conditions and tracer problems

Opening up the black box of health care brings to view a complicated mechanism with an uncountable number of components. Does evaluation mean that we must test every one of these? Evidently this is impracticable. We must choose a limited number of items for investigation, in such a way that they will give the maximum amount of information about the system as a whole. It is evident that we need to pay special attention to the input side—numbers of clients, budgets, buildings and equipment, numbers of staff—and the output side—mortality and morbidity rates and any other indicators of general health levels. But what about the mechanisms which connect inputs and outputs?

The problem is rather like that which faces the evaluator of the quality of care in a single complex health institution such as a hospital. Patients are being treated for a very wide range of conditions, each requiring different handling; how to arrive at an assessment of the overall quality of care within the limits of the resources available for the investigation? One established answer is through the use of 'tracer conditions'—a small number of conditions chosen to be representative of different aspects of health care, which can be investigated objectively and in detail. (This technique is discussed more fully in Section 5.2.) Similarly, an efficient way of evaluating the working of the health care system is often by concentrating attention on 'tracer problems'.

How can such problems be selected? The commonsense starting point is the awareness of health administrators and of the articulate public. Not all problems that take up a great deal of an administrator's time have obvious significance for the system as a whole. The fact that a senior medical officer spends much time on the phone listening to reasons why a doctor in a rural hospital should be transferred to the city may mean no more than that the doctor's wife wants to be near her family—or it may cast light on the whole personnel policy and management structure of the health services. Even trivial problems may be more significant than they appear. Many years ago the director of health services in Burma, asked by a visiting team what was his most difficult management decision, replied after consideration that it was the choice of doctors to go abroad on fellowships. Behind this limited matter lay questions about the relation between the professional conduct of the health services through the formal administrative machinery, and the influence of the Party with its insistence on ideological purity.

Thus the current preoccupations of health officials are often a convenient starting point for the selection of 'tracer' problems, with certain provisos. One is that the problems must be capable of being investigated objectively. Another is that they must, in fact, have implications for the health system as a whole. A third is that once selected, they must be followed wherever they lead—which may be into areas of the health system, and even of the political system of the country, apparently remote from their starting point. (It would have been a brave consultant who dug too deep into the problem raised by the Burmese official.) In the Jamaica Health Services Evaluation Project some of the tracer problems used were the attitudes of women towards antenatal care and towards child diarrhoea; hospital costs; the legal basis of the work of nurse practitioners and community health workers; and the level and composition of maternal mortality. Each of these led to the evaluation of wider fields—the first, of health education; the hospital cost study, of general hospital management and financing; the legal study, of the relation between the health professions; and the maternal mortality study, of the quality of technical support services and official records.

4 Basic information on health system performance

4.1 Waste not, want not: making the most of the data

It is a common complaint among health planners and administrators concerned with developing countries that their job is made difficult or (in pessimistic moods) impossible by lack of information. There is something of a paradox here; for the volume and range of data collected by the health authorities and other national agencies is often enormous. In Jamaica, for example, the administrative process gathers data, for all or part of the system, under the following heads:

(1) vital statistics: population by
   (a) total numbers
   (b) age and sex
   (c) births, deaths

(2) census: dwellings by
   (a) age and type
   (b) access to water supply, latrine, power

(3) service statistics: clients by
   (a) disease category
   (b) location
   (c) age and sex
   (d) nature of service
   (e) institution
   (f) source and destination of referrals
   (g) length of hospital stay

(4) budget system: expenditure by
   (a) institution
   (b) nature of expenditure

(5) personnel system: numbers of staff by
   (a) grade
   (b) institution
   (c) posts established versus posts filled.

Jamaica may be rather better served, statistically, than most developing countries—at least those of us who owe it allegiance like to think so. But the reporting system which generates the above data is of a kind standard among ex-British territories. Indeed, in many respects the standardization is international. There are certainly items not included above which an evaluator would like to have—for example, the outcome of treatment for hospital in-patients, or the prevalence of disability in the population. Nevertheless, the above items cover a good part of the field of health system evaluation. Why then is there a lack of information?

The short and abstract answer is that data is not information—at least if we define data puristically as the symbolic counterpart of an observed event, and information as that part of data which reduces uncertainty. More concretely, data systems like that of Jamaica fail to yield their due quota for information purposes because of certain faults—incompleteness, inconsistency, and delay (Casley and Lury 1981).

The data are commonly *incomplete* in the sense that items recorded for clients using one part of the system are ignored in others. In Jamaica, for example, the age, sex, and residence of clients are recorded for hospital in-patients, but not for out-patients or visitors to casualty departments or health centres. So far as data on residence are concerned, it happens in this case that the lack is not of crucial importance; we know from independent evidence that in Jamaica users of health centres and hospital outpatient facilities come from a quite restricted geographical area. But this would not necessarily be true of countries with lower population densities and more dispersed health facilities. The lack of data on the age and sex of clients, on the other hand, is important since it makes it difficult to generalize about, for example, the differences in utilization rates between age groups—an important consideration if one wishes to predict the changing demand for services during the demographic transition from a young to an older population.

Administrative health data are often *inconsistent* in that similar events are measured in different ways for various facilities. Usage of hospitals by in-patients is commonly measured in discharges (effectively, episodes of sickness) for hospital in-patients, but in terms of attendances in other parts of the health services. The reason for seeking health care may be given for in-patients in terms of the International Classification of Diseases (ICD) of one or another date, but for health centre users in terms of type of clinic, symptom category, or other non-ICD classification.

Administrative data are subject to *delay* in publication (and so in availability for current evaluation purposes) for many causes. One of course, is the lack of resources in developing countries with which to process them. Another, less deserving of sympathy, is the confusion between management information and public statistics. The former can be useful even if based on data which are incomplete on the national scale; the latter follow standards which demand considerable completeness, even to the point of holding up the publication of national data until reports are received from the most remote, understaffed, and recalcitrant institutions in each category.

Does this mean that evaluators should demand expansion of the system of administrative information until the reporting and processing of all items is complete, consistent, and timely? Not necessarily; there are reasons, rooted in the administrative needs of each kind of institution and of the system as a whole, why their yield of information falls short of the ideal. Sometimes, particularly in the 1970s, the number-crunching capabilities of modern computers tempted planners and administrators to demand an information system for the health sector which would be total, monolithic, and instantaneous. This is to ignore the fact that the limit on the use of computers is not the hardware, but the interface with the real world in which raw data are generated and processed data are transmitted to analysts and decision makers. There are undoubtedly ways in which the administrative information system can be modified and supplemented to make it more useful for evaluation, as discussed in a later section. But the practical problem is more often how to make the maximum use of routinely available data.

The problem is in many ways similar to that which faces economic statisticians in drawing up a country's national accounts, where also use must be made of data of varying quality and completeness to produce a consistent picture of national economic activity. Some of the principles which underlie national accounts work can be transferred to the health sector (Cumper 1986)—the use of a comprehensive conceptual framework; the pursuit of exhaustiveness, so that no event within the scope of the exercise is either omitted or counted twice; and the use wherever possible of alternative ways of estimating the same variable, so that one estimate acts as a check on the other. The application of these principles in order to prepare a model of the activities of the health sector which can form the starting point for evaluation requires a particular mental attitude on the part of the statistician—a recognition that at many points accuracy must be traded against significance and timeliness.

This attitude may appear raffish to professionals working in other fields. But it is a fact of life that different disciplines have very different concepts of accuracy. Cosmologists are often content if prediction and event agree within an order of magnitude; engineers have their 'fudge factors'. Even within a single field, standards of accuracy must be adjusted to the purpose of the work in hand. Commercial accountants would be culpable if they did not try to trace the last cent, while the builders of macro-economic models work with units of thousands or millions of dollars. Modelling the health sector in real time, as a basis for planning and evaluation, permits and even requires a slightly piratical attitude towards one's data sources, which must be balanced by realism about the accuracy of the results achieved.

The principal steps in the modelling process are the choice of the basic framework, the assessment of the available information in relation to this framework, and the filling of the information gaps through the gathering of new data, the synthesis of information from existing data and the exploitation of the possibilities of comparisons over space and time. These are described briefly in the following subsections as they occurred in the Jamaica Health Services Evaluation Project, and more generally elsewhere in this chapter.

4.1.1 Choosing the framework

What are the basic factors which need to be taken into account in building a model of the health system? One approach is to see the system in terms of two flows through time. One flow is that of the population from one health state to another—from 'well' to 'sick' of this or that condition, and then back to 'well', or to one or another state of disability, or to death, with the reservoir of the total population being continually replenished by births. In a sense, this is an extension of the demographers' model of population increase, and in principle one can measure the probability of transition from one state to another by rates which have the same form as rates of fertility and mortality. But it can also accommodate, as special cases, many epidemiological models of specific diseases, each of which yields its own set of transition probabilities from state to state.

The other flow is that of people and resources through health care institutions—defining these very broadly so that, if we had the data (which we seldom do) we could include household care and the services of traditional and informal healers. The characteristic feature of such institutions is that they change the transition probabilities from one health state to another. Preventive institutions decrease the probability of movement from 'well' to 'sick', curative institutions increase (we hope) the probability of going from 'sick' to 'well', and rehabilitative institutions affect the probability of movement between different degrees of disability.

Because of lack of data, we cannot translate this model completely into numbers, though some explorations of this possibility were undertaken in the 1970s by the UN Statistical Office. But as a framework for analysis it has two virtues. One is that it concentrates attention on the need to link two kinds of material on the health situation which are relatively abundant—demographic and epidemiological data on the one hand, and institutional inputs and outputs on the other. Secondly, many other factors relevant to health can be given perspective by locating them within the framework of the model. For example, environmental influences on health can be seen as changing, for good or ill, the transition rate from health to sickness, and the quality of institutional care as affecting the transition rate from sickness to health. For the planner and evaluator, such a model provides a qualitative and order-of-magnitude framework within which particular relationships can be identified for more exact quantitative expression.

4.1.2   A Jamaican example

Among the objectives of the Jamaica Health Services Evaluation Project was the analysis of the country's health information system. The purpose of the analysis was threefold: to construct a framework for understanding how the health care sector worked, to act as a 'tracer' problem to throw light on health service management generally, and if possible to generate recommendations about how the system might be improved. Under this last heading, some recommendations were made during the life of the project, mainly in terms of more efficient use of the data already collected, and this chapter is partly an amplification and generalization of these. Under the second heading, the health information system served the project well as a tracer problem. It led us to the physical origins of the data—medical records departments in rural hospitals that managed to be both overcrowded and understaffed, the reception counter in the main city hospital that seemed too frail to hold back the teeming 'casualty' crowd, health centres with bulging filing cabinets kept more or less orderly by conscripted community health aides, dusty rooms in the Ministry of Health where staff had to dig like terriers to unearth past budget documents. We saw how the data were processed—mainly by clerks in the rented Health Information Unit quarters which had not then been upgraded from disgusting to the merely Spartan. (It is always interesting to note which departments an institution chooses to hive off into separate accommodation, as WHO's Geneva headquarters does with 'essential drugs' and other programmes crammed into the extensions huddled under the skirts of the main building.) In Jamaica we saw how the processed data were distributed; how far they appeared as an input of information into the making of decisions (which, as so often, depended heavily on the personal management style of the decision-makers); in which areas similar data were collected twice over, and in which areas they were not collected at all. We picked up examples of the sometimes bizarre ways in which managers supplemented the formal information system—for instance, a senior manager, having completed a business call to a hospital, drawing the switchboard operator into an exposition of its current situation which he could not hope to receive through official channels. All in all, the information system, interpreted broadly to include financial and personnel information, served as an excellent tracer for management problems.

But of the three purposes for analysis of the information system, it is the first—the construction of a quantitative framework for the evaluation of the health care system—which concerns us most here. Developing such a framework was a concern from early in the project, but the choice of a model in terms of patient and resource flows and transition probabilities only emerged as successive practical problems were faced and overcome. By the time the framework was taking final shape in 1986, it was showing a good deal of convergence with a computer model developed independently by a colleague (Max Price) as a tool for district level health planning, and Price's data list and procedures served as a check on those emerging from the Jamaica project.

With only a normal amount of tidying up in the light of hindsight, the procedures used in Jamaica can be summarized as follows:

(1) *assessment* of existing administrative and public statistics against the requirement of the emerging model;

(2) *identification and filling of data gaps*—either areas completely without data, or areas where bridging information was needed between independent statistical series;

(3) *synthesis* of new and old data to fill (so far as possible) the boxes of the model;

(4) selection of information for *presentation* in tabular or diagram form for different purposes.

None of the methods used were particularly sophisticated. In particular, the work of synthesis and presentation was done manually (to give more flexibility in an experimental situation, and perhaps also as a reflection of conservatism on the part of the investigator, who was of a generation to remember the Facit hand calculator and the exact angle at which it had to be struck to clear its Swedish log-jams). The procedures finally adopted were objectively specifiable and could easily be reproduced on a microcomputer.

The assessment process suggested that if we were willing to take the last census year, 1982, as our base year, there would be little trouble about the quality of demographic information. Besides the census data on age and sex structure of the population, available to a low level of geographical disaggregation, printouts were coming forward of birth registrations by age of mother and of deaths by age, sex, and condition. But problems, mainly of inconsistency, could be expected in the use of data on service utilization and of expenditure. The most serious are summarized in Table 4.1. How could they be overcome?

The circumstances of the project did not permit large scale independent data gathering. One constraint was budgetary; a sample household survey, for example, would have required more funds than were available for the whole project. Such a survey would also have widened the bureaucratic field in which approval for the form of the study must be sought, and probably

Table 4.1   Nature of administrative statistics on health service utilization and expenditure, Jamaica 1982.

Information category	Hospital in-patients	Hospital OP clinics	Hospital casualty	Health centres	Private doctors and hospitals
Service unit	Discharge, patient-days	New/total attendances	Attendances	First/all visits	—
Location	Point of service/ residence	--- Point of service ---			—
Condition/ nature of service	ICD	Specialty	—	MCH: nature of service other: ICD	—
Curative or preventive?	—	—	—	Clinic categories	—
Referrals; source, disposal	—	Source	Source, disposal	—	—
Publication lag for utilization data	1 yr	1 yr	1 yr	1/2 yr	—
Expenditure data	---- Budget by region ----			Budget by area	—

meant the sacrifice of other branches of the operation. But three ways were left to fill the information gap (Table 4.2):

(1) *small ad hoc surveys* of critical points (for example, the ratio of new to total attenders for hospital casualty departments, a ratio needed in order to translate attendances into 'episodes' of sickness; or in a different field, the distribution of hospital staff by department and grade);

(2) *accelerated or extended processing* of existing data (e.g. the results of a

Table 4.2 Action taken to supplement administrative statistics, Jamaica 1982.

Information category	Hospital in-patients	Hospital OP clinics	Hospital casualty	Health centres	Private doctors and hospitals
Translating service unit to episodes	NAR	NAR	Sample of new attenders	NAR	Assumed as for casualty and out-patients
Location	NAR	-- Assumed residence same -- as point of service			
Condition/ nature of service*	NAR	Distribution within specialty assumed as hospital IP	Sample of new attenders	NAR	
Curative or preventive?	------ Assumed curative ------			NAR	Assumed curative
Referrals; source, disposal	—	NAR	NAR	—	Estimated from Sample Survey 81
Publication lag	Analyse sample of 1982 discharges	—	—	—	—
Expenditure data	--- Hospital cost study ---			Estimated from BUS Survey 82	Estimated from Sample Survey 81

* Translation to modified form of International Classification of Diseases.

NAR   No action required.

Sample Survey 81. Health Consumer Survey 1981 (Planning and Evaluation Unit, Ministry of Health, Jamaica).

BUS Survey 82. World Bank, Jamaica Population Project, Building Utilisation Survey 1982 (Cumper *et al.* 1982).

household survey of health care carried out in 1981 were extensively reprocessed);

(3) *assumptions*, based on direct knowledge or local discussion, concerning the applicability of relationships beyond the field for which the data were originally intended (e.g. it was assumed that in hospital out-patient clinics the distribution of attenders by condition within each specialty was the same as for in-patients).

In this way it was possible to build up a set of estimates of the volume of health care for Jamaica in 1982 in terms of episodes of sickness (or other occasions of recourse to health care, such as pregnancy) classified by health condition involved, location (even if only whether rural or urban), institution involved (including the private sector), and in many cases the age and sex of the person concerned; and so associate these categories with appropriate demographic data on the one hand, and with estimates of expenditure on the other. From the complete set of estimates it is possible to select subsets to throw light on particular aspects of the working of the health care system, in the confidence that the data sets used for different purposes are consistent with one another. Some examples will illustrate how the estimates can be exploited.

Figure 4.1 shows the estimated flow of people seeking curative care

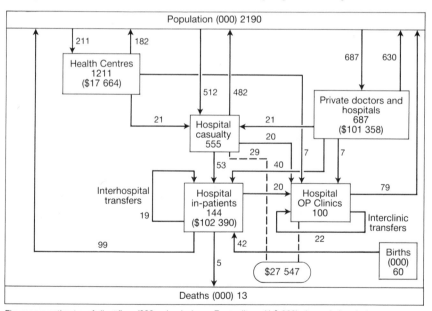

Figures are estimates of client flow (000 episodes)   Expenditure (J $ 000) shown in brackets

Fig. 4.1 Estimated client flows and institutional expenditure, curative services, Jamaica 1982.

through the health care system in 1982. The integrated form of presentation brings out features of the system which might easily be missed if the data were presented institution by institution; for example, the dominating role of the private sector as the point of first recourse, and the importance of hospital casualty departments at the hub of the referral system.

Table 4.3 shows estimates of the number of 'episodes' treated in each type of institution. Again, a consolidated presentation brings information which might otherwise be overlooked. For example, of an estimated 38 000 episodes of mental illness, only 1000 are represented by in-patients in Bellevue, the notorious (and ironically named) central mental hospital, against 3000 in-patients in general hospitals. This not only runs counter to the popular belief that mad people 'belong in Bellevue', but shows that events have long ago overtaken the stumbling efforts to implement the official policy of caring for the mentally ill 'in the community'.

Figure 4.2 shows estimates of the number of 'episodes' handled as in-patients by rural and urban hospitals, first in relation to the populations of the rural and urban areas, and secondly as a population rate after allowing for the referral of rural patients to urban hospitals. In the first case the differential in rates (57 rural as against 91 urban episodes per 1000 population) is more striking than in the second (57 as against 74). The first type of rate is that most often quoted to show the rural-urban resource imbalance in developing countries, but it is the second type of rate which gives a more

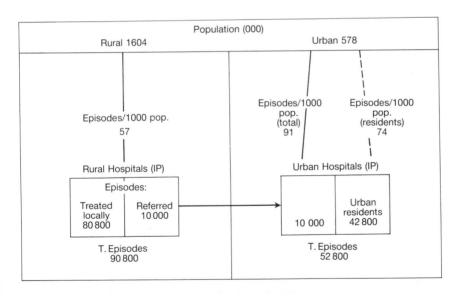

Fig. 4.2 Estimated urban and rural hospitalization rates, with and without referral between hospitals, Jamaica 1982.

Table 4.3   Jamaica 1982: Estimated health care utilization, by condition and institution.

('000 episodes)

Condition (disease, system)	Health Centres MCH	Health Centres curative	Hospital casualty	Hospital IP General	Hospital IP Special	OPD Clinics	Private GPs Hospitals	Total
Infectious and parasitic	15.5	4.2	65.2	8.3	1.9	3.9	67.5	166.5
Neoplasms	—	3.1	4.2	6.7	*	3.1	9.4	26.5
Endocrine, nutritional, metabolic	—	8.4	11.5	4.7	0.3	3.0	20.9	48.8
Blood, etc.	—	0.4	4.9	1.3	0.1	0.3	5.6	12.6
Mental	—	1.6	14.1	3.0	1.0	1.6	16.7	38.0
Nervous system, etc.	—	26.9	22.6	3.2	0.2	27.1	69.6	149.6
Circulatory	—	25.9	33.9	9.1	*	5.3	62.4	136.6
Respiratory	9.7	16.5	75.0	11.0	3.1	5.2	85.4	205.9
Digestive	—	7.6	14.7	11.0	0.3	7.7	27.7	69.0
Genito-urinary	—	6.8	37.8	12.3	0.2	9.7	48.2	115.0
Condition of pregnancy	—	5.5	11.0	37.7	15.6	5.6	18.9	94.3
Skin	—	30.3	42.7	1.9	0.2	5.2	73.2	153.5
Musculo-skeletal	—	7.2	5.4	1.9	*	7.2	17.6	39.3
Congenital anomalies	—	0.6	—	1.3	0.1	0.6	1.1	3.7
Perinatal conditions	—	0.7	—	1.5	0.4	0.7	1.3	4.6
Injuries, etc.	1.9	24.1	86.9	19.3	0.8	13.8	106.3	253.1
Other and unspecified	—	—	60.8	9.1	0.6	—	54.7	125.2
Total	27.1	169.8	490.7	143.3	24.8	100.0	686.5	1642.2

realistic idea of the rural-urban balance of amenity for the health services as a whole.

Finally, Table 4.4 shows estimates of the expenditure, curative and preventive, on each illness or condition. Not only is the total preventive expenditure small in relation to the curative component, but it is almost entirely confined to conditions connected with maternal and child health. The diseases which increasingly dominate mortality in Jamaica—metabolic (diabetes), circulatory, neoplasms—attract virtually no attention for preventive purposes. (Preventive expenditure here does not include health-related activities such as water supply and education; but this would not affect this particular comparison.)

4.1.3 Administrative statistics versus sample surveys

It has been suggested above that, in the Jamaican example and generally, one way of remedying the incompleteness and inconsistency of administrative statistics is by the use of sample surveys to get limited bodies of key

Table 4.4 Jamaica 1982: Estimated curative and preventive health care expenditure by condition.

Condition (disease, system)	Expenditure (J$ million)	
	Curative	Preventive
Infectious and parasitic	20.7	2.5
Neoplasms	9.7	—
Endocrine, nutritional, metabolic	11.9	0.6
Blood and blood forming organs	2.1	—
Mental disorders	6.9	—
Nervous system and sense organs	17.7	—
Circulatory	21.3	—
Respiratory	25.5	1.2
Digestive	14.5	—
Genito-urinary	19.9	—
Conditions of pregnancy	18.5	7.1
Skin	18.2	—
Musculo-skeletal	5.8	—
Congenital anomalies	1.4	—
Perinatal conditions	1.4	—
Injuries, etc.	39.0	0.7
Other and unspecified	14.4	1.5
Total	249.0	13.6

data—for example, the ratio of health centre visits to episodes (see, for example Borgdorf *et al.* 1988). To some statisticians, this may appear blasphemous; surely sample surveys should rank as a source of information in their own right, not as handmaidens to the administrative system?

The use of sample surveys to obtain population data on social and economic matters did not become commonplace until after the Second World War, though it built on much older foundations—classical probability statistics, and their application to experimental work in fields such as genetics and agronomy (there are still some of us around who learned our statistics from the early editions of Snedecor). In the early years the evident advantages of sample surveys for many purposes came as a Pauline revelation to many social scientists—the economy of sampling as against complete enumeration in large populations, the liberty to create links between characteristics (of persons, households, or communities) belonging to different social and economic fields, the independence of the investigator from the constraints of the administrative process. With time, in the developed countries the limitations of sample surveys became clearer and a *modus vivendi* has been established between administrative and sample-based statistics in most fields. In developing countries, with administrative statistics generally weaker and less representative, a stable balance has been slower to establish itself. In the health field, which in this as in so many respects stands at a slight angle to the rest of the universe, sample surveys have so far been confined successfully to an ancillary role. In the UK the report of a joint working group of the Korner Committee on Health Services Information and of the Faculty of Community Medicine (Knox 1987) set up to review the whole field of health care information, does not give them a single mention. But (particularly in developing countries) are we justified in assuming that this state of affairs will continue? If we want an appropriate, accurate, economical, and flexible database for health system enumeration, are we justified in taking administrative statistics as our starting point? Should not the evaluator, in particular, design and execute his own comprehensive sample survey?

It is easy to demonstrate that if we are interested in health care in general, and not simply the care provided by the official health services, we need information that cannot be generated from administrative statistics alone. Suppose we adhere to the kind of model of the health sector sketched in Section 4.1.1, in which the important variables are the transition frequencies between 'states' such as 'well', 'sick without treatment', 'under treatment' (for various conditions and in various types of health care institution), 'disabled' (to various degrees), and 'limbo' (into which the dead vanish and from which the newborn come—though we do not propose any Pythagorean relation between these two flows). Figure 4.3 shows schematically the boxes which have to be filled with data to make the model work. For simplicity,

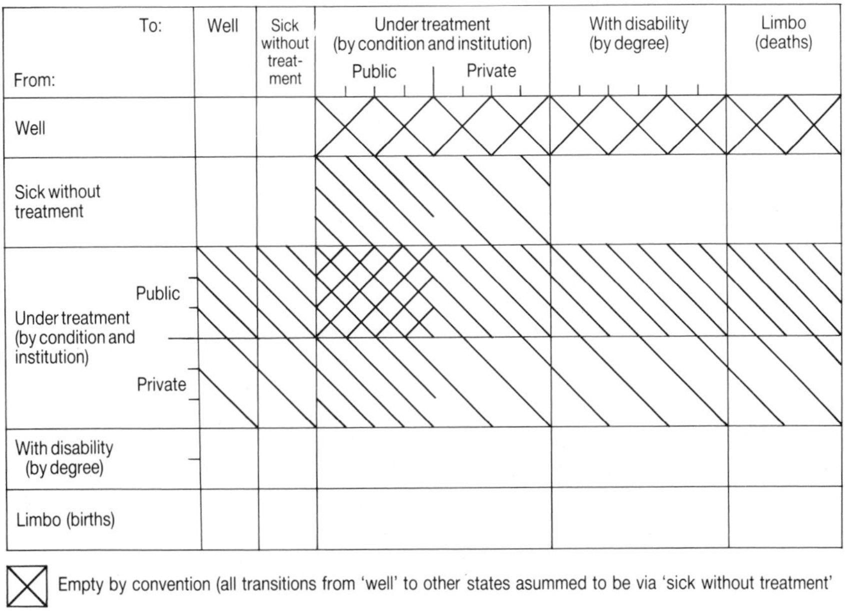

Fig. 4.3 Pattern of transitions between health states (curative) as framework for statistics.

only curative flows are shown; preventive health care would require a parallel representation.

One set of these boxes—those most heavily shaded—represents transitions within and between government institutions. This is the minimal area covered by standard hospital statistics, all these items of information springing naturally out of the administrative processes involved. It is the area in which administrative service statistics have the greatest comparative advantage over population censuses or surveys, though sampling of data— as against sampling of the population—may be useful to speed up data processing.

This central block can be extended vertically and horizontally by the elaboration of institutional data collection to cover the sources from which the admissions are derived and the states into which patients are discharged (in the diagram, the areas with the next heaviest shading). Here again, there is a comparative advantage in the use of administrative statistics.

This leaves unaccounted for a set of boxes (lightest shading) concerned with entry into and exit from private sector treatment, except in so far as this is already covered by implication through standard administrative data from public institutions (e.g. referrals from private to public hospitals).

This area could in principle be made an administrative concern by requiring that private practitioners and hospitals make minimal statistical returns about their clientele, directly or through intermediaries such as the providers of health insurance. The practicability of this will vary from country to country, and experience in developing countries suggests that the results are likely to be meagre and the cost in resources and in intra-professional conflict are likely to be high.

Finally, there remain some boxes, unshaded, relating to the 'well' population, those 'sick without treatment', and those 'disabled'. These are beyond the reach of administrative statistics (except perhaps for those forms of disability recorded in censuses and registers). Not surprisingly, this is the area which has received most attention in health interview surveys (Ross and Vaughan 1984; Teeling Smith 1988).

The field of health care information therefore divides naturally, like Gaul, into three parts; one where administrative statistics are the natural data source, one where they may need to be supplemented with population sample surveys, and one where such surveys are the only practicable recourse. In terms of the number of health events to be recorded, the balance between the three will depend on the health level of the country and the volume of health care provided by public and private institutions. Yet even if the share of public institutions in health care is small, there is still a strong argument for adapting the patterns of survey work to the conventions of administrative statistics rather than vice versa, so long as the ultimate purpose of the data is health sector management, planning, or evaluation by governmental agencies. For the administrative statistics reflect the form in which management decisions arise, and are the natural language of the health administrator.

To appreciate the strength of this consideration, it is worth taking a look at the history of statistics in a different social field—employment and unemployment. It is accepted in most countries that governments need an accurate and up-to-date estimate of the numbers of unemployed. Such an estimate can be obtained in two ways. One is through periodic sample surveys of the population. The other, only available in countries where unemployment involves administrative action (for example, the payment of unemployment benefit), is through the records of the agency concerned. The UK is an example of a country where both are available; sample data through the General Household Survey, and administrative data from records of the numbers of registered unemployed. Each approach has its own virtues. Labour force surveys permit a much fuller exploration of the different aspects of unemployment—as a loss of productive resources, as a cause of poverty and as a social stigma—and allow us to link unemployment (and employment) with other social characteristics such as level of education and household status. The data from the registration system serve as useful

indicators of unemployment as it varies over time and between administrative districts. Ideally, both kinds of data would be used to throw light on
the employment situation, with the survey results providing the analytic
framework for interpreting the registration data. The actual situation is
quite different. In Britain, public discussion of unemployment is dominated
by the numbers of the registered unemployed—an administrative statistic—
and any attempt to interpret this statistic in terms of survey data, or to
reconcile the two sources of information, tends to be seen as *lèse majesté*.
The situation is quite different in the United States, where unemployment
has no administrative significance at the federal level and therefore there
has been much greater reliance on the estimates provided by periodic labour
force surveys.

There are certainly irrational historical and political elements in the
British preoccupation with administrative statistics of unemployment.
Politicians, in particular, often seem like the man who was found searching
for his keys on the ground under a streetlamp. A helpful passer-by asked
'Are you sure you lost them here?' 'No' he replied, 'but where I lost them
there is no light to search by.' The availability of administrative statistics
may cause problems to be wrongly formulated simply to make maximum
use of the data available. But it is unlikely that administrative statistics of
unemployment would have been favoured for so long in Britain if there was
not a more solid reason—that they reflect the form in which decisions
currently arise. This, in the health field, provides a justification for shaping
population surveys, so far as possible, in the same terms as are used in
standard service statistics—or, where this is not possible, building bridges
between the two.

4.1.4 Data comparisons over time and space

It is a truism that an item of data gains disproportionately in usefulness if it
can be compared with corresponding items from other times and other
places. To the numerically minded investigator, there is nothing so mouth-
watering as a long statistical series, unless it is the availability of comparable
data from many regions or institutions, or (at the international level) from
many countries; data which are comparable over both time and space send
such an investigator into a seventh heaven. Examples of the exploitation of
comparisons over time and space are given in the following sections.
However, there are certain pitfalls in such comparisons which need to be
kept in mind. They can be labelled as the 'noise' problem, the 'systems'
problem, and the 'mote in the eye' problem.

If we wish to extract meaning from a time series—say, the number of
deaths, year by year, from a particular condition, or the number of admissions to a particular hospital—an obvious approach is to look for a trend

(the 'signal') which has to be separated from random and non-random fluctuations or 'noise'. Standard regression techniques can be used to separate the two elements; but these techniques work best when the time series is a long one and the noise is truly random. In the health field, particularly in developing countries, time series are often short—ten years or less—and the deviations from the trend may incorporate large non-random elements such as changes in the efficiency of reporting and in the classification of health conditions. For example, in Burma the introduction of ration cards for rice in the 1960s produced reluctance among the population to admit to the death of a household member and a sharp fall in the apparent death rate. Under these circumstances, too much enthusiasm for extracting the maximum information from the data may lead to conclusions which interpret as a meaningful signal what is simply short-term noise. (The same applies, *mutatis mutandis*, to comparisons between regions and countries.) The temptation to do this is especially strong in crisis situations or in matters which have a political content. For example, in the early years of the UK National Health Service a conservative American presidential candidate argued that since the UK's crude death rate was higher in the year following the establishment of the NHS than in the year before, this demonstrated the inferiority of socialized medicine. (Harold Stassen was not otherwise unintelligent; the issue of Reader's Digest in which he put forth this argument has not been traced, but the writer has never forgotten the shock of meeting so naive an argument from so sensible a politician.)

There is another reason why we should be cautious in the use of trends identified from time-series data. A trend, in the context of health planning, is an invitation to extrapolate—to assume, for example, that the rate of growth of a variable in the future will be the same as in the past. This is often a permissible simplification for key variables which have their own momentum in the real world, but in the case of variables which are tightly bound into a complex causal 'system' it can lead to nonsense results. It would be wrong, for example, to assume that because a nation's spending on health care has grown from 5 per cent of national income ten years ago to 10 per cent today, in ten years' time it will have reached 15 per cent—because of the nature of the relationship between health spending, other forms of expenditure and national income, this variable cannot be meaningfully extrapolated simply in terms of its own past performance.

The 'mote in the eye' problem is so named here in memory of James Thurber and his attempts to pass freshman biology—in particular, to adjust his microscope to see the amoebae which his instructor assured him were there. After a series of settings which showed only a blur, he found one which filled the field with convincing animulculae, and proudly reported it to his instructor. 'Idiot' said the latter, 'you have set the mirror to reflect! That is your own eye!' The statistical equivalent of setting the microscope to reflect one's own eye is the extraction from the data, often by long and ingenious analysis, of the assumptions that the analyst or others have built in. In developing countries particularly, the greater the apparent span of data over time or across space, the greater is the likelihood that at some point gaps in the data have been filled by estimation. If the data are to be used safely, it is important to know the assumptions on which such estimates have been based. For example, it is of some interest to know whether the recession of 1975–85 has been accompanied by increases in infant mortality rates in the poorest countries. Material for such an investigation of this point appears to be available in such sources as the 'World Tables' (World Bank 1983), and would suggest a highly optimistic conclusion—mortality rates appear to have continued their secular decline well into the 1980s. It has been shown, however, that the procedures used by the international agencies concerned to fill gaps in the mortality record for poor countries are based squarely on the assumption of such a continuing decline. The evidential value of the resulting data for testing this assumption is therefore zero.

4.2 Sources of information on health care events

This section reviews the sources of quantitative information on the flows of clients through the health care system in developing countries. It deals first with the standard data sources in four separate areas—service statistics, demography, epidemiology, and geography; then with data (still of fairly standard types) which represent links between these areas; and finally with possible ways of estimating the size of flows which fall outside the scope of the standard system. Many of the examples under the latter head are taken from WHO's Country Health Programming work in Bangladesh in 1976–7.

The reader is warned that this section is dull but worthy. Furthermore, to those who are specialists in the areas covered it may seem intolerably brief and superficial, while to others it may appear dense and cryptic. The aim is to give a *tour d'horizon* of the data sources needed as a foundation for objective health system evaluation.

4.2.1 *Service and utilization statistics*

At their simplest, service statistics represent a head count of the numbers of persons attending a health care facility day by day, summed over whatever period and whatever grouping of facilities is most convenient for administrative purposes. They gain most of their significance for purposes of evaluation when they are related to the demographic, epidemiological, and geographical background in the ways described in the following sequences, and to the inputs required to produce the services in question as described in a later section.

Some service statistics are available even in the poorest countries, most commonly for hospitals, where they are usually linked to measures of capacity (such as bed complement) to provide statistics for utilization. They become more meaningful when they are broken down according to the main administrative-cum-medical departments of the hospital (out-patients, by type of clinic; casualty, in-patients, by specialty; service departments such as pharmacy, X-ray, and operating theatre). Service statistics for health centres and health posts are less universal, and are more difficult to make meaningful through comparisons with capacity or through internal break-downs, though the numbers attending various types of clinic may be available.

Even at the simplest level, service statistics offer some common limitations and difficulties of interpretation. One is the fact that they usually cover only public facilities, and sometimes not all of these. It cannot be assumed that the facilities providing information are typical of the rest, but if data are hard to come by there may be a real temptation to extrapolate from the admirable statistics of a tertiary teaching hospital to all hospitals, or to assume that the often-visited demonstration health centre a convenient twenty kilometers from the capital city is typical of other rural facilities.

Another difficulty is created by the fact that the natural unit for service statistics is the contact of a client with the institution. If our interest is centred on the client, rather than the facility, we are likely to be as much interested in the number of episodes of sickness for which the client receives service as in the number of contacts. An episode may obviously involve several contacts, not necessarily with the same institution.

Hence the need, not always met, to record referrals from one facility to another, and to record the number of new contacts, each of which can be taken as initiating an episode. (To compound the confusion, it may be administratively convenient to define a new contact in terms of whether the client has previously used the facility during the current year or other accounting period, which weakens the link between 'new contacts' and episodes.)

4.2.2   Demographic statistics

Demographic statistics are important to health systems evaluation both because they provide the reference populations to which service and epi-demiological information must be related, and because two demographic events, births and deaths, are linked directly to the demand for health care. The elements of a good basic demographic system include regular censuses of the population giving its age, sex, and geographical structure; an effective registration system for births and deaths, and the recording of inward and outward migration; and procedures for combining these to permit the construction of population profiles for the intercensal years and their projection into the future at the level of the nation and of its main administrative divisions. Many other kinds of data—marriage rates, occupations, numbers of internal migrants, etc.—can be incorporated into the system, but for the purposes of health evaluation in developing countries these must be classed as 'nice to know'; the basic demographic information is a 'need to know'.

Since long before the days of Caesar Augustus, colonial administrators have recognized the importance of demographic information, so that it is perhaps not surprising that many developing countries have effective census and registration systems, in some cases with considerable historical depth. In the Commonwealth Caribbean, for example, usable vital statistics are available since the 1880s. But there are still some developing countries where the demographic system is seriously defective, and unfortunately these tend to be the very countries where health conditions cause most concern. In some sub-Saharan African countries poverty, war, and forced migration have prevented regular census-taking and registration of vital events, and demographic statistics have to be constructed on the basis of obsolete population totals and of estimates of key variables (such as infant mortality rates) which are based on small, perhaps unrepresentative sample surveys. This situation may not be apparent to the international observer because of the virtuosity with which demographers have developed methods of estimation to fill the gaps—for example, through the application of standard regional models to infer the values of missing items. It is salutary to note how many African populations are shown in international statistical publications to have identical life expectancies. Such estimation has a useful function on the world scale, but it does not provide satisfactory material for detailed national planning.

On the other hand, methods of estimation are available for inferring birth and death rates from census data which have value for planning and evaluation purposes at the national and even provincial level. For example, death rates for most age groups can often be inferred from a comparison of the numbers in a given cohort at successive censuses. For this reason, and because of their general usefulness outside the health field, censuses in the poorest countries probably have a higher priority in statistical development than registration systems.

4.2.3 Epidemiological statistics

Epidemiological information is clearly fundamental to any attempt to evaluate health care. Ideally, one would wish to know what diseases are found in the population, as well as those emergent diseases (like AIDS or haemorrhagic dengue) likely to establish themselves in the future; what are the mechanisms of occurrence and transmission; how many cases connected with each disease are found at each stage of the progression from health, through sickness and care, to restoration to full or partial health, or to death; and how widespread are the social and economic factors which influence the prevalence and severity of each disease. One would also like to have equivalent information for the problem areas which cannot be labelled as diseases—for example, pregnancy and child development—with emphasis on the distribution of degrees of positive health, rather than a simple dichotomy of presence or absence of disease (see, for example Teeling Smith 1988).

Of this ideal catalogue of information, only a small part is commonly on order in developing countries. For virtually all the diseases of importance the relevant biological mechanisms are known and can be assumed to operate in the same way in all countries—though in some cases this assumption may merely reflect our ignorance. It is salutary to remember that malaria, the best studied 'tropical' disease, is still producing tactical surprises—new vectors, emerging forms of resistance to insecticides and drugs. Similarly, recent studies in India have cast doubt on the effectiveness of the tuberculosis vaccines well established in the West (ICMR 1980; WHO 1983). It is salutary also to remember that it is only a generation since the received wisdom regarded milk and animal protein as the key elements in improving nutrition in poor countries; the US senator who earned opprobrium from liberals by opposing 'sending milk to Hottentots' may have been wiser than they knew. There may, then, still be unsuspected weakness in the biological and medical foundation for epidemiological information— particularly, perhaps, in the application to developing countries of criteria established in the developed world for the so-called Western diseases which are becoming of importance in the healthier countries of the Third World. How, for example, do West Indian women live comfortably with levels of systolic blood pressure which would set an English GP reaching for his prescription pad, at the least (see, for example Grell 1978, 1982)? But on the whole, traditional epidemiological models serve developing countries reasonably well.

If we wish to assign numbers to the population affected by each disease or health problem, the situation is much less satisfactory. Generally, it is only when diseases bring clients into contact with formal health care—a hospital discharging a patient or a doctor certifying a death—that their epidemiological status is regularly recorded. If our classification of diseases is to be based on professional diagnosis, there is an obvious and valid reason for this. But it is only in those developing countries where formal health care is available to a substantial part of the population that figures so derived can be taken as representative of the national epidemiological situation. There is a special danger to the unwary investigator in the deaths-by-cause data of countries where many deaths are not certified but which nevertheless use the full panoply of the International Classification of Diseases for their publications. In such cases a high proportion of deaths will be put down to such uninformative categories as 'senility' and 'ill-defined causes'. (Sometimes, however, it is plausible to redistribute these categories *pro rata* for each age group among the specific causes of death.)

There are various ways in which these constraints can be evaded. One is by acceptance of less rigorous, partly symptom-based diagnoses, an approach which seems to work well for India's sample certification of deaths under the Model Registration Scheme, and can also be useful for health centres and health posts. Other possible sources of epidemiological data are notification schemes and special studies of the prevalence of individual diseases, and, in rare cases, comprehensive health interview surveys of the population. None of these can be regarded as standard sources, and in many cases they may require judgemental adjustment in the light of local conditions before they can be used.

There would probably be wide agreement that it is desirable ideally to extend the concept of health beyond its narrow meaning of the absence of specific diseases to something more positive, and for evaluation purposes this seems to call for a quantitative measure of the extent to which members of a population are able to fulfil their physiological potential. In practice in developing countries there appear to be only two very partial measures in this field which are common enough to be called standard sources of information. One is a count (or sample-based estimate) of the numbers of people who suffer from specific disabilities such as blindness. The other is an estimate (again sample-based) of the distribution in the child population of measures of stature (height and weight for age), usually interpreted as a measure of the nutritional status of the population.

What of the social and economic factors which have such a demonstrable effect on the epidemiological situation in developing countries? The most important of these by general consensus are individual incomes, housing, education, and water supply. Indicators for the last three are included in many population censuses (often with data on other useful variables such as marital status and occupation), and usually remain valid for some years. Hence in these cases the census may be regarded as a standard source, even though better and more up-to-date information may be available in particular countries from special surveys or from administrative statistics. Individual or household incomes in developing countries are notoriously difficult to measure accurately, even through specialized income and expenditure surveys (and hence for statistically underdeveloped countries published indexes of income distribution should be regarded with grave suspicion (McGranahan and Hong 1979). A broad indication of average levels of income can be obtained from national income estimates, but not in a form suitable for epidemiological analysis. Realistically, it has to be said that for this important item there is no standard source.

4.2.4   *Geographical information*

While geographers may fairly claim that any kind of information that can be given in a spatial frame of reference is geographic, the main inputs into health evaluation from their discipline are maps of the conventional kinds, covering topography, settlements, communications, administrative boundaries, and population densities. Partly because colonial administrators gave mapping as high a priority as census-taking, maps of the first four kinds are widely available in developing countries, though varying in scale and up-to-dateness. Ideally, one would wish to use a range of scales, from, say, 1:50 000 for local work to whatever scale is practicable for showing the whole country. (If there are gaps in the range, it may be possible to fill them by using ingenuity and a photocopier with reduction and enlargement facilities.) Obsolescence of maps is not usually a serious problem for topography, but it may be so for settlements, communications, and administrative boundaries. In particular, the boundaries of cities (*de jure* and *de facto*) in developing countries can change substantially over a span of a few years.

Up-to-date maps of population distribution are usually obtained by marrying topographical maps with the results of a population census. This is made easier by the fact that censuses are usually organized on the basis of small topographically defined areas, but even so the plotting of the populations of census districts is a substantial undertaking for large countries and the resources needed are not always made available. This is unfortunate since the results are a basic tool for health planning and evaluation.

4.2.5   *Crossbreeding service statistics with other data*

The information base for health system evaluation becomes much stronger if data from each of the above categories—service statistics, and demographic, epidemiological, and geographical data—can be brought to bear on a single problem. Information from the standard sources is often presented so as to take advantage of this fact. However, such crossbreeding of categories brings its own problems. As in the animal world, it may generate hybrid vigour if the matching is appropriate, or chimaeras and non-viable or sterile forms if it is not.

The linking of service statistics with epidemiological categories—for example, the presentation of hospital discharges by condition—presents few problems since both types of information are generated within the same institutions. Difficulties arise when service or epidemiological information is to be related to demographic or geographical variables—for example, through the comparison from hospital to hospital of annual discharge rates per thousand of the population. The general shape of the provision of health care is that providers are concentrated while their clients are dispersed, and that the universe of clients can be divided on geographical lines into catchment areas, within each of which the great majority of clients relate to a single facility. How are these catchment areas to be defined?

The commonest approach to this problem is to say, in effect, that the catchment area of a facility is the administrative unit with which it is organizationally associated—that, for example, the catchment area of a district hospital is its district. This works well enough where the district is a well-defined geographical unit and both facilities and population are widely dispersed. Where these conditions are not met, administrative definitions of catchment areas may be unsatisfactory. In Jamaica, for example, an analysis of residence data for hospital discharges has shown that catchment areas do not always coincide with local government boundaries, that there is considerable interpenetration between neighbouring catchment populations, and that the size of catchment area differs with the level of service provided, being much wider for tertiary and specialized hospitals than general hospitals. In the Jamaican case it was possible to construct workable catchment areas in terms of 'Thyssen polygons'—polygons whose sides represent points equidistant between neighbouring hospitals of a given grade—and to calculate the populations of these areas from census data on population distribution; the results clearly showed the unequal distribution of hospital in-patient services. In other cases, different methods of defining catchment areas, perhaps on a more judgmental basis, may be appropriate. Whatever the method adopted, it is likely to require basic data on population distribution for units considerably smaller than the major administrative units of most developing countries to permit aggregation into catchment areas for different types of institutions and the relation of one to another.

4.2.6 *Statistical improvisation in Bangladesh*

In 1967 the government of Bangladesh sought the assistance of the World Health Organization in drawing up a plan for the health sector using WHO's Country Health Programming procedure. An important preliminary step in applying this procedure was the assembly and analysis of existing information on health care in Bangladesh. The war of 1970–71 which had established the country's independence from Pakistan had badly disrupted the administrative and statistical system; of the standard sources of national information covered by subsections 4.2.1–4.2.5 above, all that was available and up-to-date was a population census carried out in 1974. Methods for filling some of the gaps were prescribed within the Country Health Programming process (e.g. the identification of priority health problems through professional consensus), but it would obviously be of value to have in advance even a rough idea of the incidence of and mortality from different conditions. This justified some experiments in the kind of statistical improvisation called in French 'bricolage'.

The obvious place to look for indicators of the health situation in Bangladesh was over the country's border with India, in the states of Orissa, Assam, Bihar, and West Bengal. The latter state, in particular, was believed to be similar to Bangladesh in physical, demographic, social, and economic terms except for the greater importance of its urban population. This was of course due to the presence of the megalopolis of Calcutta, whose representatives sometimes referred to Dhaka, the capital of Bangladesh, as a village—unkindly, but at that time not altogether unjustly. While quantitative health information for the Indian states was imperfect, it was substantially better than in Bangladesh at that period. The most useful information came from the Model Registration Scheme (under which a sample of deaths were classified by cause using partly symptom-based categories) and the utilization statistics for West Bengal health centres and hospitals.

The distribution of *mortality* in Bangladesh was estimated by taking the breakdown of deaths by cause and broad age group for the four neighbouring Indian states in 1972 and applying it to the total number of deaths in Bangladesh as estimated from the census population and the best available estimates of the Crude Death Rate (19.4 per thousand population) and the Infant Mortality Rate (140.1 per thousand live births). This entailed some manipulation of the MRS categories to bring them onto a basis consistent with the International Classification of Diseases; procedures for this had been developed in earlier work with the MRS data, which had bred a confidence in the Scheme without which the extrapolation to Bangladesh would not have been justified. Table 4.5 shows the resulting estimate of the distribution of deaths by cause and age group in 1975. A feature of the distribution which appeared mildly suprising at the time was the small part played in mortality by some of the classic 'tropical' and immunizable diseases—cholera, whooping cough, leprosy, polio, measles, rabies, malaria—compared with respiratory and diarrhoeal diseases. The only immunizable diseases for which mortality estimates justify their traditional status are diphtheria and tetanus (which accounts for 10 per cent of infant deaths). Experience suggests that in this respect the estimates are realistic, at least in the context of South-East Asia. Indeed the recognition of this

Table 4.5 Bangladesh 1975. Estimated percentage distribution of total mortality by cause, for broad age groups.

ICD A List 1955		Percentage mortality—total, and by age groups			
		0	1–14	15 +	All ages
1	TB of respiratory system	0.1	1.6	7.0	3.3
12–13	Typhoid and paratyphoid	1.4	7.0	4.6	4.0
16	Dysentery	5.6	13.8	6.3	7.7
21	Diptheria	0.8	2.7	2.2	1.8
26	Tetanus	9.7	2.5	1.3	4.5
39–42	Helminthic diseases	n.a.	n.a.	n.a.	0.8
(43)	Scabies	n.a.	n.a.	n.a.	—
64	Avitaminoses	n.a.	n.a.	n.a.	1.7
65	Anaemias	n.a.	n.a.	n.a.	3.3
70	Vascular lesions, C.N.S.	0.3	0.2	2.1	1.1
(78)	Other conditions of nervous system	n.a.	n.a.	n.a.	2.1
74–6,(78)	Eye conditions	n.a.	n.a.	n.a.	0.1
79–86	Heart conditions	n.a.	n.a.	n.a.	3.9
87–97	Respiratory conditions	16.9	20.6	6.1	12.9
104	Gastro-enteritis	5.0	9.8	4.3	5.7
99–103,106–10	Other conditions	n.a.	n.a.	n.a.	6.4
115–20	Conditions of pregnancy and childbirth	—	—	4.0	1.8
124(126)	Skin conditions	0.1	0.7	1.7	0.9
132	Infections of new born	4.4	—	—	1.5
131,133–5	Other infant diseases and immaturity	22.4	—	—	7.7
136	Senility	—	—	16.1	7.1
138–50	Accidents and violence	1.0	5.7	7.1	4.7
	Total above	67.7	64.6	62.8	83.0
14	Cholera	0.6	1.8	0.6	0.9
22	Whooping cough	0.1	0.3	0.1	1.4
25	Leprosy	n.a.	n.a.	n.a.	0.2
28–30	Poliomyelitis	0.1	0.3	0.4	0.3
32	Measles	0.6	1.7	0.2	0.7
35	Rabies	—	0.7	0.5	0.4
37	Malaria	0.1	0.4	0.1	0.2

n.a.   Not available.

situation helps to account for the importance now attached to basic primary health care.

For *hospital morbidity and mortality* the main data source was a report on the state of health of West Bengal for 1966–7. The conditions in the ICD 1955 A List were grouped to give 60 categories, and the breakdown of admissions and deaths by these categories was calculated for five broad age groups. Since West Bengal is more urbanized than Bangladesh, an adjustment was made by applying to each condition a factor based on the number of admissions and deaths occurring outside the district of Calcutta. The breakdown so obtained was applied to an estimate of the total number of admissions to Bangladesh hospitals about 1975; this estimate assumed 15 000 beds and 30 patients per bed-year. In-patient deaths were estimated by applying the West Bengal case fatality rates to the estimated number of hospital admissions by cause. The results are shown in Tables 4.6 and 4.7.

The same source and procedures were used for estimates of *hospital and health centre out-patient visits*, except that no breakdown by age was possible. On the basis of fragmentary data, the number of out-patients attending hospitals in Bangladesh was estimated at 4 million per year, and the number attending rural health centres was estimated at 8 million. The results are shown in Table 4.8.

For health planning purposes it would be desirable to have some estimate for the distribution of *population morbidity* between different conditions. This would serve as an indicator of the total potential demand for health care which it is the ultimate object of the planner to meet. Where, as in Bangladesh, hospital admissions and out-patient visits account for only a small percentage of episodes requiring health care, their distribution is a very poor guide to population morbidity. The numbers seeking care for a particular condition represent an interaction between many factors, including distance from a health care provider, cost and severity of the health problem; and these factors will have different weights from one condition to another. It seems reasonable to suppose that if we imagine the availability of health care expanding from a small core of hospital facilities to a wider and wider system of health centres and other dispersed facilities, we must think of diseases of less and less severity being brought into the net according to some consistent trend. If we have some measure of severity, and if we have data on utilization at two points during this expansion—say, the number of hospital admissions and the number of visits to a restricted system of health centres, as in the Bangladesh estimates above—it should be possible to extrapolate the demand pattern to any given degree of population coverage. A plausible candidate as a measure of severity is the Case Fatality Rate in hospitals, which was known for West Bengal. Table 4.9 shows that there was in fact a consistent relation between the CFR and the ratio of in-patient to out-patient numbers. This relationship was used to extrapolate

Table 4.6   Bangladesh 1975. Estimated percentage distribution of hospital in-patient admissions by cause, for broad age groups.

ICD A List		Percentage in-patient admissions by age groups			
1955		0	1–14	15+	All ages
1	TB of respiratory system	0.3	0.6	2.0	1.7
12–13	Typhoid and paratyphoid	0.2	5.1	1.1	1.7
16	Dysentery	2.2	3.0	2.9	2.9
21	Diptheria	2.9	4.7	0.1	0.8
26	Tetanus	22.7	5.2	0.8	2.1
39–42	Helminthic diseases	0.3	2.4	0.8	1.0
(43)	Scabies	0.1	0.2	*	0.1
64	Avitaminoses	0.6	2.5	0.4	0.8
65	Anaemias	0.2	2.4	2.4	2.3
70	Vascular lesions, C.N.S.	—	—	0.6	0.5
(78)	Other conditions of nervous system	1.7	2.0	0.7	0.9
74–6,(78)	Eye conditions	0.4	1.1	3.0	2.6
79–86	Heart conditions	0.1	1.8	2.6	2.3
87–97	Respiratory conditions	14.6	9.7	3.6	4.8
104	Gastro-enteritis	9.7	5.3	2.0	2.7
99–103,106–10	Other conditions of stomach, etc.	2.9	4.4	6.6	6.2
115–20	Conditions of pregnancy and childbirth	—	—	38.3	32.0
124(126)	Skin conditions	2.2	2.5	1.8	1.9
132	Infections of new born	2.7	—	—	0.1
131,133–5	Other infant diseases and immaturity	19.0	—	—	0.6
136	Senility	—	—	*	*
138–50	Accidents and violence	3.1	20.7	10.1	11.4
	Total above	85.9	73.6	79.8	79.4
14	Cholera	0.2	0.3	0.1	0.1
22	Whooping cough	0.2	0.1	*	*
25	Leprosy	—	—	0.1	0.1
28–30	Poliomyelitis	0.2	0.2	*	*
32	Measles	0.3	0.5	*	0.1
35	Rabies	—	0.3	0.1	0.1
37	Malaria	—	0.2	0.1	0.1

* Less than 0.05%.

Table 4.7   Bangladesh 1975. Estimated percentage distribution of in-patient mortality by cause, for broad age groups.

ICD A	List	Percentage mortality— in-patients by age groups			
1955		0	1–14	15 +	All ages
1	TB of respiratory system	0.1	0.6	6.3	4.2
12–13	Typhoid and paratyphoid	0.1	2.1	1.2	1.3
16	Dysentery	1.5	3.9	4.0	3.6
21	Diptheria	0.3	7.4	*	2.1
26	Tetanus	29.9	12.9	4.9	10.0
39–42	Helminthic diseases	0.1	3.2	0.5	1.0
(43)	Scabies	—	—	—	—
64	Avitaminoses	0.3	4.1	1.9	2.1
65	Anaemias	0.3	3.4	5.3	4.2
70	Vascular lesions, C.N.S.	—	—	4.4	2.9
(78)	Other conditions of nervous system	0.3	5.4	1.8	2.7
74–6,(78)	Eye conditions	0.2	0.3	*	0.1
79–86	Heart conditions	0.1	1.4	7.4	5.1
87–97	Respiratory conditions	10.1	9.6	2.4	4.7
104	Gastro-enteritis	9.1	5.5	2.8	4.9
99–103,106–10	Other conditions	3.6	5.9	10.0	8.2
115–20	Conditions of pregnancy and childbirth	—	—	11.1	7.1
124(126)	Skin conditions	0.6	0.6	0.5	0.5
132	Infections of new born	3.5	—	—	0.5
131,133–5	Other infant diseases and immaturity	24.1	—	—	3.2
136	Senility	—	—	0.1	0.1
138–50	Accidents and violence	1.6	13.3	13.6	11.9
	Total above	85.8	82.6	78.2	80.4
14	Cholera	0.2	0.7	0.2	0.3
22	Whooping cough	*	*	—	*
25	Leprosy	—	—	0.5	0.3
28–30	Poliomyelitis	0.3	0.5	0.1	0.2
32	Measles	0.2	0.3	*	0.1
35	Rabies	—	0.9	0.4	0.4
37	Malaria	—	0.1	*	*

* Less than 0.05%.

Table 4.8 Bangladesh 1975. Estimated percentage distribution of out-patient visits by cause.

ICD A	List	Out-patients
1955		All ages
1	TB of respiratory system	0.4
12–13	Typhoid and paratyphoid	0.8
16	Dysentery	9.8
21	Diptheria	*
26	Tetanus	*
39–42	Helminthic diseases	1.8
(43)	Scabies	8.3
64	Avitaminoses	2.6
65	Anaemias	2.2
70	Vascular lesions, C.N.S.	*
(78)	Other conditions of nervous system	1.0
74–6,(78)	Eye conditions	4.1
79–86	Heart conditions	1.1
87–97	Respiratory conditions	22.4
104	Gastro-enteritis	3.0
99–103,106–10	Other conditions	11.7
115–20	Conditions of pregnancy and childbirth	0.5
124(126)	Skin conditions	6.0
132	Infections of new born	*
131,133–5	Other infant diseases and immaturity	*
136	Senility	*
138–50	Accidents and violence	5.8
	Total above	81.5
14	Cholera	*
22	Whooping cough	0.4
25	Leprosy	0.1
28–30	Poliomyelitis	*
32	Measles	0.2
35	Rabies	0.1
37	Malaria	0.1

* Less than 0.05%.

Table 4.9   Estimation of distribution of population morbidity, Bangladesh, 1975.

W. Bengal in-patient CFR/1000	Condition	No. in-patients	No. out-patients	Ratio IP/OP	Estimated ratio, Population Morbidity/ out-patients	Estimate no. contacts Population Morbidity ('000)
0–99	Venereal diseases	100	23 800			746
	Pertussis	10	51 800			1 624
	Malaria	370	12 800			401
	Scabies	350	999 600			31 337
	Other infectious and parasitic diseases	11 360	268 300			8 411
	Neoplasms	4 440	139 700			4 380
	Psychosis, etc.	1 560	7 200			226
	Eye conditions	11 850	490 000			15 361
	Ear conditions	390	370 000			11 599
	Conditions of teeth, etc.	1 090	459 600			14 408
	Other genito-urinary diseases	15 000	213 400			6 690
	Abortion	7 190	11 700			367
	Skin conditions	8 670	722 000			22 635
	Total	62 390	3 769 900	60.42	31.35	118 186

100–199	Typhoid	7 650	100 300			2 679
	Dysentery	13 290	1 180 300			31 526
	Measles	400	19 500			521
	Helminthic diseases	4 740	213 400			5 700
	Asthma	3 700	238 900			6 381
	Respiratory diseases	21 710	2 681 400			71 620
	Accidents	51 620	699 700			18 689
	Total	103 100	5 143 500	49.93	26.71	137 367
200–299	Hepatitis	1 530	13 400			281
	Goitre, etc.	10	59 800			1 256
	Anaemias	10 480	268 400			5 636
	Gastro-enteritis	12 140	361 100			7 583
	Other skin conditions	28 070	1 399 300			29 385
	Hypoplasia of prostate	550	700			15
	Senility	160	2 300			48
	Total	56 340	2 110 800	37.50	21.00	44 323
300–399	Pulmonary TB	7 800	47 600			619
	Cholera	560	2 600			34
	Diptheria	3 800	4 100			53
	Avitaminoses	3 810	312 600			4 064
	Diseases of blood	360	98 100			1 275
	Heart conditions	10 460	132 200			1 719
	Pregnancy-sepsis	810	8 000			104
	Congenital malformations	750	1 400			18
	Total	28 940	613 200	21.19	13.00	7 972

Table 4.9 (*cont.*)

W. Bengal in-patient CFR/1000	Condition	No. in-patients	No. out-patients	Ratio IP/OP	Estimated ratio, Population Morbidity/out-patients	Estimate no. contacts Population Morbidity ('000)
400–499	Other TB	2 250	13 500			116
	Septicaemia	430	4 600			40
	Leprosy	520	15 600			134
	Diseases of nervous system	4 200	117 100			1 009
	Pregnancy—toxaemia	4 660	6 000			52
	Total	12 060	156 800	13.00	8.62	1 352
500–599	Cirrhosis	1 930	5 600	2.90	2.45	14
600 +	Tetanus	9 570	2 600			4
	Poliomyelitis	210	1 300			2
	Rabies	350	7 900			11
	VLCNS	2 450	3 000			4
	Birth injuries	70	800			1
	Infections of newborn	390	1 500			2
	Other MT conditions	2 730	5 300			7
	Total	15 770	22 400	1.42	1.34	30
	All Total	280 530	11 822 200	(42.14)	(23.16)	309 244

for each condition the number of episodes which would require health care provision if total utilization were at a level of 4 episodes per person per year—a level chosen as the maximum likely to be attained in a developing country. The procedure used was as follows:

let $p_0, p_1 \ldots p_n$ = number of out-patients in disease groups with CFRs of 0–, 100–, etc. in Table 4.9

$r_0, r_1 \ldots r_n$ = ratio of out-patients to in-patients for each CFR group in Table 4.9

I = estimated number of health care contacts from all causes

then $I = p_0 (r_0 x) + p_1 (r_1 x) \ldots$
$= \Sigma p_i r_i^x$

where x is a number to be determined.

Assuming the number of health care contacts from all causes is 4 per capita per year, and using the values of p_1, r_1 from Table 4.9, x has a value of 0.84. The resulting values of the estimated ratio of population morbidity to number of out-patient visits for each CFR group $(r_1^{0.84})$ are shown in column 6 of Table 4.9, and the estimated number of contacts for each condition is shown in column 7. The resulting all-age percentage distribution of population morbidity by condition, with the corresponding distribution for in-patient and out-patient numbers and for population mortality, is shown in Table 4.10.

Were these statistical experiments justified? In Bangladesh they had a limited function—to provide a temporary framework which could be modified during the CHP process in the light of professional opinion and of the results of further information from special surveys, and superseded as the health information system was developed. Nevertheless, hindsight shows that they correctly represented the main features of the epidemiological situation, such as the much greater importance of diarrhoeal and respiratory diseases in population morbidity than could have been deduced from institutional data. But such experiments may have a longer term value for planning and evaluation in countries (hopefully fewer and fewer) where no alternative estimates are available.

4.3 Sources of information on health care resources

For the purposes of planning and evaluation, the flow of clients through the health care system, for which the information sources were reviewed in the last section, needs to be linked with the flow of health care resources. Data on resources, in its primitive state, differs in kind from data on the flow of

Table 4.10 Distribution by condition, Bangladesh 1975. Hospital in-patients, out-patients (including health centres). Population mortality, population morbidity (%).

ICD A List 1955	Condition	Percentage distribution of:			
		In-patients	Out-patients	Population mortality	Population morbidity
1	TB of respiratory system	1.7	4.2	0.2	3.3
12–13	Typhoid and paratyphoid	1.7	1.3	4.0	0.9
16	Dysentery	2.9	3.6	7.7	10.2
21	Diptheria	0.8	2.1	1.8	*
26	Tetanus	2.1	10.0	4.5	*
39–42	Helminthic diseases	1.0	1.0	0.8	1.8
(43)	Scabies	0.1	—	—	10.1
64	Avitaminoses	0.8	2.1	1.7	1.3
65	Anaemias	2.3	4.2	3.3	1.8
70	Vascular lesions, C.N.S.	0.5	2.9	1.1	*
(78)	Other conditions of nervous system	0.9	2.7	2.1	0.3
74–6,(78)	Eye conditions	2.6	0.1	0.1	5.0
79–86	Heart conditions	2.3	5.1	3.9	0.6
87–97	Respiratory conditions	4.8	4.7	12.9	23.2
104	Gastro-enteritis	2.7	4.9	5.7	2.5
99–103,106–10	Other conditions of stomach, etc.	6.2	8.2	6.4	9.5
115–20	Conditions of pregnancy and childbirth	32.0	7.1	1.8	0.2
124(126)	Skin conditions	1.9	0.5	0.9	7.3
132	Infections of new born	0.1	0.5	1.5	*
131,133–5	Other infant diseases and immaturity	0.6	3.2	7.7	*
136	Senility	*	0.1	7.1	*
138–50	Accidents and violence	11.4	11.9	4.7	6.0
	Total above	79.4	80.4	83.0	81.2

14	Cholera	0.1	0.3	0.9	*
22	Whooping cough	*	*	1.4	0.5
25	Leprosy	0.1	0.3	0.2	*
28–30	Poliomyelitis	*	0.2	0.3	*
32	Measles	0.1	0.1	0.7	0.2
35	Rabies	0.1	0.4	0.4	*
37	Malaria	0.1	*	0.2	0.1
	Numbers ('000)	450	12 000	1 482	305 567

clients, and is presented in different categories; the meeting point of the two types of data is at the level of the health care institution—using this word in a broad sense to include not only hospitals and health centres, but the offices of general practitioners, the counters of druggists and even ordinary households so far as they are providers of health care. The supply of data for resources, as for client flow, is most abundant and precise for the institutions of the public sector. The standard sources of information are reviewed below under four heads: finance (which is often what worried Ministries of Health mean by resources, at least in the short run); real resources such as manpower, buildings, equipment, and supplies; national physical infrastructure such as water, electricity, and telephone systems; and the social infrastructure represented by the community and the household.

4.3.1   *Filthy lucre*

In most developing countries, an investigation of the financial resources available for health has to depend heavily on the information which can be obtained from the government's budgeting and accounting system. The system is not loved by health professionals since it imposes on them constraints which are always irritating and may seem immoral (particularly when budgets are contracting). But it is central to the management of government health services.

The primary function of an official budget is to establish accountability for government funds. The procedures for doing this, and the information they generate, are very similar in all the developing countries which have been under British political control, and the same essential features are found also in countries with other traditions. At the highest political level, a document is approved each year which gives the permitted expenditure for the coming year of each government unit (called, for example, the 'Annual estimates of expenditure as approved by parliament'). This becomes the basis of the spending plans of government institutions, subject to the possible issuing of 'Revised estimates' during the year and to any additional procedures required for the actual release of budgeted funds. It also provides the framework for the accounting process which records the funds actually spent (usually published in the same 'Estimates of expenditure' though with a two-year time lag). The comparison of budgeted and actual expenditures constitutes the processes of control and auditing, the information from which eventually is fed back to the parliamentary level, usually through an independent auditor general. Sanctions are provided against any excess of actual expenditure over budget. Properly administered, the system provides an effective guarantee that the intentions of the political authorities are not perverted by dishonesty and indifference. Because of its political function, it is often well run even where other aspects of the government system are weak, and the information it generates is relatively reliable and timely. It is important, therefore, to make use of it for evaluation purposes. The extent to which this can be done depends very much on the possibility of linking money expenditures with real inputs to the health system on the one hand (considered in the following subsection) and with real health care outputs on the other.

If we think of the expenditure information simply as a measure of cash available, a traditional budget offers us a hierarchy of categories, from the total of all government expenditure down to the smallest operating units with full financial responsibility—for example, hospital boards and health districts. Data of this kind gain greatly in usefulness if they can be built up into time series (which can usually be done, with due regard to possible changes in the location of activities within the government system) and related to the totals of which they form a part. In this way we can answer questions such as 'has the share of the Ministry of Health in government expenditure been growing or declining over time?' or 'have there been changes in the balance between primary and secondary health services?'. Still at this general level, we can go further. We can ask whether government spending, and health service spending in particular, has been an increasing or decreasing proportion of the national income; or we can ask how much of any change in expenditure represents price changes, and how much changes in real purchasing power. To answer such questions we need to draw on basic economic statistics which may vary greatly in quality and availability from one developing country to another. One country may have a fully developed system of national income estimates and specialized price indexes; in another it may be necessary to rely on occasional estimates of national income prepared by outsiders, and on a single consumer price index. Small differences in the technical specification of economic statistics may produce large differences in the results of the analysis—for example, changes in the real purchasing power of the health services budget may look very different according to whether they are based on a general index of consumer prices or on an index of the prices of government purchases. Hence although basic economic statistics can contribute greatly to the analysis of health budgets, they must be handled with caution by those ignorant of the technical background.

As we move down the hierarchy of government units from ministries through departments to individual programmes and institutions, the possibility becomes more and more enticing of relating expenditure to particular kinds of health service output. Under traditional budgeting systems, this is only possible with budgetary units which have a single type of product. But the dominant health service institutions—hospitals, health centres, health education campaigns, etc.—produce many outputs jointly, so that budget-based costing of single outputs is not possible. Some developing countries, often under pressure from outside agencies, have experimented with forms of budget presentation which link expenditure and output, under names such as performance budgeting, programme budgeting, and even zero based budgeting. Up to about 1970 the Jamaican budget format followed the traditional dispensation; since then a mild form of performance budgeting has been introduced. There are, however, basic problems in thorough-going programme budgeting; if the accountability function is to be maintained, the presentation of expenditure according to organizational units cannot be abandoned, yet its combination with a presentation according to output becomes inordinately complicated. No universally accepted compromise has yet emerged to take its place as a standard source of evaluation material.

In spite of these problems, the budget of a country's Ministry of Health is such a rewarding source of information for evaluation purposes that there is a natural tendency to overlook its limitations. One of these is that it does not tell us about health service expenditure by other ministries (for example, the ministry for the armed forces); nor about government expenditure on health-related activities such as water supply, education, or nutrition. These must be sought elsewhere in the budget documents. Nor does the budget of the central government tell us about health expenditure at other levels of the system. In India, for example, the main public expenditures on health services take place at state level. Even in non-federal systems, there is likely to be some public health expenditure through local government units. In Indonesia, the distribution of health expenditure between central, provincial, and village levels, and between different agencies at each level, has in the past been so complicated that it has needed a major research effort to disentangle it (Wheeler *et al.* 1980).

The major limitation on the government budget as a source of financial data, however, is simply that in many developing countries the greater part of health care is not provided or financed through the government machinery. Private financing of health care may include many different elements—social security payments, private health insurance and various kinds of out-of-pocket payments. Though estimates of aggregate private financing may be available as part of the national accounts, these are not likely to provide the kind of breakdown needed for evaluation purposes; nor are the accounts of social security agencies or commercial insurance companies always available and up-to-date. To obtain a picture of private sector financing, data must be fitted together from various sources, including if necessary *ad hoc* sample surveys. Manuals to guide the process have been developed (see, for example Griffiths and Mills 1982), but their use is not yet sufficiently widespread to provide a standard source of evaluation information.

4.3.2 Men, materials, and monuments

Surely, it may be said, although the government budget is not very helpful as a way of linking expenditure with outputs, we can expect it to do better as an indicator of inputs? For expenditures, after all, can only be rationally budgeted for on the basis of the inputs—manpower, supplies, buildings, and equipment—which they are intended to purchase. To some extent this expectation is justified. Both traditional and modern budgets provide useful information on inputs to the government health services. Expenditures are divided into three broad input categories: personnel, other current expenses, and capital expenditures, their separateness emphasized by the fact that the control process allows very little *virement* of funds between them, and much detail is given under each head. But, as on the output side, the budget's usefulness is limited by the primacy of the accountability and control functions and the fact that so much of health care falls outside the government sector.

Budget expenditure on *manpower* is based on detailed personnel lists, either part of the budget document or administered in parallel with it. These are often very specific in terms of grade and institution. The concentration, however, is on those 'established' or 'permanent' posts which represent a continuing obligation of government. Much less attention is paid to temporary and part-time employment. Nor is it of great importance for budget purposes whether a post is filled, and if so whether the holder is present or away on leave or training. Hence it may be necessary to look for other sources of information about manpower inputs actually used. For this purpose, special registers (nowadays often computerized) may be maintained for professional staff. Ironically, the best data, covering both professional and other staff, is already implicit in the accounting system, since every week's or month's salary payment must be identified in terms of individual, grade, and location; and with the spread of computerized accounting it becomes more and more feasible to draw manpower information from this source.

Budgets provide a breakdown, often detailed, of expenditure on *supplies* and other non-personnel expenses, though the actual distribution between items may diverge considerably from that budgeted for. The most important category here is drugs and medical supplies; the budget breakdown here is not likely to be sufficient for technical evaluations, but there is necessarily an information subsystem based on the drug supply process (again, nowadays increasingly computerized) which can be used to supplement the budget breakdown.

Government budget and accounting systems are at their weakest when dealing with the services of *physical capital* (buildings and equipment). Capital budgets record only additions to the stock of capital year by year.

They do not provide a valuation of this stock, nor of the value of the services it supplies to the health care process. In this respect, they appear to the economist much inferior to the accounts of commercial organizations. The omission seems to stem not merely from the primacy of the account-ability function in budgeting, but from a narrow view of accountability which ignores costs like the depreciation of capital assets which do not take the form of a cash expenditure. There is no standard source from which this gap can be filled; recourse may be necessary to direct surveys of facilities, or to estimates based on lists of institutions and assumptions about their value and rate of depreciation. It may be the lack of hard information about the capital involved in health care which generates such dubious generalizations as that health care is necessarily a labour-intensive industry or—not very consistently—that hospitals are monuments to medical selfishness, 'disease palaces', and enormous eaters up of capital resources in relation to the service they provide.

For both manpower and capital in health care, we need to know not merely the current situation but something about its implications for the future—in the case of manpower, because of the long-term perspective needed by training programmes; in the case of capital, because of the durability of the assets concerned. On the manpower side, one calculation is so commonly performed as part of the planning process that it may be called a standard data source, namely a listing of the expected output from training institutions set against projected demand. Whether there is an analogue for this on the capital side depends very much on the state of health planning in each country.

When one moves from the public to the private sector, one enters an area where there are few statistical signposts. Professional associations may be able to provide lists of those permitted to practice, but these are likely to include names of those who have retired, emigrated, or died, and to make no distinction between public and private practice; for doctors, in a small country it may be more economical to check the telephone directory. On the side of supplies, in a country where all drugs are imported their volume should in principle be traceable from trade statistics; but these are often ambiguously classified, and in any case make no allowance for distribution costs which will account for the greater part of consumer's expenditure. The identity of private hospitals, profit and non-profit, is likely to be known, but not necessarily their capacity, and information about smaller institutions is likely to be even more elusive.

4.3.3 Physical infrastructure

Health care as practised in the developed countries depends for its effective-ness on a service infrastructure it shares with the rest of the economy—roads, electricity, telephones, postal services, water supplies. This dependence is not always taken into account by planners in developing countries where such an infrastructure cannot be taken for granted; hence a familiar litany of problems—health centres without regular water supply, hospital equipment burned out from voltage fluctuations, laboratory specimens lost in the mail and so on. Items of 'appropriate technology'—for example, ways of sterilizing without electrical equipment—can go some way toward meeting such problems, but the dependence cannot be entirely removed. Hence some knowledge of the efficiency of the infrastructure is necessary to health care evaluation. This information is usually obtainable in general terms from official reports, but often nothing short of direct enquiry will disclose whether water supply, power, and telephone are available at a particular facility.

4.3.4 Social infrastructure

That health care, at least of the Western type, depends on physical infrastructure is obvious. That all health care depends on a social infrastructure is a less evident proposition, but one which nowadays would receive nods of approval in any gathering of health administrators—though particularly, perhaps, those whose careers have committed them to the promotion of primary health care. The health care process functions in the presence of, and hopefully through, a system of social relations which for the most part exists independently of that process. The implications of this form a theme which will recur more than once in later sections. Here we are concerned with sources of information about a country's social structure as it relates to health care.

Such information covers a spectrum from the most formal aspects of a national society to its functioning at the local and interpersonal level; and as we should expect, standardized information is much more easily available at the former level than at the latter. A standardized description of a country's political and administrative structure and the main features of its official culture as these relate to health is not difficult to come by; for example, many WHO member countries include a summary of such information in their Country Health Profiles. Such descriptions include an account of the formal pattern of local government, but this is likely to be a poor indicator of political realities at the local level and of the social relationships on which these rest. When we come to the small units based on face-to-face relationships—the household, the rural village—or to larger scale concepts ignored by the political machinery, such as caste and class, information is likely to be abundant, diffuse, and largely unstandardized, at least as it relates to health care. For the evaluator in a hurry, there is here a real gap in the information needed for his work.

There are two groups one might reasonably expect to be able to fill this gap. One is the nationals of the country involved, and particularly the health planners and administrators; surely they are in touch with social realities? This expectation is often false. To urban middle class professionals, the way of life of the rural and peri-urban poor may seem a social chaos which they people with stereotypes convenient for themselves. Their degree of detachment can be frightening. In Nepal in the 1970s a group of devoted obstetricians expounded to visiting experts the need for all births to take place in the few health centres. How long, asked an expert timidly, would it take a woman in the remotest village to reach a centre? The answer, arrived at after some discussion, was 'three days by oxcart' . . .

The second group to whom recourse seems natural is the social scientists. Their usefulness for the present purpose seems still to be limited in developing countries by the traditional difference in function between sociologists and anthropologists. The anthropologist is invaluable in the study of small social units and in the formulation and execution of projects concerned with a specific population, but does not generally operate in categories which permit concise presentation at the national level. The sociologist is more likely to provide a quantitative framework for the study of national relationships, but has so far taken less interest in their relevance to health care. There are, however, some accessible sociological data with such direct implications for health care that they might well be made standard data items—namely, those which show the location of children, mothers, and old people, the classic 'vulnerable groups', within the household system. The data for this are almost always collected as a step in the execution of censuses and sample surveys, but are too seldom tabulated and analysed.

The pessimistic conclusion seems to be that while the evaluator, national or external, badly needs to understand the social context of health care, he will often have to operate on a rather impressionistic basis, applying a mixture of intuition and scepticism to inadequate and sometimes unverifiable data. Even this will be more useful than indifference to the social context. The following section, which applies an impressionistic approach to the social context of certain aspects of primary health care in Jamaica, is admittedly a piece of self-indulgence on the part of the writer—but hopefully it is more than that.

4.3.5   *Jamaica: inlaws, outlaws, and grandmothers*

The 1970s were exciting times for members of the staff of the World Health Organization. The organization was clearly moving further and further away from any concentration it had ever had on hospital medicine and vertical disease campaigns, and we awaited hopefully the results of the new emphasis on primary care. We thought we knew what primary care meant;

it was the level of the health system at which the client with a health problem made his first contact with a professional provider of care, and from which he could if necessary be passed on to secondary and tertiary institutions for further treatment. We also knew that primary care was organized in different ways in different countries; and we accepted that, regardless of the way it was organized, it could be good or bad. We were taken aback to learn from the Declaration of Alma Ata that we had been wrong in an important particular; primary health care was only worthy of the name if it was effective, economic, and accessible. There was no such thing as bad primary health care—or at least it was not entitled to capitalization.

In retrospect, we should have known that any policy statement from a multi-national bureaucracy must represent a political compromise between departments and between national interests—even more so if it is also intended as a campaign slogan. Yet some of us, particularly the research-minded, liked the old definition because it gave us leave to fossick around among the real-life forms of health care at the primary level without pre-conceptions about whether they were good or bad, whereas primary health care built a ring fence around our curiosity. Let us look, in Jamaica first of all, at the no man's land between a personal health problem arising and the admission of a patient to a hospital—primary care in the loosest and most non-committal sense. Let us leave aside the official channels—health centres and private allopathic practitioners—which are discussed elsewhere. What remains is three forms of health care. One is provided by the commercial pharmacists, operating professionally within, or not much outside, the law. A second is provided outside, and often against, the law by 'healers'. The third form, of which the law takes almost no cognizance, is the care provided by the members of the public—by us—to ourselves and the members of our families.

4.3.5.1 *Aspirin and oil of healing*

Forty years ago, before the wharves were shifted to the west of the city and the suburban plazas drained away the customers, lower King Street from the country bus park at Parade down to the sea was the commercial centre of Kingston. Here middle-class people from uptown came to use the department stores and specialty shops and to consult their lawyers and doctors, mingling with farmers in from the country, dockers peering out of the rumshops, and the whole anonymous population of the city's core. Midway along lower King Street was K.'s Pharmacy, a dark clean-smelling cavern opening off the arcaded pavement. Its walls then still carried advertisements for Minard's Liniment and for Canadian Healing Oil, 'good for man and beast'. The pharmacy provided prescription medicines for the clients of doctors who practised in the area, and sold a wide range of tonics and off-prescription items, from international brands such as Wincarnis to local products like Ooman Glory. But in addition—and perhaps above all—it was a centre for health advice and unofficial prescription for all those who did not have the money or courage to visit a private doctor, and who for lack of time and fear for their social status did not want to use the casualty department of the Public Hospital a mile away to the west. It was, in other words, a centre of primary care.

It was not only lower Kingston that had its K.'s Pharmacy. There were counterparts in the suburbs of the city (much smaller then than now) and in the country towns. In Savanna-la-Mar, then a sleepy appendage of the great sugar estate at Frome, one could consult Doc Martin, though he might be called away from his counter, or even from a social occasion, to draw a tooth or lance a boil. Other practitioners ventured even further over the boundaries of the pharmacist's trade, into abortion and the mysterious substances prescribed by healers under names like 'Oil of Healing'. Even small general stores sold basic remedies such as aspirin and salts (often Glauber rather than Epsom salts, because these too were good for man and beast).

There are more pharmacies in Jamaica now than in Doc Martin's day (probably about 130 for a population of 2 millions) and their nature has changed in many ways. The physical changes are the most obvious. Each suburban plaza has its drugstore; it is fronted with plate glass, instead of the decent darkness of small windows and metal shutters, and the prescription counter, which used to dominate the interior, has often retreated to a remote corner behind the showcases of cigarettes, costume jewellery, films, cosmetics, and garden supplies—even in some cases a soda fountain. The country pharmacies are following more slowly down the same path.

The content of the pharmacist's professional work has also changed. He—or, increasingly, she—is no longer called on to mix or compound remedies from a limited range of primary materials. Instead there is a much wider range of factory made products whose sale needs the pharmacist's supervision in varying degrees. Some are standardized versions of the old lotions, cough medicines, and laxatives which need only token supervision, and in fact are sold unsupervised from the shelves of supermarkets and general stores, along with analgesics and disinfectants whose use is so well understood that they present no hazard. (A cynic might ask whether some of these are not more dangerous than some of the pills so carefully guarded in the pharmacist's cubby hole; but danger in these cases is relative to the familiarity and sophistication of the user—otherwise railway passengers would be as hedged around with restrictions as air travellers).

The heart of the pharmacist's mystery lies in that cubby hole, now capacious enough to store in an orderly way the hundreds of 'drugs', the ambivalence of whose name recalls the days of laudanum and calomel. These also are factory made, and the pharmacist's task is largely to match product name, and number and content of pills with a doctor's prescription, with occasionally the substitution of one proprietory name for another or for a generic name, and very occasionally the sour satisfaction of catching out the doctor in error. To keep up-to-date with the properties and inter-actions of all the drugs dispensed, the maximum effort required from the pharmacist is very great indeed. The minimum effort required to get by, on the other hand, is very small by professional standards—no more than reading the manufacturer's leaflets and following prescriptions with care. It is suspected that in Jamaica some of the older pharmacists (and there are some very old ones) follow the minimum energy path.

There have been changes, too, in the pharmacist's clientele. There are more people to be served than in Doc Martin's day, and more money to pay for service. There are more doctors to prescribe, and among the middle class more people who pay for their prescriptions through private insurance schemes. On the other hand, the expanding use of hospital casualty depart-ments in the 1970s, and of the health centre system from 1975 on, must have withdrawn many potential customers from the pharmacies, particularly mothers and children—the woman with a sick child on her arm is no longer so common a sight. The public no doubt has a more sophisticated knowledge of its own health needs, but it is clear that to many people still the pharmacist is the first outsider to be told of family health problems. Furthermore, chance has brought a new opportunity for the pharmacist as unofficial prescriber; with rising drug import prices, clients with several items on a doctor's prescription may find they can afford to buy only some of them, and must consult the pharmacist to make a sensible choice.

What have these changes done to the pharmacists themselves? Their formal position within the health system remains as secure as it has ever been. Under the law, only they can dispense prescription drugs. They have a strong and well-disciplined professional association, and an aggressive representative within the Ministry of Health in the Director of Pharma-ceutical Services. Yet it is hard to escape the impression that they have lost status, and are aware of it. A loss of status has been common to many sub-professional groups in Jamaica in the last generation as the public level of literacy and sophistication rises and new channels to power open up; the days are long past when a researcher, entering a rural village for the first time, would be automatically referred to the teacher or the minister as the people best fitted to conduct its relationships with the outside world. Furthermore, in the last few years the real incomes of salaried professionals have fallen, particularly when compared with entrepreneurial neighbours such as unofficial importers and ganja growers.

Their status has fallen in another way. Forty years ago the typical pharmacy was owned by a pharmacist; his physical terriory, as well as his professional field, was his own. Today the trend is for the pharmacist to be an employee of a commercial concern, to whom his presence is a bait for impulse buyers of notions and a legitimation of long opening hours and weekend working. This can be a profitable role, particularly for those moonlighters who manage to combine it with a salaried job, but it is not one which would have appealed to Doc Martin.

It is hard to avoid the impression that these changes have led pharmacists as a group to adopt something of a siege mentality, constantly alert to resist any breach in their legal privileges but uneasily aware that the main battle for health has passed them by. When the matron of a small rural hospital has to break off her regular work to search for a key which fits the drug cupboard because the aging pharmacist has neither come to work nor sent a message, one becomes aware of the crucial role pharmacy plays in the hospital world and of the odd forms professional bellicosity can take. Yet pharmacists could justly complain that the other health professions have done little to draw them into the mainstream of health service development. Nurse practitioners, for example, were trained and operating in Jamaica long before any decision was taken on whether pharmacists were obliged to fill any prescriptions they might write. Nurse practitioners are associated with primary health care (though in Jamaica many of them work in hospitals); pharmacists merely meet the demands of the public, largely in ways which are neither approved, forbidden, or guided by law or plan.

Is Jamaica singular in its treatment of pharmacists? The paucity of studies—at least by health planners—of the pharmacist's role in developing countries as seen from the inside makes it difficult to answer this question objectively. Impressionistically, one can say that the forces at work to shape this role are largely universal, with Jamaica as so often being somewhere near the midpoint of an international spectrum. The old-style country pharmacy was not very different from Mr. Bajaj's establishment in New Delhi's Khan Market (or the rival establishment a few doors away set up by his son-in-law after a family quarrel). The pharmacies in the plazas are well on their way to the North American pattern which sells everything—'What do you mean, you don't sell tyres? This is a hell of a drugstore!'. (But Jamaica does not—or not yet—have a pharmaceutical industry whose marketing of its own products would offer a parallel to Boots the Chemists.)

The technical forces shaping the pharmacist's role are much the same wherever Western medicine has penetrated—which, in spite of the lip service paid to traditional medicine in the planning literature, is virtually everywhere—and are paralleled by similar developments in non-Western systems such as Ayurveda, where also the factory product is more and more displacing the bundle of local herbs. The failure to co-opt private pharmacists into the primary health care movement also appears to be universal. It would be silly to idealize them; they include surly, greedy, and stupid individuals as does any professional group, and in the poorest countries (such as Bangladesh) a large part of the public's spending on health care ends up in their pockets. But they have one virtue which should not be under-estimated; they face the demands of the public with a minimum of organizational armour, and are less inclined than most professionals to neglect what the public wants in favour of what it needs.

There can be no clearer example of the practical difference between want and need than the health literature on oral rehydration therapy (ORT) for children with diarrhoea. A WHO nurse once shocked a medical meeting in New Delhi by describing how a poor mother would use the end of the same sari to handle the cooking pot and to wipe the baby's bottom. The doctors present were convinced, and rightly, that a mother could save the life of a dehydrated baby with ORT, a procedure to which palliatives such as kaolin or opium-based medicines were irrelevant. It had not occurred to them that she might also want the baby's bottom to stop running—and that in terms of transmission to other children in the home and general cleanliness, not to mention her own patience, this desire might not be unreasonable. It is not surprising that a recent study in Bangladesh, the home of ORT, found pharmacists still prescribing medicines for infant diarrhoea which were second best in terms of objective need to ORT, and it is not necessary to conclude that their motive was merely profit.

Pharmacists, then, throughout the world, are an example of a professional group whose actual contribution to health care has been under-estimated by health planners. Their potential contribution may be wider still; the private pharmacist particularly, deals with the public face-to-face, though the pharmacist in the public sector tends to operate from behind a wire mesh window grudgingly pierced with a hole just large enough to pass a bottle or envelope of pills. Pharmacists can be a powerful agency for health education and for the triage of patients for other levels of the health services, and a force to reconcile the clients' needs and demands. But if they are to come out of the cubbyhole, co-operation will be needed from both sides of the professional fence.

4.3.5.2 *Healing in the balmyard*

Forty years ago, as one drove along a country road in the south of Jamaica, one saw from time to time a yard outside which there flew a pennant on a slender bamboo. It was the sign of an unofficial public service; it might be a point where one could buy ice or pick up the 'Daily Gleaner', but it could also be the 'balmyard' of a healer, an institution common enough to be enshrined and mocked in a popular mento song of that generation. Today the institution is rarer, and even its name is probably strange to young, street-wise Kingstonians. But the unofficial healer is not dead. A main road which winds through the hills of the centre of the island is over-looked at one point by a sprawling concrete mansion of the kind that grows new wings as its owner's fortunes soar, and the traveller will be told that it belongs to Ape Man—a character about whom stories accumulate, not least those about his supposed dressing in a monkey skin as part of a ritual to cure female frigidity. Legend and gossip cluster around unofficial healing in Jamaica, while hard information is hard to come by; is there a meaningful pattern behind the gossip?

Since the days of slavery, official Jamaica has been haunted by a fear of, and fascination with, an anti-world beyond its understanding or control. In this anti-world, strange forms of religion, politics, science, and family life were knit together into a mysterious whole. Before emancipation it had fairly precise location, racially and geographically; it was an affair of black people, located in the slave villages of the plantations and, even more, among the mountains thinly populated by runaways and Maroons. During the 19th century, when an emancipated peasantry spread to every corner of Jamaica, the boundaries between world and anti-world became blurred, racially and geographically; the official world ceased to be the exclusive preserve of whites and high browns, or to be confined to the plantations, and the racial picture was confused by the intrusion of Indians, Chinese, and Syrians. In the 20th century the anti-world has tended to be defined in cultural terms—colloquially and negatively, as the world of people who lack education and a more fundamental knowledge of morals and manners which Jamaicas call 'broughtupsy'; with antiquarian interest as a source of folksong, story, and ritual; with more serious anthropological concern as the possible repository of a hypothetical African culture; and most recently for political purposes as the incarnation of the values of the people in their struggle against injust authority. Whether the anti-world has been regarded as the work of God or devil, there have been psychological pressures at work to make people regard it as a unity rooted in transcendental forces. If this were so, unofficial healing in Jamaica would have to be understood as a part of the transcendental unity of the anti-world as a whole.

However, both the historical record and the contemporary scene suggest a different view of the institutions of the anti-world, as changing, unco-ordinated, pragmatic, eclectic, and deeply influenced by the contemporary forms and content of the official world itself. Where, indeed, would an integrated Jamaican folk culture come from? Not from some hypothetical African substrate, which would have had to survive a people's separation from its ancestral soil, its mixing with other peoples originating anywhere from Angola to Senegal and a multitude of translocations and inter-marriages within Jamaica itself. The most diligent search in the West Indies has found distinctively African patterns only in groups with a special history—the isolated islanders of Carriacou, and in Jamaica the Maroons and the descendants of African immigrants who had never experienced slavery. Even here, what survives is not a single culture but aspects of different African cultures. Nor is it plausible for political economists to expect continuity and integration of the anti-culture on class grounds in a society which is a palimpsest of plantation and peasant agriculture and all the stages of capitalism and post-capitalism. The anti-culture, whether as African survival or proletarian ideology, is literally a myth.

Correspondingly, if we narrow our perspective from the supposed anti-culture as a whole to the unofficial healer, we should not be surprised to find that he (or she) does not conform to a single unchanging type. If the class of healers has any enduring characteristics, they are two. One is that they occupy the ground which is not effectively served by official medicine. Forty years ago this ground was much wider in Jamaica than it is today, both geographically and in terms of the conditions which could be effectively treated; it included many acute conditions which now yield to the appropriate drugs (but not bone-setting, which has never emerged as an unofficial specialization in Jamaica). It is still true, however, that official medicine is relatively unhelpful for chronic conditions and for mental illness. Correspondingly, the field of the unofficial healers has narrowed down over the last forty years from general medicine to a concentration on chronic and mental conditions. There was an intermediate stage where the healers adopted what was new in the official pharmacopoeia. In the 1950s a doctor friend in western Jamaica said of a local healer 'The man is irresponsible! He is always prescribing antibiotics', and the 'penicillin doctor' was not unknown in Jamaica. But the helper appears now to have yielded this ground wholly to official medicine.

The second characteristic of 'healing' in Jamaica is that it has always been closely linked with the supernatural. It is true that the established churches—Baptist, Methodist, Anglican, Roman Catholic—accept no responsibility for the physical health of their members, delegating this to the equally firmly established medical professions. But Jamaicans do not deal with the supernatural only through these churches. There are also a multitude of small churches, from those which preserve the trappings of Anglicanism (like that which first shelters and then rejects the hero in 'The Harder They Fall', Jamaica's best film to date) to the fissiparous groups whose shouts of praise shake the walls of little wooden halls in country villages every Sunday. There are individual mystics like M.G. Smith's Dark Puritan (Smith nd) who find, sometimes to their own surprise, that their spiritual powers extend to the healing of others. There are evangelists from the States, descending on Jamaica for short campaigns with the Bible in one hand and a collection box in the other; there are groups where African gods and ancestors come down to possess the dancing worshippers; and everywhere are traces of the protean cult of Ras Tafari and its newer and slicker rivals like the so-called Coptic Church. None of these groups exist primarily for physical healing; few of them would reject opportunities for healing if these come their way.

The generalization is sometimes offered that traditional medicine is not interested in the 'why?' of sickness which describes the physical process involved, but in the 'why me?' which explains the location of this process in one person rather than another; and that the characteristic answer involves some kind of violation of the social order. To pervert very slightly the words of the Book of Common Prayer, we have left undone those things which we ought to have done, and we have done those things which we ought not to have done, and there is no health in us. Is this applicable to healing in Jamaica? Two characteristic forms of healing suggest that the generalization has to be stretched very far to cover the Jamaican case. On the one hand, Rastafarianism tends to reject Western medicine but places great emphasis on the observance of certain food tabus; these have been elaborated into a dietary scheme—'I-tal food'—which has spread beyond Rastafarians themselves and has reached the dignity of published cookbook of its own. It is typical of the difficulty of assigning sources to the practices of a syncretistic cult like Rastafarianism that elements of the I-tal dietary could plausibly be sought in kosher and halal food preparation, in the traditional diet of Jamaican farmers, in the Western cults of vegetarianism and organic food growing, and even in the culture of the Indian immigrants who came to Jamaica in the 19th century and played so important a part then in religious development because they offered a third way between the white and black churches. Whatever their sources, Rastafarian dietary beliefs clearly link behaviour and health, but in an individualistic and even rationalistic way.

A totally different approach is that of obeah. This work is often used loosely to mean magic, and in this sense a thriving branch of gossip has always been the identification of particular dignitaries of state or church with their obeahmen (the evidence is always that the dignitary's car has been seen late at night outside the obeahman's house). More narrowly, an obeahman is one who will set up a spell to bring ill-fortune (including sickness) to your enemy, or identify the enemy's spell on you and take counter-action. In the obeah framework, the cause of sickness is not physical; on the other hand, it is only social in the limited sense appropriate to an individualistic, commercial, and slightly paranoid society. Obeah has been illegal since the mid-19th century, and is condemned by both churches and doctors; if it persists, and is as financially successful as rumour says, it is presumably attuned still to something in Jamaica, even though the conflicts it feeds on are now likely to be those of politicians rather than peasants.

The professional in his balmyard, then, represents only one form of unofficial healing in Jamaica. There are many niches for the healing function, forming not a unified system but a range of independent responses to social needs and opportunities. Do these responses make a positive contribution to the health of Jamaicans? Should they be replaced as soon as possible with more respectable forms of health care?

It would be easy to collect horror stories of illnesses aggravated by unofficial healing—herbal remedies misused, referrals to hospitals delayed, people driven deeper into schizophrenia or paranoia by beatings and bushbaths. It would be much harder to measure the successes (even if only palliative and subjective) or to strike a balance between good and bad. This balance would have to depend on whether, for the clients concerned, better health care was available. For the mentally sick, for example, the main alternative to unofficial treatment was relegation to the island's one mental hospital, up to the 1970s a cold storage institution for 2000–3000 in-patients with its own brand of horror. Success in the present efforts to establish an effective community service for mental health would probably greatly reduce the scope for unofficial practitioners. But it would not settle the question of whether in their day they had played a useful or harmful role in the public's search for health.

The history of unofficial healing in Jamaica should make us suspicious of idealized versions of 'traditional medicine' in poor countries and 'alternative medicine' in rich ones. Jamaica appears to be extreme in its degree of fragmentation and lack of a common basis among unofficial practitioners; there is no agreed body of doctrine or practice, as with Ayurveda, and no group of healers is capable of holding professional conventions or negotiating with government, as in Malaysia or Tanzania. (This means, among other things, that there is little scope in Jamaica for co-opting unofficial medicine into the official system.) But the Jamaican case may be suggestive for anyone who wishes to predict how traditional medicine will evolve in a particular country as the ambitions of Western medicine expand and the population grows more urban and more literate.

4.3.5.3 *Tender loving care*

It is a reasonable presumption that in Jamaica very few of those who enter the net of the official or unofficial health care services have not already told someone of their problem, and probably received advice and assistance. There may be exceptions among the 5 per cent or so of the population who live alone. There are certainly exceptions where the problem is shameful or embarrassing—in a morbidity survey in 1981 there was demonstrable under-reporting of sexually transmitted diseases and of cancer. But overall, the first level of health care involves those nearest to us in kinship or friendship, within or, less often, outside our households. On its quality depends the working of the rest of the system.

A hundred years ago, the importance of household care could not be missed. In many country districts—for example, the valley of the Swift River in Portland parish—a prosperous and literate family might live a life as secluded as a ship at sea, eating what they grew, building their house from country boards, and visiting the store only to buy salt, cloth, and kerosene for the lamps. For such a family the recourse to doctor or hospital, by mule or pony and trap over twenty miles of unmetalled mountain roads, could only be justified by acute illness or injury. Other sicknesses must be nursed at home, with the help of the older people's memories of previous sicknesses and of one of the popular handbooks of medicine. There was the less harm in this as except for a few conditions, the nature of practical medicine at that time was essentially domestic; cleanliness, the right food, ventilation, warmth in season, and the 'tender loving care' which in modern nursing training has become a wry joke.

When, thirty years ago, McCulloch wrote the first health manual by a Jamaican for Jamaicans (McCulloch 1955), his emphasis was still on domestic matters, but now from the point of view of prevention rather than cure. Only in the last chapter of his little book does he discuss curative medicine, and then with the doctor as the patient's point of contact with the health care system; the day of the health centre has not yet come. Within these limits he gives very sensible advice about what the client can expect from his doctor. He is, however, clear that in return the client owes the doctor absolute trust, and self-treatment is mentioned only to pour contempt on its sillier items—'Can I perish a growth in my womb? Are teething powders good for my baby?'. These were the days when Readers Digest announced a miracle drug every month, and doctors were justifiably defensive about self-prescribing.

Since McCulloch's day the official health services, public and private, have grown greatly in accessibility and sophistication. It might be thought that the field of household care would have contracted correspondingly. But there is unexpected evidence that it is still of very great importance— probably the most important of the various forms of primary care. In 1981 a sample survey collected information on morbidity (reported illness in the previous year) and utilization of health services (reported use of a health facility, public or private, in the previous three months). The results showed that an individual's probability of illness and of using the health services varied inversely with the size of the household in which he or she lived. This relationship withstood all attempts to break it down in terms of other variables such as education, urban–rural residence, or the age and sex structure of the household. The differences were so great that if all households had experienced the same probability of illness as the smallest, total reported morbidity would have been doubled.

What is it that a household contributes to the health of its members? First, perhaps, the knowledge and practice of basic hygiene and dietetics of the kind McCulloch emphasized—but why should this be found in large households rather than small? Second, a socially supported definition of illness; after all, a large number of visits to practitioners (and of letters to the medical columns of the Gleaner and Star newspapers) are to answer the question 'Am I ill?'. Third, a pooling of experience on what can be done for a particular health problem within the sphere of the household, where to go for help when the household's resources are exhausted, and how to find one's way through the labyrinth of the official health services. Fourth (and this may be the most important), a shouldering of one another's burdens when these are made intolerable by illness—for example, a grandmother's care of the children of a sick mother. Finally, the despised tender loving care which relieves the emotional stress of illness and nerves the sick person to fight for health.

Given a respectable statistic to start from, then, it is not hard to think of reasons why the household should be accepted as the foundation of primary health care. But this acceptance lands us in paradox. In Jamaica very little of the time of the health services is spent on improving the effectiveness of the household for health care, what little time is so spent is concentrated on one aspect of the household—the relation between mother and child—and the emphasis is on the whole on the health virtues of small families. How can this be reconciled with the idea that large households may be healthier than small?

Part of the answer is that even in colloquial terms, family and household are not the same; and that doctors writing about maternal and child health have often used a concept of the family which exaggerates the difference. A 'family', in this sense, is held together by the bond between mother and child, with the child's father as a secondary and medically inessential component. A household may be (and in Jamaica often is) tied together by many other bonds—between the mother and her parents, between brothers and sisters, even, traditionally in Jamaica, between employer and domestic. There has been little detailed work on the composition of the Jamaican household since the flurry of anthropological studies in the 1950s and 60s, since when urbanization has no doubt blurred many of the old categories, but there is ample evidence that it is still a complex organism which cannot be understood in terms of the medical 'family'. Hence there is no essential contradiction in identifying health with small 'families' but with large households.

This, however, raises the further question of why the literature on maternal and child health in poor countries, and even that on family planning, has paid so much attention to the 'family' and so little to the household. The answer to this, at least in Jamaica, has some darkly irrational elements which take us back to the anti-world referred to above. Part of the terror of the anti-world was its fertility; irresponsible black men helping black women to breed without respect for their children's welfare or for the bonds of marriage. The focus of concern changed from time to time; once it was illegitimacy, then fertility in general, and most recently teenage pregnancy. When widespread woman-controlled contraception became available in the 1950s, it could be advocated for rational reasons of personal choice and national policy, and it has now been largely accepted as such, as appears from the statistics of contraceptive use, confirmed by MacCormack's interviews with young women in 1984–5. But an element in the early birth control campaigns was an attempt to push back the frontiers of the anti-world, and it was so understood by many of its intended recipients. A wall in Kingston still bears the 30-year-old graffito 'Birth control a plot to kill negroes'.

The Jamaican campaigns received much support from North America, which had its own international anti-world of teeming black, brown, and yellow people outside its frontiers. This is not written in denigration of the social function of family planning, but to help explain why even though much of its justification lies in its contribution to the health of mothers and children, it has tended to deal with medically controllable situations—the mother attending a clinic—and has paid little attention to the household background from which the mother comes. Yet this background profoundly influences the effectiveness of both family planning and maternal and child health services.

The importance of household health care is particularly clear in the case of children, since they are the largest group of people who cannot look after themselves or independently approach the health services. They are also the group whose care in sickness is most often shared between adults; fortunately most children in Jamaica are found in households where this is possible (in 1981 78 per cent of children under 14 were found in households with two or more adult members). Also dependent on household care are many of the 7 per cent of the population aged 65 and over, and of the unknown number of mentally ill and mentally and physically handicapped. Urbanization has driven many of these from their sheltered niches in country life. Papine was once a village which tolerated characters like the bent old lady who danced along the roads quarrelling and head-butting with the long-gone rivals of her youth; it is now a busy suburb of Kingston where only the sharp-witted can survive. But the city has not yet developed effective public institutions to deal with the old and the handicapped (if it ever can); and so their care becomes increasingly a household matter.

Household care, then, is inevitably the first recourse of those whose health demands are greatest. How well equipped are Jamaican households to provide this care? Once more, a paradox; we must be doing something right, since the infant mortality rate is about 25 per thousand live births and other indicators are (by the standard of poor countries) similarly favourable. But this cannot be put down to official health education, which (except for family planning) is starved of resources and lacks penetration beyond public situations. The most admirable poster on oral rehydration therapy is of little use if it is only seen in the waiting room of the health centre. Part of the answer is that most Jamaican homes now have the minimum physical equipment to be healthy: water, if not piped into the house, in a standpipe only yards away; a WC or pit latrine; walls and roof that keep out the weather; floors that can be kept clean; and over-crowding mitigated by that greatest boon of a kind climate, the power to live half one's life out of doors. But this equipment is of no use without the knowledge of how to use it. Where does this knowledge come from?

Part of the answer is the experience of older people. For some purposes this is irreplaceable. No amount of book knowledge alone will enable one to change a dressing without creating more damage than relief, or to deal without panic with a baby's convulsions. But experience alone has its drawbacks, tending to reflect the health standards of one or two generations ago. McCulloch's emphasis on the doctor as the first professional recourse in illness is still strong among older Jamaicans, even when the health centre would be cheaper and as appropriate. Belief in the universal virtues of calomel, senna, and castor oil no doubt goes even further back. Current knowledge about health in Jamaica must be assumed to come largely from the media, bearing in mind however that in Jamaica the most powerful of the media is gossip, including gossip about other people's illnesses and what the doctor did for them. The media, too, have their drawback as an educational force. Ben Casey, St. Elsewhere, and commercials for Tylenol are not the best guide to primary care. But they do, at least, carry some general ideas about the concepts of illness and its rational prevention and cure, and there have been some admirable Jamaican programmes on paediatrics and family planning. The paediatric programme was especially effective because it was presented not by a professional educator or broadcaster but by an identifiable practising doctor who had the gift of clear and uncondescending expression.

It is unfortunately still true in Jamaica that health education is much more concerned with what the doctor and nurse can expect from the patient than the converse. This leaves two great gaps in the household's health knowledge. One is the lack of guidance about when and through what channel to seek professional help when the household's resources are exhausted—health centre, of one grade or another? hospital casualty department? private doctor? In Jamaica the choice is unconstrained, and all the more confusing for that. This confusion may help to explain the continued popularity of the general practitioner, who takes the burden of such decisions on himself. Further, how does one conduct oneself in the various health institutions? Jamaican hospitals are as little user-friendly as those of any other country, and there is always a minority of staff prepared to take advantage of the fact, from the porter seeking a tip to the junior doctor working off his hangover in bullying a confused old countryman. The other related gap is in the public's knowledge of what standards of care and communication it can expect from its health professionals, including those in private practice. It would be pleasant to be able to record that the professions discipline so effectively that minority of their members who mistreat their clients that the public could take standards of care for granted. But this has notoriously not been so in the past, and there is a place in any health service system for informed public complaint.

One would expect that generalizations about household health care would rarely be transferable between countries; the household is an institution which differs from culture to culture, group to group, and period to period. But it is worth keeping in mind that some of the underlying forces in Jamaica operate in many other poor, and even rich, countries. The importance of the household as the first line of primary care is probably universal. So may be the conflict between the health knowledge of different generations—how many Indian children's health is ruled by their grandmother rather than their mother? The indifference of the official health services to the household's needs and functions, except in terms of a narrow mother–child relationship, is certainly not confined to Jamaica. Once stated, the importance of the household seems not only commonsensical, but an intellectual challenge which brings together themes from medicine, environmental health, and social planning. Economists have become increasingly aware of the productive function of the household, in health care and otherwise (Becker 1981). Sociologists have devoted considerable study to the vulnerability of those socially isolated (Bowling 1987). It is exasperating to find the household virtually ignored in the literature of health care, and from the applied point of view almost unresearched in poor countries.

4.4   Sources of information on organization and management

For evaluation purposes, it is important to know how the inputs into the health sector are organized and managed so as to produce a given level of health care. The management picture is a complex one since it covers institutions with different fundamental objectives—governmental, commercial, and private non-profit—and the first step is to identify the activities which belong to each of these categories. Furthermore, in each category the pattern of management is strongly affected by the special nature of health care. The most obvious manifestation of this is the presence within the management system of large numbers of health professionals—doctors, nurses, pharmacists—whose relations with each other, and with the public, are regulated by law and influenced by their professional training. More fundamentally, health care is not, like so many products of commercial and even public industries, something given or sold to the consumer item by item at arm's length; for many kinds of health care, the so-called client is an integral part of the production process. In principle, therefore, he or she is as much part of the concern of management as the workers in health institutions, and for some purposes can be regarded as a co-manager.

It is not easy to find information which summarizes a system of management of such great (and often unrecognized) complexity. Some generally available sources of information are set out below under three heads: the organization and management of the government health services, the contribution of the medical professions to management, and the legal framework within which the health care system operates.

4.4.1 Organization and management of the government health service

A standard way of summarizing the organizational structure of a government health service is in terms of an organogram—a diagram in which posts and units are arranged hierarchically, with those enjoying the greatest authority at the top, and lines are drawn from superior to inferior to show the channels along which authority is exercised. One organogram may be used to show the relation of the Ministry of Health to other ministries and to the highest political authority; another may supplement this with the relations between the Minister of Health and his subordinates. If organograms are available and up-to-date, they convey succintly a great deal of useful information. (If they are not available, of course, this also is informative.) It is even possible to begin the process of evaluation simply by noting whether the diagram shows certain common weaknesses—for example, too wide a span of control or a confusion of line and staff functions. But organograms have very definite limitations.

A simple organogram can only be a full description of organizational structure in a situation where all the significant relationships are incorporated in commands flowing 'downward' and reports flowing 'upward' along the same channels, with each unit under the authority of a single superior. Real organizations do not conform to this pattern. Inferiors often report to their technical, as well as their administrative, superiors (and organograms are often elaborated to show this); for example, hospital matrons may report for some purposes to the chief nursing officer as well as to the hospital manager or senior medical officer. Power relationships and informal connections may distort the formal authority structure. The more important these factors, the less satisfactory is the organogram as a description of reality. Generally, the closer one gets to the operational level, the more important the informal relationships, and the less informative is the organogram. This may be why the diagram often peters out at the level of individual hospital and health centre. For the internal structure of these institutions, vital to real-life management problems, there is usually no summary source of information.

At its best, the organogram gives us only the anatomy of the management situation. For its physiology—for the content of the relationships indicated by the lines of the diagram—we have to turn to two other sources. One is the management implications of the training of health professionals, dealt with below. The other is the code of regulations which governs the conduct of public servants, and which is usually available in documentary form. The code is, however, as much a definition of standards aspired to as a record of what is actually achieved, and it is considered further from that point of view in the following chapter.

While organograms and regulations have provided the basis for public sector management for generations, specialized planning procedures are a newer element in the government system of most developing countries, and have been more slowly adopted in health than elsewhere. By now, however, there can be few developing countries which do not have an accessible health plan. For evaluation purposes it is desirable not only to be aware of the plan document, and any associated policy statements, but also to know its status —is it a serious commitment of the ministry, or merely something to be shown to potential aid donors?—and the location of the health ministry's planning activities in the overall national planning system.

4.4.2 *Management and the roles of health professionals*

In addition to its technical content, the training of doctors, nurses, pharmacists, and other professional health workers provides two elements of organization and management without which the working of Western medical services is incomprehensible. It is this training which defines the area of competence of each profession, and establishes the authority relationships between them. Nominally these relationships apply only to technical matters, but in practice they supplement, and sometimes conflict with, the administrative relationships summarized in the organogram.

In all countries where Western medicine is taught, the management content is much the same—similar definitions of the role of doctor, nurse, etc., and similar definitions of the relations between these roles, with supreme authority in the hands of doctors and a conventional distribution of this authority within the medical profession. Because of this uniformity, and because much of the relevant teaching is implicit, the curricula of medical schools, while an accessible source of information and therefore not to be neglected, leave a great deal unsaid from the point of view of the evaluator.

It is important, therefore, to be alert for signs of departure from the standard professional model in particular countries. Some of these may be matters of conscious policy—for example, recognition of the role of formal non-Western systems of medicine such as Ayurveda and Unani in India and Sri Lanka, or a redefinition of the authority of the doctor as part of the promotion of Primary Health Care. Others may emerge unstated from the social context; in countries where nurses are scarce because of limitations on the opportunities of women, there is likely to be some redefinition of their roles in relation to other health workers.

Note must also be taken of the professional associations which play a part in maintaining the status of their members after training is ended. These are commonly of two kinds: those with legal status, such as national medical and nursing councils, whose main function is the registration of those qualified to practice and the enforcement of discipline; and less formal associations whose objectives may include the maintenance of professional standards but which also represent the material interests of their members, functioning as lobbying groups and trade unions. Information on the nature of these associations, and their degree of activity, is relevant to the evaluation of health service management.

4.4.3   *The legal framework of health care*

The provision of health care involves such special relationships between health workers, their clients and the social and physical environment that it requires a specific legal framework. This framework can be ignored by most health workers so long as the objectives and background of health services remain static, but it nevertheless limits the organizational and management possibilities, and is particularly important in times of change.

To make a Western medical system work, legislation is required in the following fields (the acts cited as examples are drawn from Jamaica, and will of course vary in detail from country to country):

(1) the registration of health professionals and their special rights and responsibilities vis à vis the public (dental, medical, nurses and midwives, opticians, pharmacy, and professions supplementary to medicine acts);

(2) the status of health care institutions which are outside the government health service or are to be given some degree of independence within it (family planning, hospitals, nursing homes, and university hospitals acts);

(3) the powers of the government and the obligations of the public in relation to communicable diseases, nuisances, and public health in general (public health act), with specific provision for various specialized fields (pesticides, clean air, and food and drugs acts).

The specific acts will often include provisions which have implications outside their particular subject. Thus in Jamaica the mental hospital act (hopefully soon to be superseded by a mental health act) makes some provision for the rights of patients deemed not to be capable of valid judgements about their own health. The public health act incorporates a particular pattern of health care administration, defining the relative roles of the central and local government systems. There may also be aspects of more general statutes and common law which have implications for health in the criminal field (e.g. abortion) or the civil field (medical negligence).

The laws of a country, being public documents, have the merit of ease of access (at least in physical terms—but their meaning, particularly if they have been much amended, may not be easy to construe). But they may have to be implemented through regulations, and amplified within the government service through standing orders, which are often harder for an evaluator to locate.

5 Standards for health system evaluation

5.1 Norms and standards: some basic problems

5.1.1 *The nature of norms and standards*

Evaluation requires not only that we assemble information on how the national health system performs, but also that we find clear and appropriate norms and standards against which its performance can be judged. (We use 'norm' and 'standard' here as roughly equivalent, the former being more often quantitative—'three hospital beds per thousand population'—and the latter qualitative—'the mother's blood pressure to be checked on each ante-natal visit'.)

Since the distinctive function of a national health system is the improvement of health, it might seem that the most useful norms for evaluation purposes would be those most closely related to measures of health status such as mortality and morbidity. Some of the problems with this approach have been indicated briefly in chapter 3, where it was argued that evaluation must concern itself not only with the output side of the 'black box' of health, but with the inputs and the mechanisms within it. What this means in terms of the setting of norms can be seen more clearly in relation to a specific problem—the variations in Infant Mortality Rates (IMR) between the countries of Europe.

These variations have for some time been considerable. In 1976 the IMRs of the Scandinavian countries lay between 8 and 10.5 per thousand live births, against 14 for the UK, 15.5 for the Federal Republic of Germany, and 38.9 for Portugal. There were comparable differences between socialist countries; 13 for the German Democratic Republic, 28 for the USSR, while Albania admitted to 57 per thousand. It is not surprising that in both the lay and the professional press the Scandinavian levels of IMR were treated as norms for other health care systems. In Britain, as in other countries, the national performance was compared with this norm and found wanting.

It may be that those who made and publicized such comparisons believed that they left to the national health authorities no course of action except a massive increase in the resources available to the health care system (and in particular to the institutions making the comparison). If so, they were much deceived. It was pointed out that the increase would indeed have to be massive; in 1976, for example, the Scandinavian countries' per capita health expenditure was two to three times that of the UK. Was the necessary expenditure to come from the government budget? If so, it would be necessary either to withdraw funds from some other kind of expenditure, or to increase taxes; what was the evidence that the public was willing to pay this price for better health? If, on the other hand, the additional expenditure was to come directly from the pocket of the client (or his/her parents), this would almost certainly compromise the principle that basic social services should be available to all regardless of income; what was the evidence that the public would choose to sacrifice this principle for the sake of better health? As the controversy renewed itself from time to time, the form in which these counter-arguments were put varied somewhat, but the essential result was the same; what had seemed a straightforward evaluation of the performance of the British health care system, based on a comparison with Scandinavian health levels as norm, lost its emotional force in a morass of qualifications. Many of these qualifications concerned the difficulty in specifying norms of health independently of the available resources, and therefore fell to be voiced by economists. (This confirmed the opinion of many senior health professionals that economists were not to be trusted.) However, if economists had been less pre-eminently articulate, more attention might have been paid to other kinds of objection which could have been raised to the naive use of mortality rates as norms of health care. Sociologists and political scientists, for example, might have asked questions about the degree of social control of the individual's lifestyle which must be accepted to reach Scandinavian levels of mortality. These would have led to a broadening of concern beyond the narrowly economic to cover the trade-off between physical health and other individual and social benefits.

Beyond this lies the field of the theologian and the philosopher on which the health planner may trespass without realizing it. In discussing infant mortality in developed countries, we can usually treat a fall in the IMR simply as a reduction in suffering; the fact that in the medium term it also slightly raises the rate of population increase is of little importance, or even counts as a positive factor. Concern may arise from the possibility that lower mortality has been achieved through the survival of some children whose health and development may never, or not for a long time, meet normal standards; but this remains a marginal problem of medical policy. In many developing countries, on the other hand, the possibility cannot be ruled out that lower infant mortality may mean a population which is significantly larger than it would otherwise be, and may be, on average, significantly poorer. There are all kinds of ad hoc arguments which can be used to fend off the recognition of this problem. We may believe that in the medium term lower IMRs lead to lower fertility; or that a healthier population will be productive enough to cope with its own increasing numbers; or that any impoverishment created by too rapid population increase can be easily offset by diligence, planning, or revolution. These arguments may cushion the dilemma in particular cases; but the fact remains that to plan to save the life of a child in a poor country is to accept the onus of choice between more people and richer people. This is not a choice on which medicine has anything to say, nor indeed any scientific discipline. If anyone accepts intellectual responsibility here, it must be the theologian.

In summary: the norms by which a health system is to be evaluated cannot have regard only to health, nor can they be justified wholly from within medical science. This is the fundamental reason why the present chapter discusses norms of many kinds and origins—relating to medical processes and inputs, to the financial and administrative framework, to the policy, planning, and budgeting processes and to consumer expectations— all of which have a contribution to make to health system evaluation.

It might be thought that for medical inputs and processes, at least, it would be possible to identify norms which were independent of outside considerations and could be justified solely in terms of the professional disciplines of health care.

Certainly norms are often stated as though this were so. A recent report of the Royal College of Physicians, for example, laid down the staffing norm for an intensive care bed as five nurses, without economic or other qualification. But consideration shows that this can be a norm only for a certain type of intensive care unit staffed by a certain category of nurse and certain supporting staff; the task, and the organization, of an intensive care unit reflects its social and economic, as well as its technical matrix, and the associated norms may change when any part of this matrix changes. Subsection 5.2.2 below gives an example of the derivation of norms of process and input for some tracer conditions in Jamaican hospitals in the 1980s; the procedures used made explicit allowance for the fact that these norms were to be conditioned by the local availability of resources.

5.1.2 Problems in norm setting; an international example

It would be a tidier world if norms relating to health care could be set up on an international basis so as to provide a universal frame of reference for national health system evaluation. Something like this has been attempted by WHO as a mechanism for evaluating progress toward 'Health for All' (see, for example WHO internal paper EB83/PC/WP/6 21 September 1988 *Second report on monitoring progress in implementing strategies for health for all*) and the resulting successes and failures are instructive—particularly so since 'The Organization has consistently emphasized the use of the common frameworks as monitoring and evaluation tools to support countries' managerial processes for national health development' (EB83/PC/

WP/6 21 September 1988 Second report on monitoring progress in implementing strategies for health for all, p. 5, section 18). WHO's Executive Board had approved 12 'Global Indicators' of progress, in most cases couched in terms of the number of countries reaching an approved standard:

(1)   degree of commitment to Health for All (HFA);

(2)   degree of community involvement in health care;

(3)   spending of more than 5 per cent of Gross National Product (GNP) on health;

(4)   devoting a reasonable proportion of national health expenditure to local health care;

(5)   similar Primary Health Care (PHC) inputs per capita between population groups and areas;

(6)   international action in support of HFA;

(7)   presence of elements of PHC (safe water, sanitation, immunization against Expanded Programme diseases, health care available within 1 hour's travel, staff available to care for pregnant women and children);

(8)   minimum standards of infant and child nutrition;

(9)   Infant Mortality Rate (IMR)—especially if <50/1000;

(10) life expectancy—especially if >60 years;

(11) percentage literacy among adult men/women;

(12) national GNP per capita.

These indicators are the result of a long sifting process during which many appealing measurements have been rejected for one or another reason. In many cases the problem has been the unavailability of data, particularly for the countries most in need of health for all. In other cases it has been difficult to find terms to define an indicator which have the same meaning from country to country, or to identify those persons who in different countries perform the same function through under different names. The eventual list of global indicators still bears traces of these difficulties—some indicators (e.g. 1, 2, 6) are still uncomfortably qualitative, while others (e.g. the parts of 7 which relate to mothers and children) have had to be worded carefully and periphrastically in order to be applicable in different national contexts.

For all the care that has been taken, there is one weakness that has not been overcome since it is inherent in the use of a series of independent indicators. This is the fact that the significance of a nation's 'score' on one indicator may depend on another. Global indicator 3, for example, implicitly condemns a nation which does not spend 5 per cent of its GNP on health care. But the proportion of national income spent on health care is well known to vary systematically with income per capita (see, for example Cumper 1984); 5 per cent of GNP would be a modest expenditure for a high income country like Sweden or Switzerland, but virtually unattainable for a poor country like Bangladesh. Similarly, it would be impossible to construct useful independent norms for doctors and nurses per hospital bed since one can to a considerable extent be substituted for the other.

There is another kind of difficulty in the establishment of international standards, one perhaps too little discussed because it casts no flattering light on the health research community. In many fields where international norms would offer great practical advantages—for example, the nutritional requirements of children and pregnant women in the third world—the pressure of demand from practitioners has made a little investigation go a long way. Too often, so called norms in such fields, though enunciated with authority (which in the medical world has often been used to extend science as soya meal can be used to extend hamburger), have rested on drastic extrapolations from results obtained in developed countries or in limited areas of the third world (McLaren 1988). Once established, such norms resist reexamination for personal and institutional reasons. Not many of us have the courage of Professor Waterlow, who has recently (Waterlow 1988) disavowed in the light of new discussions a view of child mortality in countries which he helped to develop.

If it has proved difficult for WHO to develop a useful set of international norms for the highly specific purpose of evaluating progress toward 'Health for All by the Year 2000', it is fair to assume that in evaluating a national health system more broadly we shall get very restricted help from explicit international standards. Our emphasis will have to be on standards set at the national level. These will often require identification and clarification, and much of the following sections relates to how this can be done.

5.2   Technical standards and the quality of care

5.2.1   Technical standards for the health care process

We deal first with the identification of appropriate national technical standards of health care. If we think of the health care system in terms of the tripartite division *inputs*, *process*, and *outputs*, this section is concerned with process. To the patient, it is a striking and, on the whole, reassuring fact that the technical standards of health work differ little from country to country all over the world. A doctor (at least, a Western doctor) will follow the same paths of diagnosis and management in Burma as in Birmingham, England or Birmingham, Alabama, with minor differences according to fashion and the availability of drugs and facilities. How does this unanimity come about?

Certainly not, it must be said, through any formal international machinery. In a few fields, usually inherently disputable ones such as radiation sickness, standards are set by the technical reports of general health agencies such as WHO and specialized agencies such as the International Agency for Research on Cancer (IARC). There is presently an increasing vogue for 'consensus meetings' in fields where serious differences of opinion exist on the prevention, diagnosis, or management of health problems in order that these differences (and, cynics would say, the patient) may be decently buried. But these cover only a small part of the technical field.

The international uniformity of health care standards is in great part a product of the institutions of medical training and research—not only medical schools and research institutes, but also publishing houses, professional associations, and the much maligned pharmaceutical industry. It should not surprise us that the scientific base of Western medicine is international, but it is perhaps rather remarkable that the application of science to such diverse populations has resulted in so little in the way of medical Lysenkoism.

('Ah!' says the voice of conscience at this point, 'aren't you exaggerating the uniformity of medical practice? Are you sure you have been fair to alternative medicine—and folk medicine—and Ayurveda, and Chinese medicine?' The writer wishes to place on record his belief that we have all been fair to non-Western medicine for long enough. The only items in the alternative-medicine shopping list which can be shown to have had a positive effect on health are those which have absorbed some part of the Western scientific apparatus—for example, osteopathy and chiropractice in the West, or the rigorous pharmacological study of Indian and Chinese herbal drugs. We shall therefore concentrate our attention in this section on technical standards derived from Western scientific medicine.)

It is evident that within a national health system there is a tremendous corpus of medical standards, of which a formal evaluation can only take account of a fraction. The practical question then becomes 'how is this fraction to be selected?' The answer may well be a compromise between what is desirable from the point of view of the evaluation as a whole, and what is easily and cheaply available.

The criterion of availability suggests that special attention should be paid to health problems for which appropriate action has already been codified —for example, through national practice protocols. But such protocols in developing countries will probably exist only for a minority of conditions, and these may not be the most important from the point of view of system evaluation. It is very probable that it will be necessary to devise ways of articulating standards in a form in which they can be explicitly tested against actuality at the national level. This is not the same task as the case by case evaluations afforded by peer review and medical audit, though these are admirable components of medical management and their existence will facilitate system evaluation. The techniques required will vary from country to country according to local and national health priorities and the institutional setting. Rather than attempt an exhaustive survey of the possibilities, it is proposed in the following section to trace what was done in Jamaica as part of the Jamaica Health Services Evaluation Project.

5.2.2 Establishing standards for quality of care: Jamaica 1987

5.2.2.1 The background of quality of care assessment in Jamaica

Jamaica has a well-developed system of primary and other health care. In recent years the government health services (which account for about 60 per cent of health care expenditure) have come under increasing financial pressure, and in 1984 a restructuring of the public health system was implemented as part of an effort to contain government expenditure. Increased attention was given to improving the efficiency and cost-effectiveness of health services. A corollary of this was a concern to ensure a reasonable quality of care within the tight financial constraints. Hence an increased interest in quality of care assessment (the measurement of the quality of services in relation to some standard) and assurance (the steps taken in the light of this assessment to improve the provision of services).

Over the past decade or so there had been many examples of *ad hoc* quality assessments usually carried out by clinicians at the hospital level and relying upon informal mechanisms to diffuse good practices to medical and other workers. This had been supported by several in-service training programs and many medical scientific meetings where the results of evaluative studies had been presented. The most notable of these were the annual meetings of the Commonwealth Caribbean Medical Research Council.

There had also been considerable progress toward developing criteria and standards for the care of high priority groups (e.g. pregnant women and children) and particular conditions (e.g. gastro-enteritis and malnutrition in children (see for hospital care Picou *et al.* 1978, and for management in the community Gueri 1980)). Texts had also been produced, principally for medical students on diagnostic issues (such as examination of the acute abdomen in adults and inguino-femoral hernia) and patient management problems (such as analgesia in labour). To clarify the practice of nurse practitioners a set of over 20 diagnostic and management protocols had been prepared together with legislation to formalize their status.

In addition, to assist with appropriate therapeutics, a National Formulary had been produced, and this formed the basis of listings of *vital, essential,* and *necessary* drugs (VEN lists) for hospitals and for primary health care.

A review of primary health care in Jamaica, carried out for the Pan American Health Organisation (PAHO) in 1983 (Figueroa *et al.* 1983), identified a need to increase efforts to systematize health care, and as part of this to continue work on the development of standard management schedules. Studies had also been initiated to clarify linkages between primary and secondary care, since the junction between these two was known to be a point of weakness in the maintenance of the quality of health care.

In 1983, as part of the Jamaica Health Services Evaluation Project, it was decided to develop and test a methodology to assess the quality of medical care for a wider range of health conditions. The framework for this has been described elsewhere (Walker 1983) and was based on the tracer methodology (Kessner *et al*. 1973). This examines the adequacy of care for a group of conditions which are selected to cover both sexes and all major age groups in the population served, and various aspects of the components of medical care (prevention, screening, diagnosis, management, and follow-up). Criteria for acceptable medical care are set by peer or expert consensus. They should preferably be based on the results of randomized controlled trials and clearly related to variations in the outcome between patients. In applying the methodology in Jamaica, attention was concentrated on care provided at first referral level hospitals, but as will become clear later, for several tracer conditions the assessment extended to care provided at the basic and primary level and at tertiary levels.

5.2.2.2 *The selected tracer conditions*

Discussions were held with personnel in the Ministry of Health and others at government hospitals and the University Hospital. With their agreement, a set of 12 tracer conditions were selected for consideration. These were chosen to reflect important health problems in Jamaica and to represent various age and sex groups and aspect of medical care.

In Jamaica the relative importance of infectious diseases as public health priorities has fallen markedly in the past two decades (Cumper 1983). Mothers and young children remain a priority target group and form about 35 per cent of the total population. But with the reduction in importance of communicable diseases and with decreasing fertility rates, the management of chronic diseases of middle and older age groups (particularly diabetes mellitus and hypertension) and routine in-patient hospital care have become more important (see Florey *et al*. 1972; Grell 1978; Ashcroft 1979; Alleyne *et al*. 1979; Morrison 1982; Grell 1982; PAHO 1983; Fraser 1984; Grell 1987; Alleyne *et al*. 1989). The tracer conditions selected for study were acute gastro-enteritis in children under five years; measles; appendicitis; diabetes mellitus, initial presentation and management, keto-acidosis and peripheral gangrene; hypertension, initial presentation and management; stroke; abortion; maternity care; pelvic inflammatory disease; and inguinal hernia repair.

The intention was that criteria for the medical care process would be established on the basis of consensus for 11 of these tracers (excluding maternity care), ensuring that these criteria were appropriate to the resource and practice constraints in Jamaica. Process is taken here to include what a health worker does on behalf of a patient (diagnosis—history, examination, and investigations—and therapeutic interventions) and patient compliance. The assessment of care was designed to concentrate initial investigations upon a subset of the tracers for which both process and outcome assessment could be used—acute gastro-enteritis, hypertension, and maternity care— and two where only process would be used—appendicitis and incomplete abortion. It was decided that outcome assessment was not suitable in these two conditions as case fatality was known to be very low. The inclusion of other outcome variables such as return to normal functional state, infection rates, or satisfaction with care, would have required prospective studies. As it had been decided that because of the limited funds available, investigations would so far as possible be based on routine data, the possibility of prospective studies was not pursued.

The criteria used in choosing the subset of tracers were the same as those for the fuller group of 12 conditions. Gastro-enteritis was chosen to cover important aspects of medical paediatrics; appendicitis to illustrate surgical care in mainly young adults; maternal mortality to throw light on obstetric and maternity care; abortion, for gynaecological care; and hypertension, for general medical care in a chronic condition.

There were 24 government general or acute specialist hospitals in Jamaica, including the University Hospital of the West Indies, Mona, Kingston, which was largely funded from government revenues but did not come directly under the control of the Ministry of Health. As it was not possible to include all the hospitals in the review of performance it was decided to undertake this in a sample of hospitals to reflect various levels of sophistication and geographical and economic differences between hospital catchment areas. Selected for study were two of the 15 small rural hospitals (grade C), Alexandria and Black River; one of the five larger general hospitals (grade B), St. Anns Bay; and two or three (depending on the tracer condition) of the large tertiary care acute (grade A) hospitals in Kingston— Bustamante Childrens, Kingston Public, the University Hospital, and Victoria Jubilee.

5.2.2.3 *The development of consensus criteria*

In order to establish criteria against which the process of care could be evaluated, two issues needed to be addressed. First, process care items had to be identified which were considered important for the care of patients with the tracer conditions. Second, these items should be such that if performed they would be likely to be recorded in the case notes of most patients. Furthermore, it could be assumed that physicians tended to record positive or abnormal findings more consistently than negative ones; the choice of items had to take into account the frequency of recording negative as well as normal findings. Thus a criterion item would have to be one not only considered essential for the care of most patients, but also perceived as likely to be recorded under most circumstances, regardless of the nature of the finding.

In addition, several studies have shown that quality of care correlates very closely with the completeness of the medical record. Where several people are involved in the care of patients it is important that critical elements in the diagnosis, investigation, and management of patients are included in their case records, in order that knowledge of these elements can be taken fully into account when decisions are taken on the progress of the patient's condition.

Questionnaires were developed for the agreed conditions after a review of the relevant literature and discussions with Jamaican physicians. In format, though not in content, the questionnaires were similar to those used by Hulka and Cassel (1973). They were designed to elicit information about candidate criteria, and included two main types of statement about each history, physical examination, laboratory investigation, and management item. The first was in the form 'Asking about . . . is' or 'Examining . . . is', followed by a rating scale divided into seven equal intervals from 'essential' to 'completely unnecessary'. The second statement was a question asking 'Would you record your findings?' followed by a space to check 'yes', 'no', or 'only if abnormal/positive'. The participating physicians were instructed to rate each item with regard to its importance for the care of most patients with the respective study condition, in the light of current practice in Jamaica. Questions were also included for the physicians to indicate where absence or shortages of basic equipment and supplies hindered the carrying out of specific procedures.

For each of the 11 conditions (maternal care was not included in this part of the study), 20 questionnaires were distributed to physicians working in all government hospitals in the country. No physician received more than two questionnaires, dealing with different conditions. The hospitals and physicians to receive the questionnaires were selected by the Principal Medical Officer (Secondary Care) of the Ministry of Health so as to be representative of the major types of hospital in the country and of the physicians responsible for the care of patients with the specified conditions. Of the 220 questionnaires distributed, 165 (75 per cent) were returned.

The individual questionnaires were analysed to prepare lists of consensus criteria which included all items rated in the two spaces nearest 'essential' on the seven-segment scale and to which a positive response was made on the question about recording of results. Consensus criteria were those items for which at least two thirds of physicians responded in the two spaces nearest 'essential'. The choice of two thirds (corresponding to 10 of the 15 respondents per questionnaire) was based upon work by Wagner *et al.* (1978) which suggested that two-thirds was a strategic cut-off point between important and less important items of care. The number of consensus criteria items for reasonable care in each condition varied from 15 (inguinal hernia repair) to 50 (stroke).

5.2.2.4 *The results of the quality of care assessment*

Were the consensus criteria, arrived at as described above, effective for the purpose of evaluating the medical process? In this subsection the results of the assessment of the quality of care are presented for the subset of five tracer conditions.

1. Acute gastro-enteritis in children   In the mid-1980s in Jamaica acute diarrhoeal disease or gastro-enteritis was the leading cause of death in children aged 1–4 years and the second-ranked cause of death (after conditions of the perinatal period) among infants aged under one year. In 1979, the most recent year for which analyses of deaths by cause were available from the Registrar General, gastro-enteritis accounted for 19 per cent of deaths in infants and 26 per cent in children aged 1–4 years. In 1982 it was the leading cause of admission to hospital among children aged under five years, accounting for 36 per cent of admissions.

Several studies in Jamaica have demonstrated the appropriateness of using oral rehydration therapy for the treatment of most children with acute diarrhoea (Harland 1978; Nalin *et al.* 1980; Ashley *et al.* 1981; Swaby-Ellis 1984; and Ashley 1983*a*). In 1980 a phased national programme for the control of diarrhoeal diseases was started (Ashley 1983*b*; Ashley 1984). This concentrated on the out-patient use of oral rehydration therapy initially at two hospitals and five health centres. The programme included training of health workers involved in the care of children with gastro-enteritis, and emphasised the development of skills required for oral rehydration therapy. The mass media (radio and newspapers) were used to disseminate information on the prevention and management of acute diarrhoea, and pamphlets were distributed at health centres and out-patient departments (Ministry of Health 1982*a*).

In the light of these developments it was decided that assessment of the quality of care of infants treated in hospital for gastro-enteritis should be undertaken to establish consensus criteria for the management of these children. Actual performance in five hospitals in 1984 would be compared with the consensus process criteria, and with outcome in terms of hospital-specific case fatality rates in the years 1979 to 1983 (covering the period from before the introduction of the national control program until after its wider dissemination).

The questionnaires circulated to paediatricians and general medical officers had covered 49 care items for gastro-enteritis among infants. Of these the doctors considered 25 items (51 per cent) as being essential and locally relevant for good quality care, and thought they should be, and were likely to be, recorded in the case notes of patients.

The level of performance, in terms of adherence to the consensus care criteria, was established by a review of the case notes for a random sample of 40 infants admitted to each of the study hospitals with uncomplicated acute gastro-enteritis during 1983–84.

There was quite wide variation in the extent to which the care of infants with gastro-enteritis conformed to the consensus criteria. At certain hospitals the performance was consistently worse than at others. The case fatality rates for children admitted to all the study hospitals were far higher among the very young. While only just over a half of the children aged under five admitted with gastro-enteritis were aged less than one year, 85 per cent of deaths occurred among them. The case fatality rate for infants with gastro-enteritis varied significantly between the study hospitals. But before conclusions can be drawn about the likely connection between poor performance on the consensus criteria and high hospital—and age-specific case fatality rates, it is necessary to consider the possible role of an important additional variable; can the differences be accounted for by variations in severity in the case mix of patients dealt with in different hospitals?

The study considered selective populations with gastro-enteritis and not total populations—i.e. only infants admitted to the study hospitals and not all infants with gastro-enteritis in the hospital catchment areas. The probability of death among young children with gastro-enteritis is known to be related to the severity of the illness (Hirschhorn 1980). Consequently it is important to know whether the groups of infants admitted to the various hospitals differed with regard to the severity of the hospital case mix. In acute gastro-enteritis there are various aspects of severity which are known to be related to the probability of dying. The most important are the degree and type of dehydration. Infants with dehydration resulting in 10 per cent or more loss of body weight have higher mortality than those with less severe dehydration (Nalin 1985; Ironside *et al.* 1970; Medical Research Council 1952), as also do those with hyponatraemic (Samadi *et al.* 1985) and hypernatraemic (Samadi *et al.* 1983; Finberg 1973) dehydration.

The case dockets of the infants included in the samples at the study hospitals were reviewed to determine the severity case mix. The two A grade hospitals were admitting a far higher proportion of moderately (5–9 per cent) and severely (10 per cent and over) dehydrated children with acute gastro-enteritis. These hospitals also had substantial numbers of children with both hyponatraemia (23 per cent) and hypernatraemia (21 per cent)—serum electrolytes were not determined at the other hospitals.

So the evidence on adherence to consensus criteria and the age-specific case fatality rates (for children aged less than one year), taken with the severity case mix at the various study hospitals, suggested that:

(1) quality of care was significantly poorer at hospitals C1, C2, and B1 compared with hospitals A1 and A2;

(2) hospital A2 performed significantly better than the other hospital.

Several deficiencies in care, as measured by compliance with the items identified by the consensus process, were identified (Walker *et al.* 1988). The most important of these at hospitals C1, C2, and B1 were:

(1) the failure to weigh infants on admission;

(2) incomplete physical examination;

(3) not undertaking serum electrolyte and urea determinations;

(4) infrequent estimations of fluid requirements particularly over the first 6 to 12 hours after admission;

(5) the failure to record fluid taken;

(6) the giving of antibiotics for acute non-specific diarrhoea;

(7) the giving of other drugs to control diarrhoea.

When we compare care between the two A grade hospitals, performance was better at A2 than at A1 with regard to the following care items which had been identified by the consensus process:

(1) weighing infants, and in particular repeating this at regular intervals during the hospital stay and recording this on a weight-for-age chart;

(2) undertaking biochemical estimation of serum electrolytes and urea.

These inadequacies were mainly due to resource constraints and to limitations in the awareness of the importance of performing certain procedures, and doing so adequately.

So far as resource constraints were concerned, scales for weighing children were available in all hospitals but were not always in working order. Forms for recording the weight-for-age of children were seldom available and forms for recording fluid intake were often in short supply. at C grade hospitals. Even at the B grade and A1 hospitals, serum laboratory services were irregularly available and inadequate. Many laboratory investigations could only be undertaken during daytime and even then often had to be sent to the central government laboratory in Kingston.

Several of the problem areas identified involved the perceptions of nurses and doctors of the importance of the care items identified by the consensus process for the management of children with acute gastro-enteritis. There was a lack of appreciation at the C and B hospitals of the need for adequate clinical assessment, including the weighing of children to calculate fluid requirements, which is crucial in dehydrated infants. There were also inadequacies in monitoring the fluid intake and in assessing the progress of dehydrated children, and a reluctance to refer severely dehydrated infants and those not responding to initial fluid replacement to A grade hospitals which were more able to care for them. In addition there was not sufficient recognition of the inappropriateness of giving antibiotics, antidiarrhoeal absorbent drugs, or drugs which reduced intestinal mobility.

2. Management of appendicitis and of incomplete abortion   Consensus criteria were established for the diagnosis and management of patients admitted to hospital with appendicitis or with incomplete abortion. The performance of care in relation to these consensus criteria was established for a random sample of 40 patients admitted to each of the study hospitals during 1984 for each condition.

For appendicitis, 19 care items, out of 32 contained in the questionnaires sent to doctors at all hospitals in Jamaica, were considered essential and termed consensus items. For incomplete abortion, 26 care items were identified as essential out of a total of 34.

The performance, measured in terms of adherence to the consensus criteria, varied between the study hospitals. The smaller hospitals had lower average scores than the larger, more sophisticated ones. The essential care items that were most frequently omitted for incomplete abortion were related to *clinical examinations* (examination of mucosa for anaemia, of heart and lungs, and speculum vaginal examination); *investigations* (haemoglobin and blood group); and *management*—no antibiotic was given (and where antibiotics were prescribed there was a wide range used and many combinations), and no advice was given regarding contraception. For appendicitis the main deficiencies identified were the failure to take a menstrual history, no rectal or vaginal examination, no examination of the inguino-femoral region or of the heart and lungs, and no haemoglobin or white cell count differential (Walker and Wint 1987).

3. Diagnosis and management of hypertension at health centres   At each of six health centres all newly diagnosed patients with hypertension aged over 25 years registered in one week were identified and the management they received over one year was reviewed. The patients who attended regularly had significantly lowered blood pressures at the end of the year compared with those who attended regularly. Inadequacies were identified in the information given to patients about the importance of regular hypertensive therapy and of follow-up of defaulters.

4. Confidential enquiry into maternal deaths While data from death registrations suggested that maternal mortality in Jamaica was at a relatively low level (4.2 maternal deaths per 10 000 live births in 1979), obstetricians at Victoria Jubilee Hospital were concerned that there were many potentially avoidable maternal deaths.

It was consequently agreed by the Ministry's Maternal Mortality Committee that a systematic confidential review of the circumstances surrounding all maternal deaths occurring in Jamaica during the three years 1981 to 1983 should be undertaken. Information on maternal deaths, including deaths occurring at home, was obtained from a number of sources— registrations, hospital records, police records, etc. For the three years, 193 women dying while pregnant or shortly afterwards were identified, giving a maternal mortality rate of 10.8 per 10 000 live births. Information on each woman was assembled in a standard format. This included age, parity, gestational age, whether delivered and where, details of antenatal care, and precise circumstances leading up to death, in the form of a case summary showing, for example, whether admitted to a hospital, time of admission, whom she was seen by and when, details of clinical management before death, and cause or causes of death.

In order to identify avoidable factors in the death of these women, the case summaries were assessed by obstetricians from a panel of seven Jamaican specialists. Each case was independently assessed by two obstetricians. For 80 per cent of the women there was sufficient information to make a detailed assessment. For 68 per cent of these, it was considered by both obstetricians that there was one or more avoidable factors involved (Walker *et al.* 1986).

The relative nature of the concept of a 'reasonable' quality of care must be emphasized here as the assessments were carried out by practising Jamaican obstetricians using their knowledge of what were relevant acceptable standards of care. Appropriate standards in this sense can legitimately vary with time and place. This can be illustrated from the situation in England and Wales, where confidential enquiries into maternal deaths have been undertaken regularly over a period of 32 years. The report covering the years 1976 to 1978 noted that '. . . there has been a rise in the generally accepted standards of satisfactory care over the same period . . . It is therefore not surprising to find that the proportion of deaths associated with avoidable factors has not decreased as have the absolute numbers of deaths and the mortality rates' (Department of Health and Social Security 1982).

In the Jamaican study the assessors apportioned responsibility for the avoidable factors among those involved in the care of patients as follows:

Doctor alone	39%
Doctor and patient	24%
Doctor and midwife	17%
Patient alone	14%
Doctor, patient, and midwife	4%
Midwife alone	2%

The specific avoidable factors varied with the complication leading to death, e.g. eclampsia, haemorrhage, sepsis, or pulmonary embolism. However the largest groups of similar avoidable factors were:

(1) inadequacies in ensuring that the delivery of women with high risk status took place in hospital, particularly primiparous and grand multiparous women;

(2) delays in taking action when signs of complications developed before, during, or after delivery;

(3) delays in responding to acute emergencies, e.g. haemorrhage and seizures.

More specific instances of problems in dealing with avoidable factors were:

(1) non-availability of blood for transfusion in some hospitals;

(2) unsystematic and inadequate use of drugs to control eclampsia and severe pre-eclampsia;

(3) inadequacies in the administration of general anaesthetics.

5.2.2.5 *Conclusion*

The results of the assessment of the quality of medical care for the subset of five tracer conditions (acute gastro-enteritis in children, high blood pressure, appendicitis, abortion, and maternity care) showed that the methodology was feasible for use, particularly at hospitals. Consensus criteria were established which could meaningfully be compared with performance as measured from routine data sources. In particular, the information contained in patients' case records enabled an assessment to be made of the conformity of care to the consensus criteria (it was noted that in most hospitals the records of nurses were more complete and detailed than those of doctors).

Variations in the adequacy of care between the study hospitals were clearly demonstrated for the subset of tracer conditions. The demonstration was particularly convincing for acute gastro-enteritis in children, where differences in performance in terms of carrying out critical processes in the management of these children were associated with variations in age-specific case fatality rates, even after allowance was made for differences in case severity. The review of maternal mortality provided a further dimension of assessment since it covered not only deaths in hospital but also those occurring at home.

The results of studies like these can be used in two ways. First, they can be used to provide quality assurance at the operational level. At this level, there were in the Jamaican case various uses to which the results might be put. For example, the initial results of the confidential enquiry into maternal deaths were considered by the Ministry of Health's Maternal Mortality Committee. Measures to reduce the likelihood of certain avoidable factors related to maternal deaths were identified. These included the need to encourage women to attend antenatal clinics for care at an early gestational age, and regularly thereafter; the referral of high-risk women for hospital delivery; the definition of standard procedures for dealing with certain complications (e.g. severe pre-eclampsia and eclampsia, anaemia, and postpartum haemorrhage), and criteria for referring patients to hospital or transferring them from smaller to tertiary care hospitals; and review of the arrangements for provision of blood and plasma for transfusion in acute emergencies. Senior obstetricians also recognized the need to review regularly obstetric practice at smaller hospitals which did not have an obstetrician.

For the hospital care of young children with gastro-enteritis and for health care of adults with high blood pressure, the findings of the assessments indicated several areas where action might be taken after discussion between the Ministry of Health staff and others involved in the care of these patients. In other cases the termination of the study came at a point where the operational action to be taken had not yet been decided. The assessment of the quality of care for patients with appendicitis and those with incomplete abortion measured performance in terms of the performance of the recommended process items, without the possibility of checking these against outcomes. The findings here needed to be discussed with surgeons and obstetricians before decisions were made about the action to be taken to improve performance.

For the remaining tracer conditions (measles; diabetes mellitus, initial presentation, keto-acidosis and peripheral gangrene; stroke; pelvic inflammatory disease, and inguinal hernia repair) it was felt that the consensus criteria developed from the questionnaires completed by hospital doctors should be discussed by relevant groups. Such a 'modified Delphi' technique could be the preliminary to undertaking detailed quality assessments for these conditions.

Thus at the operational level, the foregoing study showed the feasibility of developing standards of quality of care which, by comparisons with available data on performance, can yield quality assessments. Following on from this, one can envisage a series of actions which could form a strategy for a quality assurance program. Initially attention could be concentrated on implementing actions arising from the studies with the most immediate results (the gastro-enteritis and maternal mortality studies). Many of these actions would have considerable spin-offs for the care of patients with other conditions as they are of general relevance. Thus improvements in monitoring patients' condition and the clarification of criteria for referring patients to hospital and transferring seriously ill patients from basic secondary to tertiary care hospitals could have general beneficial effects. When these changes had been implemented, a further round of quality assessment might be carried out over a wider group of tracer conditions.

However, at this stage we are beginning to pass beyond the immediate operational level, and quality assessment through the use of tracer conditions needs to be seen from a slightly different point of view, since it is generating information about the quality of the health care system as a whole of the kind required for short- and long-term planning. For this purpose the distinction between avoidable and unavoidable defects of care changes its significance. Avoidability is no longer to be defined solely in terms of the actions of the individual professionals (doctors, nurses, midwives, etc.) but in terms of the working of the health care system. From this point of view, if it is a criterion of quality of care at the individual level that a certain action be taken (e.g. blood in certain cases of haemorrhage), it is a criterion at the system level that the required blood be available. Thus provided the tracer conditions are properly chosen, quality assessment can make a substantial contribution to overall system evaluation.

5.3   Input norms

5.3.1   *The significance of norms in input*

If we think of health care in terms of inputs, process, and output, it is evident that the quality of the output—health care—depends indirectly on both process and inputs. If we are assured of the quality of the process, we can take the output to be governed by the level of the inputs; and hence for evaluation purposes it makes sense to try to identify norms of input against which the actuality can be measured. Such norms offer certain advantages as a basis for evaluation, but they also present some intellectual booby-traps around which it is necessary to tread carefully.

The concepts of input, process, and output seem to be taken from the world of industrial economics, in which they can be applied naturally to situations where current inputs in the forms of labour, materials, and supplies are combined, in accordance with the rules of a specific industrial process, with the services of capital equipment to produce a physical commodity (or an impersonal service which has many of the characteristics of a commodity, such as telephone service). When these concepts are applied to health care, they are used slightly differently, though the differences are not always apparent or conscious.

First, emphasis is usually placed on those inputs which have a specifically medical connotation—on the labour side, doctors, nurses, pharmacists, etc., but not usually janitors or maintenance men; on the supplies side, drugs, dressings, etc., but not usually water or stationery. This reduces the relevance of input norms in situations where the medical inputs are not the source of the constraints on output.

Second, service inputs are usually measured in terms of their potential providers, not of the services actually made available—numbers of doctors, rather than sessions worked; number of hospital beds, rather than bed-days of actual occupancy. This weakens the connection between input levels and outputs which provides the rationale for fixing norms of input.

Third, the industrial concept of inputs does not allow for the special position of the stream of clients in any process which provides personal services. The public which uses, or wishes to have available for use, health care services is not in the industrial sense an input to the process; for one thing, we usually want to minimize true inputs in order to save costs, whereas we may want to maximize the number of actual or potential health service clients. Yet any account of the health care process would obviously be incomplete without some mention of the number of people served. One way to preserve consistency would be to say that the output of the health care services is an improvement in health which is independent of the numbers of the population treated, so that these numbers enter neither as an input nor an output. But this is a solution which is remote both from the way we normally think about health care and from the purposes of health care system evaluation. Is there not a more practical solution?

The answer is to create a set of variables—coverage, various kinds of access—which relate directly to the number of clients the health services do and can cover, and which have some of the characteristics of both input and output measures. Norms for these variables—percentage of children immunized, percentage of households within one mile of a healthy facility, etc.,—are commonly used as tools of evaluation.

Another way of looking at these measures of coverage and access is to see them as special cases of the rule that to arrive at useful norms of input, we must relate the quantity of an input to some meaningful denominator. We want to know the quantity, not as an absolute number, but in relation to the task to be done. This task can be measured in various ways. We may take as our denominator the population to be served—nurses per thousand population, for example. Alternatively, we may look at the input in relation to the population actually served—the number of nurses per in-patient in hospitals, or per patient-day. Or we may measure the input in relation to another input—the number of nurses per doctor or per hospital bed.

Input norms have certain advantages as a basis for the evaluation of national health care systems. As generally used, they relate to a limited number of input elements (those considered critical from the medical point of view) for which information in most countries is easily available—the numbers of professional personnel (though the actual number of doctors practising is often surprisingly hard to discover), the volume of supplies such as vaccines and contraceptives, the stock of capital assets such as hospital beds and health centres. These categories are meaningful both to health administrators and to those whose contact with the health care system is at the level of overall social planning and budgeting. Input norms therefore fit easily into government planning processes, and in some countries (e.g. Russia) play a very important part in planning and evaluation. On the other hand, reliance on input norms has its dangers. One, already referred to, is their remoteness from the output—improved health, or at least satisfactory health care—which is the ultimate object of interest. It is true that inadequate inputs strongly suggest that health care is likely to be unsatisfactory. But the fact that inputs conform to norms is no guarantee that output is satisfactory, unless we can rely on the quality of the intervening processes for producing health care. A more subtle danger is that a concentration on input norms tends to confirm the health professional in a view of the health care production process which, to the economist, seems unduly rigid. We are dealing here with one of the many cases where professionals from different disciplines can misunderstand one another woefully because their viewpoints are not made explicit. Both the health professional and the health economist accept that the production process is one in which inputs of various kinds are combined to yield a certain output, even though they may express this in different languages. Where they tend to differ in substance is over the question of the proportions in which the inputs are mixed.

Putting their positions in extreme terms, one can say that the health professional thinks in terms of *fixed proportions*—there should, for example, be a fixed number of nurses per hospital bed or of doctors per thousand population. The economist thinks in terms of *variable proportions*, and believes that inputs are *substitutable* for one another—so that, for example, the same output of hospital in-patient services can be produced from the combination of many doctors and few nurses, or conversely. In fact neither party sticks rigidly to the extreme form of its position. From time to time, the health professionals discover the economist's concept of the substitutability of inputs—for example, that community health workers can sometimes be profitably substituted for nurses and midwives (as in primary health care) or that the services of complex labour-saving machinery can sometimes be replaced by the use of simpler machinery with a greater input of labour (as with appropriate technology). These innovations usually appear (and, economists would say, should appear) when there are great disparities between the prices of inputs and their relative marginal contributions to output. But once such conspicuous examples of the advantages of variations in input proportions have been recognized, they tend to establish as norms a new set of 'fixed' proportions—primary health care must always include the use of community workers even if these are not particularly cost-effective; no developing country should buy CAT scanners even if it is far shorter of nurses than of foreign currency. Why, asks the economist, cannot the doctors accept the simple principle that the efficient production of health care requires not fixed norms of inputs, but the adjustment of the input mix to local patterns of scarcity and abundance?

Even the economist will admit, however, that the input mix is much easier to adjust in the long run than in the short. In the short run (which is what concerns most health service managers) some degree of fixity is necessary, first because the supply of many services is limited, and second because out of the many conceivable patterns of input mix it is necessary at any given time to give preference to one as an instrument of management and a basis for operational planning. Hence if one is irenically disposed one can see a certain convergence of views between the health professional and the economist—the former treating input proportions as fixed unless there is strong reason to change them, the latter treating them as variable unless there is special justification for fixity.

What matters, from the point of view of the evaluator, is first the fact that input norms exist and can be used as an instrument of evaluation; and second that evaluations based on such norms must often be taken with more than a grain of salt. The main sources of such norms, and the flavour of salt appropriate to each, are discussed in the following subsections.

However, there is in addition a problem about how we conceive of the overall relation between health care inputs and health outputs which has been little regarded by either health professionals or economists. Both parties have tended to think of this relation as one of a fairly simple type where changes in inputs can be linked directly with resulting changes in outputs of health care or in health. It has been implicitly assumed that a given level of inputs corresponds, other things being equal, to a given level of output; if inputs are increased, the level of output rises, and if inputs are diminished, the level of output falls. We assume away two kinds of complications—the existence of time lags between changes in inputs and changes in outputs, and the possibility that changes upward and downward are not symmetrical. There is ample evidence that in the health field these complications are real, and that they have a bearing on health system evaluation.

The existence of lags (even of several decades) between cause and effect in the health field hardly needs demonstration. For example, at the statistical level it is commonly assumed that smoking, occupational exposures, and other factors which provoke cancers manifest themselves over periods of many years. At a rather different level, in the 1970s there were a number of oil-rich countries which spent heavily on health care in order to bring their morbidity and mortality levels into line with their incomes; their health situation improved only slowly, and even in the 1980s is in some cases far from satisfactory. It is as though when faced with new opportunities, health services must follow what in industrial economics has been called the 'learning curve'—with increased inputs (for example, new buildings or equipment) output follows a course which, plotted against time, rises rapidly at first, then more and more slowly, becoming asymptomatic with the planned long run output level. The learning involved is not only that of individual workers, but also the whole process by which an organization adapts to new ways of achieving its objectives.

All these examples involve the question of reversibility. In classical physics the arrow of time can point either way and any process can run backward, and the assumption of reversibility tends to carry over to other sciences, even such very applied ones as medicine where it would be difficult to apply it to real life situations. But it is obvious that in practice there are elements of irreversibility in many public health problems. The speed at which the numbers of cancer deaths are likely to change with changes in the incidence of smoking is not symmetrical as between increases and decreases. Sharp decreases in health care budgets do not simply reverse the effects of previous increases; and so on. It is not surprising, perhaps, that the question of the reversibility of health changes was little studied in the 1960s and 1970s, when budgets were booming and it seemed that the only way for inputs to go was up. It is less easy to understand why so little attention has been paid to this problem now the health care dream-time of the 1970s has been followed in many places by budgetary contraction.

This is particularly so since so much of the distinctive 1970s improvement in health care in developing countries was based on the expansion of measures of traditional public health—immunization, sanitation, etc.—and on primary care for mothers and children: these are activities whose effects we would expect to follow a learning curve, particularly since they depend on the adjustment of the behaviour not only of health workers, but also of the general population, to new ideas, procedures, and institutions. But this type of learning curve implies a certain degree of irreversibility; new behaviour, if it is genuinely health-promoting, is not abandoned when the budget items which led to its establishment is cut, but maintains and propagates itself from year to year and hopefully from generation to generation.

This is in addition to the element of irreversibility created by technical factors in some fields—for example, the attainment of local or national non-transmission levels for a communicable disease.

One reason why this problem has been so little recognized may be that for the health services to be explicit about the irreversibility of some of their achievements would be a sacrifice of their bargaining power in a period of budget pressure. This power rests partly on the public assumption that a reduction in health care inputs means a proportionate deterioration in health services. A recent UNICEF study *Adjustment with a human face* (UNICEF 1987), designed to constitute that agency as the voice of the world's poor as against the hard-hearted International Monetary Fund and only slightly softer World Bank, was directed specifically toward the collection data to show that budget cuts in the 1980s had led swiftly to a deterioration in the health of the poor in developing countries. To some readers, at least, the evidence collected was unconvincing, and could equally have been used to demonstrate the robustness of health improvements, at least in the short term, in the face of contracting health service budgets and static or falling incomes. If we accept the reality of lags in the process which produces health care, and of some degree of irreversibility, this has the inconvenient implication that the standards of inputs we should ideally set up for evaluation purposes should not be those for a single point in time, but should have a time dimension to correspond to the lags involved. We should ideally set up a norm for, say, the input of immunizers required not merely in a single year, but over a series of years, past, present, and future. This would in effect constitute part of a plan for an immunization program; so that at this point we are approaching from a different point of view the concept of norms as emerging from the planning process (subsection 5.5 below).

5.3.2 *Internationally derived norms of input*

In principle, input norms for health care can be international in two senses —they can be enunciated by international bodies, or they can be deduced from comparisons of input levels between countries. In practice international bodies have been chary of laying down norms of input except where these could be medically or epidemiologically based; it is possible to find precise guidance in the international literature on desirable levels of immunization (which implies certain inputs of vaccines), but not on the numbers and types of personnel required for a particular type and level of health care. This is probably fortunate since there are formidable difficulties in the way of laying down international norms, as explained elsewhere. Perhaps the nearest approaches to an attempt to define input norms have come from highly standardized campaigns against specific health problems undertaken on a worldwise basis—malaria, for example, and the earliest approaches to smallpox eradication.

Comparisons between countries do not formally yield norms of input, but they provide an informal mechanism by which the experience of one country influences the ambitions of another. 'Is the Minister aware' says the opposition member, 'that in Chaconia there are three doctors to every thousand people, whereas in Barataria we have only two?'—while, perhaps in Chaconia the junior doctors are bitterly criticizing their Minister for his failure to prevent medical unemployment. We have already indicated that such comparisons can be highly misleading because they take no account of the national availability of resources in general, as measured, for example, by national income per head. Nor do they take account of special reasons for greater or less availability of particular resources; for example, some countries may possess a stock of hospital accommodation which they have inherited from the colonial period, and which it would be wasteful to ignore, even though this may apparently bias their input pattern in comparison with other countries similar in income level and health problems. Thus south Yemen, whose capital, Aden, was formerly a military and naval base, had in 1976 1.5 hospital beds per thousand population; north Yemen, with a similar income level and mix of health problems, but no such colonial legacy, had only 0.5 beds (Cumper 1984). Nor do such comparisons take into account the substitutability of inputs discussed above, nor the efficiency with which inputs are used to produce health care. There is evidence, for example, that in 1976 the cost of attaining a given level of health service effectiveness in West Germany was some 20 per cent greater than in the UK.

In spite of these limitations, there is no doubt that casual acquaintance with input levels in other countries is an important influence on the (usually unexpressed) norms that health planners and administrators apply to their national scene. But the resulting norms are not precise enough to stand by themselves as a basis for evaluation.

5.3.3   *Nationally based input norms*

At the national level, there are a number of sources from which one can draw statements of the desirable level of health care inputs which, to some extent, can serve as norms for evalution purposes. Many of these are likely to be by-products of the policy–planning–budgeting process (which is discussed in more detail in Section 5.5 below). Thus budgets incorporate, at least implicitly, statements of the expected levels of all the inputs which generate current expenditure (though not of the value of the services of existing buildings and equipment, which do not). Plans incorporate a great deal of information about projected levels of inputs—capital inputs for plans which concentrate on the physical aspects of development (as many still do), inputs more generally for plans with a wider scope. The input side of such plans is likely to include standards of population coverage for various types of health care service. Policy statements may afford further, broader statements of norms of service. Manpower planning is likely to yield staffing norms for various health institutions. Moreover, such material may emerge not only from comprehensive national planning, but also from partial planning for particular areas and programmes. In a sense, therefore, there is usually no dearth of national material on which to base standards of health care inputs.

However, if such material is to be used for evaluation purposes it is necessary to keep in mind the possible distortions and biases which may be introduced by the functions other than evaluation which it is designed to serve. The input levels incorporated into a budget may be deliberately kept low to control expenditure—for example, in times of financial stringency the allowance for postponable items like maintenance may be set at a quite unrealistic level. Establishment lists may be out of date, reflecting past technologies and bargaining situations which through inertia have not yet been adjusted. Hence caution is necessary in using such material for national evaluation.

On the other hand, because of its strong base in administration and planning this material may well provide information not merely at the national level, but also for smaller units—districts, individual institutions. If performance data are also available for these units, evaluation can be pushed further than if it were necessary to settle for national or regional averages, and can include an assessment of the degree of equity in the distribution of health care inputs.

5.4 Financial and administrative standards

This chapter takes the view that health care programmes, in addition to their contribution to better health, must be evaluated in accordance with financial and administrative criteria. This could be argued on very general grounds; if such criteria are valid, any departure from them represents a misuse of resources which must detract from the potential welfare of the society. But in fact this is not necessary; few people would dispute in practice that health services have certain financial and administrative obligations.

These obligations are reasonably clear so far as they concern the health services run by government. They are in general the same as those accepted by any department of government, and usually embodied in the appropriate regulations. Standards of this kind are discussed in the following section.

The situation is less clear about that part of the health services (in many developing countries the greater part) which falls outside the government sector. The extent to which private health care is obligated to follow financial and administrative standards, and the way in which these can be defined, are explored in the last part of this section.

5.4.1   *The standards of the public sector*

It is easiest to look first at the government sector where standards are often given a specific form. Two sets of standards are almost universal; those for accounting, budgeting, and financial transactions embodied in the financial regulations, and those for general administrative work embodied in one or more sets of civil service regulations. Government health service officials are usually continuously aware of the pressure on them to conform to these norms, and would not be surprised to find this conformity treated as a subject for evaluation—indeed, it is all too often the only type of evaluation which their employers take seriously.

These general regulations may be condensed in some areas and amplified in others to serve the special purposes of the health services. Thus Jamaica has among other such documents a manual for the running of the smallest (Type I) health centres and a guidebook for the use of doctors in the government service. This is particularly useful to new graduates (who receive little relevant formal instruction) and to foreign doctors coming to work in Jamaica (though it must be mentioned that among Indian immigrant doctors there exists an informal network which serves the same purpose very efficiently). However, the existence of such documents does not exempt the evaluator from all further enquiry. They may well be out of date, since their preparation is not usually a continuous activity; if so, this is a fact important both in itself and for its implications about management. The difficulties which may be encountered in constructing an up-to-date set of financial and administrative guidelines constitute one reason for the existence of Subsection 5.4.3.

It should further be remembered that the overall financial and administrative codes only exist by virtue of their legislative framework. It is this, ultimately, which gives authority to the whole, even though members of the government health service staff may be ignorant of it or even act in contravention of it. This framework tends to follow the same lines for all countries which have been within the British tradition; in Subsection 5.4.3 it is examined in detail for the not untypical case of Jamaica. It may be necessary to pay particular attention to a country's personnel system as it is applied to health workers. In the colonial period proper, systems of job classification, on which depended salaries, promotional prospects, and much of the national budget, tended to be informal and even simple, being based on a few categories with elementary qualifications so far as local recruits were concerned, helped out in the case of the few more highly qualified people with appointments in the imperial (not local) service and by special 'super-numerary' posts. As the time for independence drew near, the tasks of government became more complicated and called for a greater range of qualifications; so, too, did the range of jobs open to dark-skinned locals. There was a proliferation of salary grades; several pages of the budget document might be taken up with variously named, overlapping pay scales. By reaction, in the postwar period these were often rationalized (rather on the model of the United States public service) by grouping together jobs with similar entry conditions (e.g. all non-medical graduates in the arts and sciences), jobs with similar functions *vis à vis* the public, and so on. In this way the miscellany of jobs might be reduced to twenty or so, each with half a dozen salary grades—this in spite of the fact that extended scales were often broken up, and proficiency bars replaced with transitions from one category to another. In the short run, this was a very useful facility for budgeting purposes. But it also emphasized the uniformities, and relative differentials, between jobs in different fields. It therefore made it difficult to adjust health salaries simply on the grounds of the market situation of a single category, without providing grounds for increasing or decreasing (usually the former!) the salaries of other workers. This is one of the points brought out in Subsection 5.4.3.

5.4.2 *Jamaica: the legal framework of the government health service*

In 1974 the Government of Jamaica published a Green Paper containing proposals for a national health service, 'Medicare for Jamaica'. It contained both a review of the past and proposals for the future, and ranged, untypically for such documents, over all aspects of health care. It even included a comment on the legislative framework of the health services: 'The legal framework of the Health Services is defined in laws enacted before the acquisition of independence. The purposes, objectives and machinery of the Health Service changed thereafter and many of the laws are inadequate for day to day management, but no comprehensive efforts have been made to bring existing legislation up to date.' (p. 59). Following this, efforts were made to modernise particular pieces of legislation, but for different reasons, most of these have remained functionally inoperative. The need for a comprehensive overhaul of the legislative framework of the Health Services is, if anything, more necessary than it was in 1974. In the last ten years there has been a change of emphasis, as well as considerable development, in the delivery of health care. New cadres of workers have been trained and placed in the field. Throughout, the legal framework has remained virtually unchanged. Experiments with the introduction of various types of health workers had been taking place in Jamaica for many years. In 1954 two theatre nurses were trained in the USA as nurse anaesthetists, beginning a programme which has gone through various metamorphoses and is now settled in the School of Nurse Anaesthesia at the Kingston Public Hospital. Community health aides, school dental nurses, mental health officers, pharmacy technicians, and nurse practitioners have been introduced into the Health Service at various times during the last twenty years, but except for the school dental nurse, no attempt was made to provide those delivering services of a professional nature with either legal recognition or protection. Problems in practice arising from the lack of a legal status began to be apparent, especially affecting nurse practitioners and mental health officers.

Jamaica is not alone in its difficulties. Problems such as these have become widespread following the change of emphasis to primary health care in the delivery of health services. At the Fifth Commonwealth Medical Conference in 1977 it was recognized that there was an urgent need to regularize the legal base of the new cadres of health workers which were increasingly being introduced by various countries to improve the spread of the delivery of health care. Follow-up action was taken by making this one of the subjects considered in Workshops on Medical-Legal Issues held in Barbados in June 1979 and in Malawi in October 1979 (Commonwealth Secretariat 1978*a*, 1979*a*, 1979*b*). Governments were urged to review the legal arrangements which affect the selection, training, authorization, practice, and supervision of new cadres of workers, and provide not only legal recognition, but protection for workers and for those whom they treat, appropriate to their status and function. In spite of such urging, progress on this front appears to be slow.

Because of the existence of these cadres of health workers without legal recognition or status in Jamaica, it seemed timely and appropriate to extend the PEU/EPC Jamaica Health Services Evaluation Project (see Appendix) to focus on the legal problems arising from their practice, and their integration into the legal framework of the delivery of health care. The close link between this and other aspects of the functioning of the health services became apparent as the study proceeded, highlighting the restraints which lack of attention to the legislative framework in Jamaica had imposed on the delivery of care. This subsection is based on the Jamaican experience, but while its specifics apply to that country, the general points made apply much more widely.

Legislative framework of the health services The laws governing the delivery of health care in Jamaica are as follows:

    Dangerous Drugs Act   cap 90 Laws of Jamaica
    Dental Act   No 13 of 1972
    Family Planning Act   No 22 of 1970
    Hospitals (Public) Act   cap 150 amended by Act 30 of 1963
    Mental Hospitals Act   cap 242 amended No 5t of 1974
    Medical Act   No 22 of 1972 amended No 28 of 1975
    Nurses and Midwives Act   No 35 of 1964
    Nursing Homes Registration Act   cop 263
    Opticians Act   cap 269
    Pharmacy Act   No 5 of 1966
    Professions Supplementary of Medicine Act   No 49 of 1965
    Public Health Act   passed 1974, promulgated Feb. 1985
    University Hospitals Act   cap 400

A Pesticides Act and a Clean Air Act were also passed in the year 1974, but neither has yet become operative. The administrative machinery needed under these Acts was not put in place. The Food and Drugs Act is only partly operative.

As can be seen, the legislation covers three main areas—public health, hospitals and nursing homes, and the registration of the various professionals recognized as delivering health care. The balance between these elements does not reflect the importance attached to the delivery of Primary Health Care which has dominated the development of the health services during the last twenty years. The history of attempts to bring the Public Health law up to date provides an apt illustration.

The Public Health Act In 1974 a new Public Health Act received parliamentary approval. The provisions of the new law embodied the changes that had already taken place in the management of public health. It gave legal recognition to the change in executive control of public health, from the Central Board of Health to the Minister of Health, which had followed upon the acquisition of independence, and it brought within the law matters that had come to be regarded as properly belonging to public health. The parishes, as local Boards of Health, retained the right to make regulations about, and control, sanitary matters, nuisances, licences for trades people and the like. The Minister was given the power to make regulations on a number of, mostly new, topics. To notifiable and communicable diseases, vaccination and inoculations, were added air, soil, and water pollution, collection of epidemiological data, occupational disease and employment, health hazards, and pest control.

Because of a series of administrative misunderstandings, compounded by union representations and a change of government, this Act remained on the Statute Book for ten years without being brought into effect. During this time where a topic was covered by previously existing regulations, these continued to apply. Where there were no regulations, staff initiatives and responses to crises determined the level of the work carried out. This ten-year legal hiatus coincided with a period of intense reorganization and development of primary health care and public health matters generally. It also saw a decrease in the numbers of Medical Officers of Health—the effective heads of the local public health system—with consequent changes in the responsibilities of other staff, such as the public health nurses and public health inspectors, and in the exercise of powers of the local boards of health. By the time, early in 1985, that the Public Health Act was brought into effect by notice in the Gazette, substantial policy changes which would necessitate change in the law were already being debated. At issue was the effectiveness of the traditional responsibility for public health matters exercised by local government bodies. The emphasis being placed on primary health care has seemed to give a new meaning to the term 'Public Health' carrying indications that the Ministry of Health should have the responsibility for it.

Problems with the operation of the Kingston and St. Andrew Corporation, which is the capital's Local Board of Health, provided a test for the new approach. On past occasions when the operations of the KSAC were suspended, management of its affairs passed to designated Commissioners. On this occasion, following the procedure laid down in the new Act, i.e. after enquiry, finding the Local Board in default of its duties, the Minister by Order in the Gazette divested the Board of its health functions, and transferred these to the Permanent Secretary of the Ministry of Health.

The provisions of the Public Health Act 1974 make it clear that without this procedure Parish Councils which remain in existence cannot be divested of their public health responsibilities. A change in the law is necessary if this is to be done. Directions that public health staff employed by the Parish Councils are to be transferred to the employment of the Ministry of Health have caused considerable confusion. The legality of the proceeding is in question and this has consequences in practice for the staff who try to carry out duties imposed on them by Local Board regulations as representatives of the Board.

There is no way of quantifying with any certainty how much the ten year lack of an operative Public Health Act affected the administration of the service and the morale of staff employed in public health work. The uncertainties voiced by both health staff and administration show that it has not been without considerable effect. The present confusion can only worsen staff morale, and it can be no comfort to reflect that much of this could have been avoided by a little attention to the law.

Mental health Mental health demonstrates another aspect of the legal problems besetting the Health Service. Here it is the absence of legislation that creates difficulties. The law on the treatment of mentally ill persons is set out in the Mental Hospital Act which dates back to 1881, with amendments in 1973 and 1974. Naturally enough, it does not reflect the considerable changes that have taken place in the recognition and treatment of mental illnesses and the management of rehabilitation where this is possible in the community. The only indication of these changes is in the 1974 amendment which allowed regional hospitals to care for some of the mentally ill who would normally have been sent to Bellevue Hospital, and provided for the appointment of mental health officers to assist in the process of providing care in the community. It was acknowledged that this rather rough and ready amendment was only intended to provide interim coverage until a Mental Health Bill, then actively in preparation, could be enacted. This bill suffered the same fate as the three previous attempts to change the old Mental Hospitals Law. It never reached the stage of being drafted. As a consequence the hospitals throughout the island have no clear and standard policy on the management of mentally ill patients and the status and practice of mental officers have many ambiguities. Neither recruitment, training nor practice is the subject of regulation, and the recognition provided by the 1974 amendment is far from adequate. As a result what is achieved in the way of working relationships either with others in the health services, or with the police, judiciary, and social services, depends heavily on the personal resourcefulness of the individual MHO. The need of a Mental Health Act is acutely felt (Ministry of Health Jamaica/PAHO 1984). Even more urgent is an up-to-date Mental Hospitals Act which will reflect those changes that have already taken place, albeit uneasily, outside the law.

The professional councils Legislation providing for the registration of the professional deliverers of care in the health service is a necessary part of its legal framework. It not only regulates recruitment, training, practice, and discipline in each professional group but it provides the basis on which the interaction between them in the delivery of care is built. Within the terms of the Acts and the regulations made under them, both the practitioner and the patient are legally protected. The Councils set up under the various pieces of legislation are charged with the responsibility not only of seeing that standards of competence are met, but of ensuring that proper standards of professional conduct are maintained. It should be noted, however, that this latter has usually been interpreted to mean waiting on complaints before action is considered.

The list of laws show that most professional workers are covered. Doctors are registered under the Medical Act, dentists and school dental nurses under the Dental Act. Registered nurses, enrolled assistant nurses and midwives come under the Nurses and Midwives Act. Pharmacists, but not pharmacy technicians are registered under the Pharmacy Act, opticians under the Opticians Act and radiographers, medical laboratory technicians, physiotherapists, occupational therapists, and dieticians working in public hospitals and registered nursing homes are registered with the Council set up under the Professions Supplementary to Medicine Act. But, by and large, new cadres which have been trained and put in the field to fill gaps in the delivery of professional services have not been either legally recognized or protected. They are mostly nurses who have received training in certain post-basic specialties and are functioning in ways not covered by their registration under the Nurses and Midwives Act. Nurse anaesthetists, nurse practitioners, and mental health officers all deliver care but neither they nor their patients are legally protected.

In addition, the lack of legal recognition for their training and competence makes it difficult to integrate them satisfactorily into the health services. Legal regulation of training and practice provides the only generally acceptable way of defining areas of practice, levels of competence and the exercise of responsibility.

New cadres: some problem areas   The new cadres of health workers were developed, not only because of a shortage of doctors and pharmacists, but in response to changes in medical practice, drug therapies, and the perceived social and political need to extend the delivery of health care, both preventive and curative. The new cadres function in both primary and secondary care. Nurse anaesthetists work in hospital, mental health officers and pharmacy technicians work in both hospitals and health centres, nurse practitioners provide significant amounts of the curative care in Type II and Type III health centres, and their use in hospital out-patients is being considered. Without the recognition and protection given to these workers by registration, the question of who must accept the legal responsibility for their practice becomes an important one. For the pharmacy technicians, the answer is clear. He cannot function except under the direct supervision of a registered pharmacist. That this requirement severely limits his usefulness is apparent. He cannot provide assistance where the need is greatest, in the health centres, where dispensing continues to be done by nurses not trained in pharmacy, to the disquiet of all concerned. For the other three cadres, the problems arising from a lack of a legal status had by 1983 become obvious and increasingly difficult to ignore.

Nurse practitioners   The inability of nurse practitioners to prescribe drugs for the treatment of their patients because of the lack of a legal status focused attention on the matter. The Pharmacy Act limited the duty of pharmacists to fill prescriptions to those of registered practitioners named in the Act. The nurse practitioner was not among these, and was, moreover, not a practitioner known to the law. Questions about training, competence in practice and supervision were raised. A paper describing the work on a legal status for the nurse practitioner was prepared and made available. In brief, the decision was taken that the Nurses and Midwives Act be amended to give the Nursing Council power to open registers for certain post-basic specialties concerned with the delivery of care beyond the competence of the registered nurse, thus providing the needed recognition and regulation of their recruitment, training, practice, and discipline. Different regulations would have to be drawn for the different specialties. The immediate need was for the registration of nurse anaesthetists and nurse practitioners who already had acceptable training courses and for whom codes of practice had been prepared.

Mental health officers   A legal status for the mental health officer will be rather more difficult to achieve. There is no mental health (as against mental hospital) legislation and therefore no generally recognized and accepted framework for his training and practice. Some of the problems faced by mental health officers demonstrate how the ambiguities of their position affect their functioning. The 1974 amendment to the Mental Hospital Act provided for the appointment of mental health officers who were persons so designated by the Minister of Health. They were given the power to enter premises where they reasonably believed there was a person of unsound mind not receiving proper care. The purpose of the right of entry was to make an inspection. If, on inspection, such a person were found, and would not of his own accord accompany the officer to seek treatment, the officer could request a constable to effect the removal to the nearest clinic or hospital. This is a situation calculated to satisfy neither the patient nor his relatives, the mental health officer nor the police. Mental health officers became even more concerned when upon enquiry from the Law Officers of the Crown they were told that as the MHO had no legal authority beyond that of inspection, the government could not accept liability for injuries sustained while assisting a constable to take a person of unsound mind for treatment, though an ex gratia award might be payable depending on the circumstances.

It was thought that the mental health officers could be used to take up from the streets persons of unsound mind wandering around and take them to the nearest hospital or clinic. It has been pointed out to them that they have no legal status under the Town and Community and the Vagrancy Acts and cannot act without the assistance of a constable. It is obvious that the procedures used by MHOs for initiating treatment of involuntary patients need careful consideration, as they may well involve infringements of the rights of patients that may be unauthorized. MHOs are expected to be the effective agents of community care for the mentally ill. It is not at all clear in the present circumstances how their work is expected to integrate with that of other health workers whether in primary or in secondary care. Attention to the legal basis of their operation would go a long way to providing the answers.

Public health nurses   The development of new cadres of necessity changes some of the roles of existing health service workers. Nowhere is this more apparent than in primary health care where the key worker in the system is the public health nurse. The shortage of Medical Officers of Health, whether at the district, parish or regional level has effectively increased her day-to-day responsibilities. Ironically, this is the only group of established health workers that has always been without even legal recognition. This has created some tension between the public health nurses and the new cadres of nurses with post-basic specialties, often with trainings that overlap theirs, who come within their supervisory responsibilities in the field. A legal status for the new cadres with no change in the status of PHNs is likely to intensify the problems.

The delivery of health care is a co-operative activity involving large numbers of trained personnel. One important factor in its functioning is that each worker knows the level of skill, the area and methods of practice and the level of responsibility of the others. This necessary condition is made possible through the legal regulation of practice. Thus the worker, the patient and the public interest are all protected. Stated like this, it is obvious that all trained professionals in the health service whose work involves the exercise of a duty of care should have their training and practice legally regulated.

There has however been a noticeable reluctance to consider this aspect of planning when decisions have been taken to introduce new categories of workers into the health services of Jamaica. The difficulties in practice and the frustrations that can result have already been indicated in discussing the problems of nurse practitioners and mental health officers. The undermining of the confidence felt by these and other new cadres of workers is visible in Jamaica in the rapid turnover of staff.

The planning process has usually included great attention to job descriptions and sometimes prolonged negotiations about where in the establishment scale the new cadre of worker should be located. This may inform workers about what they are expected to do, but is of very little help in providing a basis for their integration into the work of the health services. A more useful way of doing this, where the Ministry of Health is the sole employer of a cadre of worker who works only with others similarly employed, is by the issuing of Standing Orders. These can cover matters such as qualification, conditions of service, and area and methods of practice which would include directions on referrals and supervision. Issued over the signature of the chief medical officer, these have the authority of a ministry directive. It is important, however, to be clear that where these cover new cadres of workers, they amount to recognition, but do not confer a legal status.

Such a status can only be conferred by legislation—whether in the words of the acts themselves or by regulations made under their authority. It is obviously not necessary to pass a new act every time a new cadre of worker comes into existence. Amendments to existing acts may serve just as well, depending upon the circumstances of each case. It is in the regulations setting out the requirements for recruitment, training, practice, and discipline that differences between cadres have to be carefully spelled out, for this is the basis for the determination of legal responsibility.

Due largely to the efforts of the public health service, Jamaica now has a population which is reasonably well-educated in health matters, with rising expectations about the competence of those who deliver health care. In such circumstances it is necessary that the health services have a legal framework which enables the system of delivery of care to function properly. Given the present state of things there is much that needs to be done before this can be achieved.

It would be helpful if, when policy decisions involving new services and new cadres of workers are being taken, such matters as legislation assigning powers, rights, and responsibilities and the legal status of workers were considered right from the start. These matters could be dealt with as integral parts of the planning process, and should go on to inform the process of administration at all levels, and not be, as now, *ad hoc* responses to the emergence of problems of practice in the field.

5.4.3   *Jamaica: problems of the administrative foundations*

In defining the administrative norms for the health services, much of the detail must be drawn from the regulations and usages of each individual country. But there are certain fundamentals which it is specially necessary to get clear. These concern the relations between the technical and administrative senior staff of the services. They are discussed here in relation to Jamaica (which in this book is used, unhappily, to exemplify so much that is problematical in management), but they occur so widely, particularly in governments committed to the 'Westminster' system, that they clearly have an importance beyond any single example.

Jamaica began the political process of change from a colony to an independent nation state in 1944, and completed it in 1962. While public attention was paid mainly to some obvious aspects of parliamentary democracy, like universal suffrage and the adoption of a written constitution, it was accepted among the cognoscenti and those hungry for office that an important administrative element was the introduction of ministries. In the colonial period each functional area of government had been in the charge of a director, subject to the governor, while the basic administrative framework was provided through the office of the colonial secretary, who was also subject to the governor. With political independence each area became the responsibility of a politically appointed minister, whose policy decisions were given administrative effect through a Permanent Secretary representing the highest rank of the intendedly non-political civil service.

Since neither ministers nor permanent secretaries could be assumed to be able to provide technical guidance in fields such as health and education, it was necessary to find some way in which technical specialists could be given an appropriate place in the structure of the ministries. This is the problem which in Jamaica has haunted the Ministry of Health since political independence in 1962.

Figures 5.1 and 5.2 represent different and extreme attempts to solve this problem, both being approximate representations of the structure of the Jamaican Ministry of Health at different dates. Figure 5.1 shows a situation in which the Chief Medical Officer and the Permanent Secretary are equals, subordinate only to the Minister of Health. This is a workable administrative system so long as the programmes to be administered are of a routine kind, continuing without much change from year to year. In such a system the Permanent Secretary controls the supply of resources (necessarily, since by an immutable law of public administration he is the officer responsible for expenditure under the budget); the Chief Medical Officer controls the technical inputs to the health services; and only slight changes in either respect are required from year to year.

Such a system purportedly minimizes the administrative role of professional health workers, whose function appears mainly advisory to the Minister. It is realistic, however, only so long as no substantial initiatives are required. It needs no argument that since 1963, the year to which Fig. 5.1 relates, the initiatives have been many and important. Some are technically based—for example, on the availability of new drugs and contraceptives. Others represent new (or newly popular) organizational ways of tackling old problems, such as the availability of clinics for the care of mothers and children. Each initiative tends to force the technical person involved into the role of the manager of a programme, developing its organization and controlling the necessary inputs. But this control is difficult for a medically qualified manager to ensure within the ministerial system, where for most items it belongs properly to the Permanent Secretary's side of the organization. Hence the years since 1963 have seen a proliferation of programmes and a struggle by professional staff to establish these in the budget and to

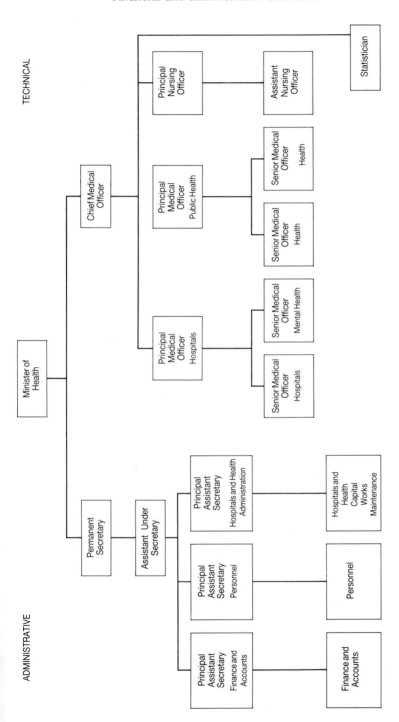

Fig. 5.1 Ministry of Health, Jamaica: organogram, about 1963.

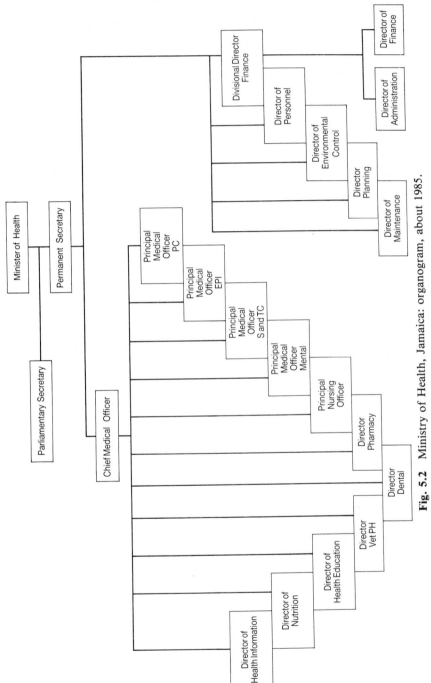

Fig. 5.2 Ministry of Health, Jamaica: organogram, about 1985.

secure for them outside funds not under ordinary budgetary control. These problems could perhaps be overcome by a Minister strong enough to knock together the heads of his co-equal Permanent Secretary and Chief Medical Officer; but no one of quite this calibre appeared.

At the opposite extreme is the structure of the Ministry of Health as it appeared in Jamaica about 1985 (Fig. 5.2). Here the Chief Medical Officer is nominally the meeting point for no less than eleven programme-oriented divisions, each of which draws on the resources provided by an additional five administrative divisions (finance, personnel, environmental control—what is it doing in there?—planning and maintenance; the Permanent Secretary controls these latter directly, and the programme divisions through the Chief Medical Officer, to whom he is definitely superior in authority. The Permanent Secretary therefore has great (but in practice unused) opportunities for programme planning and management, while the Chief Medical Officer is reduced, through the multiplicity of activities for which he is in some sense responsible, to the status of an assistant and adviser to the Permanent Secretary.

The comparison of the structures shown in Figs. 5.1 and 5.2 is not meant to highlight all or even the commonest administrative problems of the health services. There is, for example, the need (obviously ignored in Fig. 5.2) to limit each person's span of control so as to provide a feasible management structure. There is also the widespread tendency for the heads of certain programmes to become the representatives for certain groups of professionals—so that the director of pharmaceutical supplies comes to stand for the pharmacists, and the principal nursing officer for the registered nurses. It would be gratifying if, as part of our evaluation, we could lay down an ideal administrative structure and ask whether the actuality conformed to this ideal. But this evidently we cannot do. The fact that the British National Health Service is currently once again under fundamental review confirms that developed countries are still struggling to find the right allocation of management functions between different kinds of medical and non-medical professionals and the right structure within which a state-supported scheme should operate. But if we cannot lay down a universal ideal, we can at least, as part of our evaluation, ascertain as fully as possible what is intended by a particular organizational structure like those shown in the figures, and by comparing this with the actual achievements of management, evaluate their administrative performance.

5.4.4 *Administrative standards in the private sector*

So far we have discussed mainly the standards of health care management in the public sector. But it is easily forgotten that in many developing and also developed countries a substantial part of health care is provided through the private sector. For Bangladesh in 1977, for instance, this proportion was estimated at 80 per cent in expenditure terms, much of this being accounted for by the sellers of drugs who were also one of the health professionals of first resort (WHO/Ministry of Health Dacca 1977). The quality of national private health care is therefore important for evaluation.

In some respects—for example, in relation to technical quality—the private sector can be evaluated along the same lines as the public sector, though it is likely to show an enormous variability. But this is evidently not true of administration and finance, where the demands on the public and private sectors differ fundamentally. One can indeed ask whether there are any administrative and financial norms which apply to the private health sector.

At first sight the answer seems necessarily to be 'no'. What norms can be applied to a doctor's one-room office opening off an Indian market, or a Sri Lankan ayurvedic's veranda, or the crowded and easily purchasable plenty of a Thai drugseller? But the field for administrative evaluation is not as blank as it seems at first.

To begin with, in most countries the basic health laws presuppose a minimum of administration. To the stranger seeking to buy without question a dose of tetracycline or even of a narcotic, the informal Bangkok pharmacist may appear as a champion of freedom. But laws exist governing the records he should keep and the extent to which he diagnoses and prescribes, and he might be a better pharmacist if he observed them. Similarly, the private doctor should conform to the legal framework in such matters as the notification of diseases, which imposes its own administrative load. The extent to which such laws are in practice observed is a legitimate subject for evaluation. So is the extent to which the non-health public operates under the protection of planning and factory acts which have a health component, and also the extent to which these are observed. It should not be forgotten that some of the most gruesome health emergencies of recent years, such as Bhopal and Chernobyl, arose from violations of acts and regulations whose primary purpose lay outside the health care sector. Deaths at Bhopal, for example, would have been far fewer if the houses of the poor had not been allowed to cluster round the factory walls. In the second place, there are health institutions in every country which, though private, approximate in function to public facilities and are subject to the same expectations to observe high standards in their administrative and financial procedures, whatever their legal status—for example, mission hospitals, and the larger commercial hospitals.

In the third place, there is the very wide field of health care which is privately provided but publicly financed. In some countries this accounts for only a minor part of health care—for example, the Indian scheme by which employees of the central government consult private doctors who are reimbursed from public funds. In other countries a large share of health care is provided in this way—among the developing countries, the social security institutions of some south and central American countries are famous and even notorious. One of the weaknesses of such schemes is their difficulty in meeting norms of administrative and financial economy or even sometimes probity, manifested in their swollen overheads and inflated building costs which have helped to make them one of the least efficient ways of providing national health care. It is the evaluation of the administrative and financial quality of these schemes, as much as of their medical effectiveness, which has produced the current movement in the Americas toward truly public health care systems. Yet such schemes offer to an active central government a unique means to raise the standards of the private health care provider through the incentives which can be offered to him under schemes of public payment. This has been exemplified in the United States by the attachment of standard levels of treatment cost to Diagnosis Related Groups as part of the attempt to contain expenditure on Medicare and Medicaid, an approach which is believed to have had a substantial effect on the procedures of health care institutions. It should be remembered, also, that within the British National Health Service the general practitioners have the status of independent private contractors whose choices between different forms of medicine—curative, preventive, rehabilitative—and of office organization are affected by the range and form of the payments which reimburse them for their services. The evaluator should pay attention to the extent to which the health care system of a developing country exploits opportunities of this kind.

Finally, few countries, developed or developing, seem to have exploited fully the openings offered to central regulation of health policy by the growth in private health insurance. In some middle income countries this means of financing is an important contributor to health care, providing the moderately prosperous with something better, or at least more comfortable, than the basic care obtainable from government institutions. Generally, health insurance is subject only to the general requirements imposed on all forms of insurance, even though its conventions of payment may influence the nature of what is offered by health care providers—for example, the chargeability of immunizations and check-ups may influence the balance of health care provision between curative and preventive.

There is of course an uncomfortably idealistic flavour to any suggestion that the government of a poor country, perhaps already struggling with economic problems that cannot be entirely blamed on the International Monetary Fund, should extend its concern to the private health field. After all, the medical associations, the traditional guardians of the private health field, have seen off invasions of their territory in countries like the United States (till recent years) with far fewer competing problems. But one must accept that this is an area with definite possibilities of improving health care through administrative action, and should attempt some evaluation of the extent to which the available opportunities have been used. Ironically, the medical and nursing councils which almost everywhere act as nominal guarantors of the standards of Western medicine in developing countries receive subventions from public funds, but do not acknowledge even the obligation to maintain an up-to-date roster of active health workers. (As so often, the administrative record of the nurses is in this respect somewhat better than that of the doctors.)

5.5   The policy–planning–budgeting system: hero or villain?

It has already been pointed out that the policy, planning, and budgeting system of a country's health sector offers in principle a unique opportunity for health care evaluation. In effect, we can regard this system as a means by which the intentions of a country's government (and hence its people— for simplicity we assume democracy) are translated stage by stage into specific health care activities. For, at least so far as the government health services are concerned, the extent to which they carry out their duties can be evaluated by comparing their observed performance with their budget. The adequacy of the budget, in turn, as a single year's statement of the resources available for health care and how they are to be applied, can be evaluated by comparing the budget (financially and in its real-life implications) with the health plan from which it is presumably derived. This plan, in turn, can be seen as an actualization of the policies on which the plan is founded, and can be evaluated in terms of the extent to which it correctly represents them. Thus the whole management system of the health services can be evaluated in terms which should make easy the corrective task of management.

This approach is implied in much of the recent work of the World Health Organization on health service management, though that body prefers the word programming to planning and has other peculiarities of terminology. For example, stress is currently laid on the proportion of plan, budget, and actual activity devoted to primary health care as a test of the political commitment and planning competence of countries which have accepted the policy of Health for All by the Year 2000. The approach has brought to the fore the need for a more consistent definition of policy, a variable before often taken as independent and beyond analysis but in practice given varying degrees of specificity. For example, if we define policy as a statement of the desirable objectives of the health care system in general terms, in 1971 the new state of Bangladesh could legitimately have adopted the policy of making basic health care available to the rural population. In fact by stating as a matter of 'policy' that this would be done by establishing a health centre in each thana (subdistrict), it took a long step toward planning; and by specifying the exact establishment of the thana health centre and the details of its duties, as the then Secretary for Health wished to do, it stretched the word policy in a way which was inconsistent with good management—and whose vanity became apparent as soon as the 'policy' was compared with the available resources of that unhappy country. It has had of course to be quantitatively modified; and since it was a 'policy', this could only be done by reference of every detail to the highest levels of government.

But even when policy, planning, and budgeting are carefully defined, there are serious difficulties in using the relation between them as the principal form of evaluation. These arise from the concept of planning itself, and are not unique to health. They can be seen more clearly if one considers the history of general social and economic planning in developing countries.

The idea that the government of an undeveloped country can meaningfully plan the development of its economy and society has a complex history. In part it derives from the example of Stalinist Russia, with its five-year plans from the 1920s onward and its specialist system of production planning under Gosplan. The Russian example had an early, though brief influence on the health care field in developing countries since it influenced Sigerist to become an evangelist for national health systems, and Nehru in India to see national planning as the path to postcolonial independence; the convergence of these influences produced the Bhore Committee report in 1947, which foreshadowed in many ways current ideas about primary health care. But health planning as it has been practised recently is much more the product of the period of general economic and social planning which began in the developing countries after the Second World War. This form of planning did not depend on the government's having complete bureaucratic control of the economy, as did that of Russia; rather it was heavily influenced by the experience of countries which appeared to have profited from planning in a context which was at least partly commercial—the war economies of Britain and the United States, and the purposeful reconstruction of western Europe under the Marshall Plan. French *dirigisme* (technocratic rather than theocratic, social democratic rather than socialist, dependent on accord between a few major investors) was particularly influential.

This form of planning dominated the development of the poor countries (and, even more, the development literature) during the 1960s and 1970s, except only for those countries which preferred a Russian model, like Cuba, or like China originated their own. It was a period during which the western industrial countries found in it a means of purging their colonial past by the sacrifice of nothing more vital to their well-being than capital, while the governments of newly postcolonial territories sought continuing, but if possible politically neutral, sources of investment. By and large, up to 1973 the system was successful, in the sense that on the average national incomes grew faster than population—in some cases, such as Singapore and Taiwan, enormously faster. It is not surprising that from the 1970s the essentials of economic and social planning were extended to the sphere of health care. Here too, why should not a technically correct specification of the steps to be taken to achieve the agreed ends of policy, backed by a firm statement of intent on the part of the government, be an adequate basis for achieving the required improvement in health care? It was accepted that other elements of the managerial process were also required for health development, but the health plan was central. This approach to the problem produced valuable results (e.g. Gish 1975, 1977). Yet even in the 1970s the development planning process was not without its critics. India, a country much planned against, naturally developed its own brand of cynicism. In the 1970s was published a prospectus for the next five-year federal plan, including a detailed timetable of steps to be taken. Critics noted with pleasure that the last step was, not 'implement', but 'publish' the plan. For it was only too true that there was now a tendency, even in the government of India itself, to see the plan as a document to be brandished rather than a course of action to be followed.

About the same time a report circulated of a conversation between civil servants. Said the older 'what are you reading?' 'See' said his junior, 'it is the current plan'. 'But' said the senior, 'do you not know that we are forbidden to read works of fiction in office hours?' For India had by this time a growing experience of proposed government activities which had lost touch with reality before any plan could be realized.

These two stories encapsulate the main defects of development planning as practised in the postwar period. There was a widespread belief that the plan was important because it represented a commitment of government. If this were so, the plan would only have economic value if implemented by government. But its real economic value may have been rather different; it was to reduce the uncertainty of economic affairs by providing a common framework of action. In Indian terms, for example, the plan tried to ensure that the demand for electricity by the new factories of Tata and Birla would bear some relation to the supply of electricity from the central authority (or, in French terms, that Citroen could go on producing the 2CV for the farming community without having to fear competition from Peugeot or Renault). All economic factors face uncertainty of two kinds—that which arises from their ignorance of the intentions of other actors within the economy, and that which arises from outside causes. There is normally a great increase in economic efficiency attainable if uncertainty of either kind can be reduced. This reduction is one of the positive functions of national planning. It requires not only that a government shall implement a plan for its own actions, but also that it shall negotiate it with and publicize it to others.

But a national plan cannot fully protect the actors in the economy against external events; the most it can do is to offer them an improvement in the quality of the available predictions of these events. The Indian planning authorities by the 1970s had had all too much experience of their inability to control the environment; not only were external markets untrustworthy, but the Indian economy had been buffeted by droughts, floods, and wars which not only constituted elements of uncertainty in themselves, but generated unpredictable behaviour in local producers, distributors, and consumers. Hence it had become necessary to recognize that there were strict limits to the functions of planning as a way of limiting uncertainty. These limits were even narrower for countries whose economies were more outward-looking than that of India.

The Indian experience suggested another characteristic of planning which was to limit its usefulness in developing countries; no sooner was the importance of the planning *function* realized, than it was incorporated in a planning institution—in the Indian case the important and, in its own terms, admirable Planning Commission. Though this permitted a high level of technical expertise, its effect was to segregate a function which should pervade all levels of management, and to burden it with a certain institutional jealousy.

It may be asked why, if economic planning had such unavoidable limitations, did it appear so successful for two decades after its first application to the new generation of developing countries? The answer may well be simply that the world was in a long period of expansion in which almost any form of economic management could claim success. But in the 1970s the post-war boom was nearing its end, and the defects of development planning were becoming obtrusive. In the 1980s planning in the older, uniformly optimistic sense has been losing credit. In a world economy which is no longer consistently expanding, it has given place to terms of art like 'structural adjustment', which connote, in practice, planning without the hidden assumption of an expanding environment. This is, of course, the point at which international and national health authorities have adopted with enthusiasm the concept of health planning. We have therefore the paradoxical situation that agencies such as UNICEF are firmly in favour of planning in the social sphere (including health) but are straining every statistic (in studies such as those appearing in *Structural Adjustment with a Human Face*) to discredit general economic planning because of the resource limits it imposes on the health sector.

This means that the formal policy–planning–budgeting process no longer offers us the same simple comparisons between successive stages as a short cut to health care evaluation. If the health plan does not correctly incarnate the country's declared health policies, this may not be from lack of technical competence or political toughness. Rather it may reflect a shift in circumstances since the policies were formulated which has not yet been recorded in a formal document. Similarly, if the budget does not correctly represent the plan, this may mean that the latter has been made obsolete by unforeseen events. The failure to update policies and plans is of course a legitimate subject for evaluation, but these do not have the same significance as providers of norms and standards which they would have in a kinder and more predictable world.

If plans, health and other, are subject to rapid change from outside, this produces pressures to abbreviate or abolish the classical somewhat leisurely planning process. Instead of plans being formulated every five years (with longer term perspectives covering periods of fifteen or twenty years), they may be subject, in small and unstable economies, to changes almost from month to month. These will be recorded, not in formal planning documents, but in the minutes of committees and the less public records of the upper reaches of the administrative system. This pattern represents a reversion to the days before purpose-built planning institutions and documents. It is a trend to be treated with respect in so far as it acknowledges that the planning function (in its broadest sense) should enter into all management decisions. But it is a pattern which imposes on the evaluator the burden of identifying the planning content in the administrative process which is not conveniently incorporated in named documents. Similar problems may arise at other levels. Currently effective policies must be disentangled from those nominally approved (but if policy is correctly formulated, at an appropriate level of generality, it should hold fast in spite of quite large changes in available resources). Funds actually released for spending must be distinguished, in amount and pattern, from those allocated under the annual budget—an onerous requirement since health services are not good at keeping track, day by day, of their actual expenditure.

In spite of these difficulties, many developing countries use, in some form, the policy–planning–budgeting–implementation process as a management framework. It can therefore legitimately be evaluated as an element in health care management. But under current conditions, it is much less useful as a means of evaluating health care *per se* than appears at first sight. It is tempting, and often useful, to short circuit the process by comparing the system's actual performance directly with policy. This is one of the functions of policy analysis. But to do this one must translate general policies into standards according to one or other of the sections of the present chapter.

5.6   Standards based on consumer demand

5.6.1   *Giving the consumers what they want*

After all the professionals—medical, administrative, financial—have had their say, it is still possible to turn to the consumer—to the actual or potential user of health care—for further standards. To the economist this order of proceeding seems bizarre; for most commodities, it would seem more natural to begin with the consumer, as the original shaper of the good in terms of form and price, and only later consider how far this pattern must be constrained by standards formulated in other ways. Standards of passenger transport, for example, depend primarily on the choices of many individual passengers concerning where they wish to travel, at what speed and in what comfort; it is only secondarily that we impose standards of vehicle maintenance, operating hours, and safety (which travellers in country buses, market trucks, and pirate minibuses in developing countries, swaying, sweating, and rattling along ill-made roads, often wish could be more strictly enforced).

The primacy of the medical professional has resulted in a specific distortion of the standards in the health care field. It has already been suggested that his primacy results in an assessment of the public *need* for health care, professionally assessed, rather than of the public's *demand*. Hence where consumer reactions have been assessed, they have often been as an irrational element interfering with need rather than a source of standards in their own right. This is discussed in the following subsections.

On the other hand, there has been much discussion among health economists of the extent to which health care, looked at in terms of the demands of the public, conforms to the pattern of the conventional consumer good. There is general agreement that many kinds of health care, and expenditure in this category overall, show one critical characteristic of an economic good—more is demanded at a lower price to the consumer, and less at a higher price (and conversely for variations in incomes). This conformity is not so direct and demonstrable as in the case of a good taken from the supermarket shelf at a marked price. Nor is the concept of price a simple one, since it must include not only the money paid for a service, but also the other costs to the consumer—travel time and cost, employed or household time lost and social inconvenience. But for consumers in the aggregate, the underlying reality of the relation between price and quantity of health care demanded has to be recognized.

On the other hand, economists have had to realize also that the public's demand for health care presents special features. There has been a tendency to concentrate attention on two of these. One is the fact that for health care, more than for most other commodities, the ordinary member of the public is capable of making a choice not only about his own health care, but about that which should be available to others generally. Another special feature is the relative lack of information of the consumer about health technology and the consequent need for him or her to entrust many decisions to someone better informed—in developed countries usually a doctor. This problem is not avoided even by the most scrupulous delegation of decisions from the doctor as agent to the consumer, since it is the agent who most often defines the field over which decisions must be made. No matter how conscientiously the agent performs his role, he constitutes an independent economic actor with his own incentives, a worthy subject for the attention of the makers and distributors of health care commodities—just as in Britain in the heyday of resale price maintenance the manufacturers of confectionery adjusted their product and terms of sale to be attractive to the owner of the little corner shop rather than the customer.

But even after introducing these complications, there are certain naiveties about the model of the consumer demand for health care which underlies the discussion of both doctors and economists. There is a tendency to assume that the typical consumer is aware of specific symptoms which either are painful or keep him or her from normal social functioning, and that the consumer's demand is for prompt curative action which will restore the previous situation. This ignores many things—the desire for certainty as good in itself, the wish to retain control of one's choices concerning treatment and cost, and above all the importance of operating within a defined social context peculiar to one's household or community. All these are relevant if we are trying to envisage what the public conceive to be the desirable standards of health care. The following subsections suggest how the evaluator can glimpse—though not usually in a systematic way—some of these factors which enter into the public's standards of health care but not necessarily that of the health professional, doctor, or economist.

5.6.2   *Consumer satisfaction; making the system work*

Since the public does not express directly its standards for the health care system, most of these must be elicited or deduced. They can be elicited, most practicably, through interviews and questionnaires (see, for example Ross and Vaughan 1984), and these have been used widely, with their accompanying apparatus of sampling and analysis, to find out what choice people make between health care alternatives. Almost always, these alternatives are thought of as being subordinate to an overall plan, and the information involved is collected primarily so that the basic objectives of this plan may be efficiently fulfilled. For example, members of the public who do not attend the health centre which is their nearest facility may be asked why not. Have they had no need of medical attention? Would they expect to be referred elsewhere whatever the outcome of their visit? Is the staff unhelpful? Are drugs regularly available? The answers will hopefully suggest changes which will enable the health centre to play its part more effectively in the health care system, though they are not expected to lead to fundamental changes in that system.

It is clear that in such cases the public is providing us with information about the standards of health care it desires and the priority it gives to one aspect over another, as well as of the degree to which the actuality as they know it meets these standards. As it is, such information usually relates to limited parts of the health care system. Cannot this method be used to give us a comprehensive picture of the consumers' standards? An attempt at this would be a very interesting exercise. But the transition from the particular decision to the nature of a whole system would pose difficult problems for the evaluator. Do we allow the consumer to design his ideal health care system, or do we require him to work within a framework of limited resources? and if the latter, how do we impart to him an understanding of the limits within which to work? It will soon become clear that using a direct approach to provide one with a picture of the consumers' standards of health care is more difficult than appears at first sight, and it is not therefore surprising that so far as is known this approach has not been tried in any developing (or developed) country.

5.6.3 *Deductions from consumer behaviour: voting with their feet*

Another source of information on the public's standards is simply the consumer's own behaviour—particularly where this behaviour is unexpected, either because it goes against the assumptions of the official health care system, or because it seems to violate the consumer's own interests as assessed by the outsider, or because it is in some other way counter-intuitive. A common example concerns the consumer's frequent refusal to use the health facility nearest to him as his point of first recourse when sick. It is well established that there is an inverse relationship between the distance of a client group from a health facility and the proportion of the group who will use that facility (see, for example King 1966). It is therefore rational to design health care systems, and to site individual facilities, so that the consumer is as near as possible to some simple form of professional health care. He will then supposedly bring all his health problems to this facility, which constitutes the lowest level of a hierarchy of institutions, arranged in ascending order of level of care and of distance from the average consumer. Each individual client, having entered the hierarchy at the lowest level, will be referred upward according to his need until he reaches the institution which can deal with this problem. This model is a logical one, congruent

with Western patterns of medical specialization and with the epidemiological background of curative medicine, and from the point of view of the
provider appears so obvious that it is hardly ever discussed.

Yet consumers in all countries are embarrassingly reluctant to act in
accordance with the model by carrying their health problems to the physically nearest facility. In England, instead of going first to a general practitioner, they often find ingenious reasons for going first to the casualty
department of a hospital. In Jamaica they avoid the lowest level of health
centre in favour again of a hospital, or at least of a centre of a higher grade.
Similar reports come from other developing countries. In each case there
may be some rational reasons for the choice—access to a better grade of
medical care in terms of personnel or drugs, a more or less justified belief in
the accuracy of self-diagnosis and self-referral—but one can also plausibly
deduce that the public generally does not accept the hierarchical model with
its emphasis on professional referral. Their ideal medical system would be
one that took them as directly as possible to the institution where adequate
care was available.

There are other examples of apparently irrational behaviour by consumers
of health care which suggest that the public has standards not taken into
account by professional need-based systems. Examples are the recourse to
commercial medicine by poor clients who, on a rational calculation, would
be better off using free government facilities; and the way in which women
seek family planning advice, and even child care, some distance from their
own community. Anthropologists have had (literally) a field day with
examples of the insensitivity of the official health services to the real
demands of their public. But health planners could fairly retort that while
these examples are amusing and even useful as criticisms of existing services,
we are still waiting for someone to deduce from them a coherent statement
of the public's concept of the appropriate norms of health care.

5.6.4   *Consumers and political action; writing to one's MP*

In the poor developing country of Bufoto, the health services are in financial
crisis. Over the last few years the Ministry of Health has cut down on
maintenance, trimmed the budget for drugs, and postponed paying its
suppliers almost to the point where they refuse to do business; garages
refuse to mend broken down ambulances till last year's bills are paid, and
the food going into hospitals is scarcely enough to feed the staff and their
families. Even the Minister has become convinced that a final solution is
necessary. 'We must close a hospital!' he announces, while the Director of
Finance looks on in relief. 'Mr. Permanent Secretary, I rely on you and the
Chief Medical Officer to tell me which one.' 'No question, Mr. Minister'
they reply. 'It must be Mount Misery. The Matron is near retirement, no

doctor will stay there except foreign volunteers whom no one understands, and the occupancy rate for years has been below 40 per cent. Furthermore, there is a good new hospital only ten miles away, erected to commemorate your predecessor. Mount Misery is the obvious choice.' 'You have convinced me' says the Minister. 'I will hold a political meeting in the district and announce the closure next week.'

The morning after the meeting the Minister summons his Permanent Secretary. 'I have to tell you' he says, 'that Mount Misery stays open. I gave them your reasons for closure. I assured them that the hospital would remain open as a health centre; that, in fact, they would have the most luxurious health centre in Bufoto. I do not blame you for briefing me wrongly. You could not know that my election agent quarrelled in primary school with the matron of the commemorative hospital, and has sworn never to go near her again; or that in the district around Mount Misery six people have been taken to the hospital with machete wounds in the last three weeks, while eighteen swear they attend regularly for the dressing of ulcers; nor that I would already have received thirteen letters, all in the handwriting of the pharmacist, expressing the community's grief at the loss of their hospital. Our party needs those votes. Mount Misery stays!'

It is not in all countries that health services are as frankly political a subject as in Bufoto. But it is very widely true that the public feel entitled to use the political machinery not merely to choose an overall health care system, but also to secure or preserve specific facilities for themselves and their communities. This is a legitimate political function and we can learn something about the public's standards of health care from the priority they accord different items, whether dealing with MPs, writing to the Press, or participating in the electronic town meeting provided by radio phone-ins. Once again, it appears that what the public desires is not wholly in agreement with the medical model, and in some ways is positively reactionary. There is above all else a desire for health services as a recourse in emergency —serious accident, acute illness—available promptly and within one's own community. Such public preferences politically expressed have to be respected, since they offer useful insights and criticisms of the orthodox view. But, as with the materials referred to in the previous section, they do not offer a comprehensive view of the consumer's norm of health care.

5.6.5   *The mentally ill; a crucial group*

It is implicit throughout this section that the norms and standards by which a health care system is to be judged emerge from a complex interplay between the members of the public and the professionals (usually doctors) as their agents. For some sections of the public (children, certain old people) a natural agent (parent, relative) intervenes between them and the doctor as professional agent. Since the fact of agency does not mean that children and old people have no independent valuation of the health care they receive, there is here considerable room for conflict between the legitimate interests of principal and agents. In cases where it is recognized that this conflict may become acute, laws have been passed to regulate the situation—for example, the complex of laws relating to the duties of parents and guardians in relation to children, as extended by such devices as bills of the 'rights' of the child. It is worth considering specifically one group of the population who are peculiarly vulnerable to the ill effects of conflicts of interest between agent and client, and between different agents, and for whom specific legal provision is made in most countries—namely the mentally ill.

These are people to whom increasing attention is being paid in health care, for various reasons. One is that they are much more likely to require specific provision in the towns which are becoming the dominant form of social organization in many developing countries, than in more traditional rural societies. Aloysius Hobson, Hugo Winckler's spendid creation (Winckler 1988), is happy in the country eating wild fruit, conversing with trees, bushes, and stones and playing slow bowler for the village cricket team (he also talks to the ball). In a city setting he would be merely a scruffy wanderer sleeping in boxes and under culverts, eating from garbage cans and terrorizing (without intending it) shopkeepers and tourists. Then, too, more mental conditions have become amenable to conventional medical treatment—lithium for manic-depressive illness, tranquillizers for some types of depression. In spite of the current revulsion against their long-term use, these give the doctor something effective to do in situations where he was formerly helpless. With our rapidly increasing knowledge of the biology and genetics of brain function, the medical role in this field is likely to increase. A third reason for special attention to the mentally ill is their vulnerability, from the halfwitted woman bearing children for any unscrupulous man to the inmates of the Bedlams which pass for mental hospitals in some developing countries.

In relation to some of the mentally ill, the concept of agency has to be defined with care. For most physical illnesses, it can be assumed that the sick person is of sound judgement and in general agreement with the mores of his society, and that he delegates to the doctor as agent a specific aspect of his life—what is normally called health—on which he and the doctor are in general agreement. Thus though we may, as in previous sections, assume public standards of health care which are not exactly those of the medical professions, there is broad agreement between patient and doctor about the limited nature of the decisions which are being delegated by one to the other. This delegation is usually voluntary except in the case of certain infectious diseases where it is assumed that the public has to be protected from the naked self-interest of its individual members. In this respect the emergence of AIDS has given new life to what seemed to be a dying problem —for example, Cuba has announced a massive programme of compulsory testing and virtual segregation for those found seropositive for human immunodeficiency syndrome. For some types of mental illness the concept of agency is more complex. Where the client is willing to delegate responsibility for the care of a limited condition, the situation can be fitted into the same box as for physical illness. But what if the client is incapable of delegation? This situation is in many countries covered by laws and procedures for compulsory treatment or commitment to an institution, particularly justifiable if the illness threatens violence to the patient or others. But the model is already being strained; commitment often means not merely the acceptance of medication, but co-operation in a wholesale revision of the patient's way of life. The most difficult cases, however, come if the principal evidence for a patient's mental illness is a difference of lifestyle from that of the people around him. Many solid citizens would consider a man mad who had made a conscious decision to limit his involvement with the material world—to wear the same clothes till they fall to rags, and to possess no more goods than can be contained in a plastic bag—rather than burden himself with a house, car, and family. Many Stalinist-minded Russian psychiatrists have been notoriously willing to take a rejection of scientific socialism as evidence of mental illness. Here we must consider (as we need not for physical illness) what must be the level and nature of a client's intellectual and behavioural deviance to make him a legitimate concern of public health. But even in a case where the degree of deviance makes commitment fully justified, it must not be forgotten that there will be many aspects of a patient's health, not involved in their specific condition, for which they have valid standards of care. The schizophrenic patient, for example, will be more sensitive than others, rather than less, about the quality of the care he receives for a chest infection or a broken bone.

Thus, as has long been recognized, for mental illness the problems of the reconciliation of the standards of the client and the health professional are varied and serious. It may well be worth the evaluator's while to review the status of mental patients, in theory and practice, in a given national system not only for the technical quality of the health care available, but also as an indication of the pains taken to give proper recognition to the independent interests of the public and their standards for health care.

6 Evaluation: Process, priorities, techniques

6.1 Making the evaluation process work

The comparison of standards with performance provides the formal logical structure of health, as of other kinds of evaluation. It is therefore analogous with the comparison of experience with hypothesis which gives the structure of an experiment in the natural science—at least in its published form. But it has now become a commonplace that the testing of hypotheses against experience through experiment is only a small part of the process of science, telling us little about the choice of field for investigation, the emergence of hypotheses or the way experiments grow from rough conceptions to their final form. Similarly the process of evaluation is more complex and approximate than the formal structure would suggest. If it were not so, the task of evaluating a national health care system would be a daunting one, involving the comparison of performance and standards item by innumerable item, and we should have no useful answer to the first-time investigator who says 'But how do I set about this?'

First, in evaluating a health care system we may aim at greater or less profundity. We may be concerned to evaluate the system taking for granted its short term, narrow constraints, or to ask how its performance compares with the ideal if we admit all the long-term possibilities of improvement through policy change, system redesign, institutional expansion, and manpower training. To a large extent the choice of viewpoint is dictated by the nature of the organization requiring the evaluation—national as against international, for example. This is dealt with in the following chapter on the implementation of evaluations, since the nature of the originating organization is a critical factor in determining how the results of an evaluation exercise are applied.

Even if we confine ourselves, as here, to national systems, and if we accept the limitations imposed by the purpose of the originating organization as discussed in the following chapter, there is still a difficult choice to be made about the priorities which are to guide the process of evaluation. It is impracticable to tackle the job (or publish the results) on all fronts simultaneously. Where does one begin?

In addition to the purchase of the present book, two steps are self-evident:

the examination of previous evaluation documents, and the discussion with the national health body of their current preoccupations. There can be few developing countries now which do not have an impressive body of previous evaluation work, and this, so far as it is available, must be perused. But it has certain drawbacks. First, it is often repetitive; it is depressing to find the same (often well founded) analysis and set of recommendations recurring in report after report. Before this is put down to lack of 'political will' on the part of governments and administrators, the possibility should be considered that old recommendations were not implemented because their analysis ignored important features of the situation, of which a shortage of resources is often one. It may be salutary, even if not strictly necessary, to look for classic documents from an earlier period, such as the Bhore Committee report for India or the Moyne Committee report for the West Indies which have set the framework for what has followed even if they were not implemented in detail.

Second, a large part of any literature on previous evaluations is likely to relate to limited and urgent problems, and to make equally limited recommendations ignoring the background against which the problems should be placed since these are no part of the investigators' remit. It may well be, therefore, that the hares which have been started but not pursued recur from problem to problem and are more important on the national scale than the actual recommendation.

One meets rather similar limitations if one takes the current preoccupations of health officials as one's priorities for investigation. In their day-to-day work they must necessarily take a good deal for granted, trying to deal with pressing problems with a minimum of disturbance to the rest of the system. In particular, administrators are unlikely to question the nature of the professional cadres whose training has provided the management framework for so much of Western type health care. Thus a problem of health care administration is likely to be presented in terms of the relationships between fixed categories of professionals, with a solution in the same terms. It is only recently that international health organizations have begun to take seriously the possibility that these categories themselves should be re-examined in the light of the tasks to be carried out, with a reassignment of roles between categories rather than the addition of marginal categories such as the village health worker. But it is this kind of more fundamental re-examination which is needed for a satisfactory national evaluation.

Whatever the starting point, such an evaluation requires an understanding of health care as a system in its actual and potential functioning, rather than a collection of discreet parts. In a way such system understanding is analogous to the body of theory from which springs the actual experiment in the national sciences. But as in science, to arrive at such an understanding we must make heavy use of intuition, as did, for example, Crick and

Watson in arriving at a plausible structure for DNA. Such intuition is a necessary part of the equipment of the evaluator.

To the extent that system understanding is intuitive, one cannot provide the evaluator with rigid rules. But there are certain techniques which are helpful in guiding the investigator from the problem to the system level. Some of these have been already referred to. An example is the use of the 'tracer' problem which if properly chosen (and this again is partly a matter of intuition) leads the investigator to wider and wider levels of generality. These levels can also be reached through a group of techniques which, essentially, enforce generality by taking a single system-wide variable and studying it in all its ramifications. The variable may be the flow of health care clients; the flow of finance; the degree of conformity with some aspect of social policy; or the geographical basis of health care services. The first of these has already been discussed above in relation particularly to Jamaica. The rest are studied in the following sections. Each is a useful aid to system-level understanding, but each may also be a useful planning approach in its own right.

6.2   Developing system-level understanding: some techniques

6.2.1   *The health care system and geographical access*

In at least one ministry of health, a wall of the main conference room is covered with a topographical map of the country; on it government health facilities are symbolized by coloured pins whose location (when they are not borrowed by the users of neighbouring offices) is intended to show at a glance the state of access to the health services. The same map shows roads, railways and urban areas, and gives at least a broad indication of the distribution of population. Its presence shows both how widespread is the concern of health administrators with geographical access to services, and indicates one very simple way of displaying the health care system in these terms.

But it is clear that if one moves beyond a very superficial presentation, such a picture can and must be elaborated in various ways (see, for example Kemball-Cook and Vaughan 1982). Some difficulties are common to many forms of social mapping, and the techniques for dealing with them are well established. For example, it is obvious that the straight-line Euclidean distance between two points on the map does not correctly represent the actual distance to be travelled by a health care client from home to health facility. The client must use existing means of communication by road, rail, or river, with all the sinuosities caused by natural obstacles and established settlement patterns. At the extreme of elaboration, this problem can be dealt with by preparing special maps showing the distribution of features around each health facility in terms of travel distance or time. More simply, it can be treated in terms of the intriguingly named 'taxicab geometry' which assumes that all travel on the map takes place along the lines of the rectangular map grid. This has advantages in that it simplifies the mathematics of some access problems as well as fitting well with normal map references and computer coding. But experience suggests that in practice travel times and Euclidean distance are highly correlated, so that the more esoteric possibilities have not so far found a place in health care analysis.

Also common to other forms of social mapping are the problems posed by the degree of concentration or dispersal of population. For one form of settlement, that in which the population is found in well marked centres—villages, towns—separated by largely uninhabited countryside, the problem of access is relatively straightforward in terms of conception and measurement; travel distances within the centre can be assumed to be zero, while intervillage distances can be unambiguously mapped. This is the model which appears to underlie some of the early work on Primary Health Care in an East African setting; and it gives a special meaning to the idea of a community, which is assumed to be the population of a village centre acting in their social and political capacity. But this settlement pattern is not universal. In the Caribbean, for example, though a rural district may have a village as centre, its population may be quite widely dispersed on individual holdings. In Bangladesh, as shown below, more complicated patterns of settlement occur. Ideally, therefore, we should measure access in terms of the distance of each separate individual from a health facility. A possible shortcut is to assume a known gradient of population density about each inhabited centre. But while there is evidence in some settings for such gradients, based perhaps on a relation between population density and some less-than-unity power of distance, the assumption may break down at certain scales or in the presence of marked natural obstacles.

There is another problem of the analysis of access which shares some features with social mapping in general but is in other respects distinct. Any consideration of access to health care will show that it is not a unitary thing, but varies with the type of care provided. A client may be near to a health centre, but far from a tertiary hospital; and the second level is to the client just as much a matter of access as the first. (Health professionals, on the other hand, sometimes appear to feel that since all clients are assumed to make their first contact with organized health care through some peripheral institution from which they will be passed by some time- and distanceless process to more sophisticated levels, only access to the local institution counts.) So far, the mapping of access may be compared with the delineation of catchment areas for market, social, or administrative services. One naturally expects these areas to be different and larger for more specialized services. There is a village in the English counties which has half a dozen small provision stores, each serving a few streets, but one highly specialized purveyor of leather goods and hunting clothes who is not surprised to receive customers from the next county. One might expect access to different kinds of health care to follow this pattern.

But health care has certain special features not usually found in the definition of market areas, which can be summed up by saying that the various types of facility are strongly hierarchical in their relationships. The English saddler does not expect to advise the corner store, or provide it with administrative services, or insist on taking his customers only on referral from it; if he thinks his business professionally and socially superior to that of the grocer, he is too smugly tactful to say so. But the health service hierarchy, from tertiary hospital to peripheral worker, displays all these relationships. Hence often we cannot talk of independent access to the different levels of care, but rather of access to a system.

It is a further complication that the levels of the system tend to correspond to different diseases and health problems. Some problems can be met by diffused care, others require intensive help which is necessarily concentrated at a few institutions. Thus access is differentiated not only by type of institution but also by disease problem. Hence the common observation that clients travel further for serious conditions than minor ones, both willingly and of necessity.

If, then, the evaluator chooses the examination of the degree of equity in access to health care as his way to a better understanding of the health care system, he will be driven to face certain complications not at first apparent. These in turn may cause him to look again at the very concept of equity in access. This clearly does not mean equality in terms of distance from a health facility. So long as the health care resources required for some conditions remain more concentrated than the client population, some groups of people will have less access than others. So long as these resources are located (for the sake of efficiency) in population concentrations, or generate such concentrations, inequality of geographical access will have an urban/rural dimension, which means in most societies an income and educational dimension. The nature of geographical access to health care dictates that equity in this respect should not be a simple arithmetic concept, but one involving social policy and requiring positive social action. This is discussed further in a later subsection.

6.2.2   Geography and health care; a Bangladeshi example

In 1977 Bangladesh requested help from WHO in preparing a health plan using the procedures of Country Health Programming, the first step in which was an evaluation of the current health care situation. The programming exercise was carried out in 1977–8, yielding an Information Document and a Programme Proposal, and these were later reviewed at WHO's South-East Asia Regional Office. This subsection draws heavily on that review as embodied in the background papers for a consultation which followed.

At this time Bangladesh was a newly independent country of about 80 million people, the former East Pakistan, still recovering from the effects of the war of liberation in 1971 and the famines of which the worst had been in 1973–4. Its economic state was unhappy and its political and administrative apparatus severely damaged. In particular, its health services were in disarray and its health indicators unfavourable. Basic data on the health care situation were only gradually coming forward again, so that an evaluation of national health care could not always call on what might seem essential statistics. For example, the number of doctors who had remained to practise in the country was subject to even more doubt than elsewhere. In these circumstances, it was necessary to use all possible shortcuts to an understanding of the health care situation in Bangladesh.

It was at this point that the then Secretary for Health put forward an ambitious scheme for developing health services in Bangladesh at the thana (local) level which would complement the surviving structure of central, regional, and subdivisional hospitals. This scheme would establish a health centre in each thana with a wide outreach which would greatly reduce the problems of health care involving the village populations, for curative, preventive, and also statistical purposes. To calculate the feasibility and cost of such a scheme, information on access was essential, and it was in this field that shortcut methods had to be urgently sought.

Bangladesh may be seen as a central area of high density of population, with lower density areas in the hill and delta areas on its edges. Over most of the area the density does not vary greatly from thana to thana (in 1974, 60 per cent of the thanas outside the Chittagong Hill Tracts had densities between 1000 and 2000 persons per square mile). The transport pattern is basically one of radial roads centred on Dakha, but these are much interrupted by the river system, whose trend is mainly north–south. An account of the settlement hierarchy, and of geographical settlements at the lowest level, is given in the Country Health Programming Information Documents (based on material prepared by the Government of Bangladesh for the UN Habitat Conference in 1975).

The greatest distances are those between the centre and the district and subdivision headquarters; however, these correspond roughly to the best (metalled) roads. Distances between district or subdivision and thana are less, but the roads here are unmetalled, though with some all-weather capability. Succeeding units are the union, village, household, and individual; here distances become progressively shorter but means of transport slower, movement within the village area being mainly on foot.

An important link is that between village and household. There are generally assumed to be about 60 000 village tracts in Bangladesh, averaging a little under one square mile each. Within a tract, settlement patterns vary greatly in the degree of nucleation (the proportion of the population concentrated at a central point or along the line of a road or river) and the dispersal of the households outside the nucleus (i.e. whether they are located singly or in clusters).

For evaluation purposes, this situation simply could not in 1977 be studied in detail thana by thana. But the nature of the population distribution made it possible to model the pattern of access in a simple form without too much loss of information. Each village tract could be represented by a hexagon (Fig. 6.1) with the average area, population, and socioeconomic situation of rural Bangladesh. Within this hexagon all movement

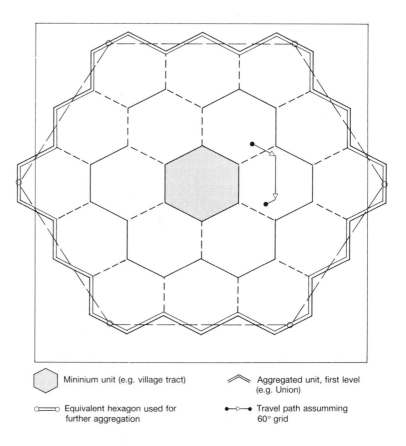

Minimium unit (e.g. village tract)

Equivalent hexagon used for further aggregation

Aggregated unit, first level (e.g. Union)

Travel path assumming 60° grid

Fig. 6.1 Modelling settlement patterns, Bangladesh, 1976.

was assumed to take place along the lines of a 60° grid. The choice of a hexagon as the basic shape is obvious in view of its space-filling properties; the assumption of movement along grid lines rather than directly allows for the excess of actual over Euclidean travel distances; and the use of average as 'typical' is made possible by the special conditions of Bangladesh. It happens that in Bangladesh hexagonal village tracts can be realistically aggregated to represent the next highest administrative unit, the union, which again can be approximated by a hexagon; and the same procedure can be followed for larger and larger units until we meet the national level.

Such modelling can be used to obtain average values for critical quantities in understanding the problems of health care and planning for their solution. These are most obvious for questions of geographical access. We can measure approximately, for example, the distances to be covered by a client of the health care system as he moves up the hierarchy of institutions from household to thana health centre and to successively higher levels of hospital. We can also measure how the distances to be travelled vary within the village tract with different patterns of settlement. It was proposed, for example, that for some conditions the clients' travel distance should be reduced to zero by having each household visited regularly (say, once per month) by a health worker from the local health centre. The model shows that while with a totally nucleated population the worker's travel distance is, by assumption, zero, with an evenly dispersed population this distance rises to a minimum of 14 miles. This would considerably increase the outreach costs of the health centre.

But the same approach can be used to construct other characteristics of the typical village. It can give indications of the typical situation regarding all those variables, other than the availability of health services, which have an influence on health. This would include the economic and nutritional state of the 'typical' village, the availability of water supplies of different kinds, and also the frequency with which households would need to be visited by a health worker if any effect was to be produced on the 'typical' disease pattern. For example, diarrhoeal episodes among children, while frequent, are likely to be of short duration; and thus if a monthly visit by a health worker was to produce any good effect, only a fraction of episodes would be caught by direct contact, and special techniques for the detection by the health worker of past and future incidence of such episodes might be required. Similarly, by examining the disease pattern of a typical village one could distinguish those conditions which would require referral to higher echelons, and estimate their number, the distances to be travelled, and the load likely to be imposed on health centres and hospitals.

As a further example, one could attach to the typical village tract the available data about water supply. In 1977 the average tract contained 5 tube wells (of which 2 or 3 would be working at one time) and a number of rim wells. Where households were scattered, the distance to be travelled to get water from clean wells was not negligible, particularly when paths were broken by flooding. Hence much water for all purposes would be taken from streams and standing water, in which pollution leading to gastro-intestinal infections was common. Thus access to water supply, very relevant to health, could be modelled on the same basis as access to health services.

It is not argued here that this particular access model would be optimal in other countries and other planning situations. In fact, about the time of the Country Health Programming exercise in Bangladesh more detailed information was beginning to come forward both from routine statistical sources and from sample surveys. A most interesting survey at this time of the sources of health care used by the general population—including druggists, ayurveds, and faith healers—showed how relatively insignificant were the official health services at this time, information which could probably have been obtained in no other way. But this case shows the way in which a careful consideration of problems of geographical access in a particular context leads to a greater understanding of the health care system at a general level.

6.2.3   Finance and the health care system

The study of money flows in the health care system—of the community's expenditure on health care, and the sources from which it is drawn—has a long history. On the one hand it is an obvious exercise for the health administrator operating a fixed budget. But he can afford to take a narrow point of view, concentrating his attention on those payments for which he is directly responsible. From a broader point of view, it is desirable for the health planner and the general planner to know how much the community is spending on health care of all kinds, both public and private, and where the money is coming from. Work on these lines, at an approximate level, has no doubt been part of the estimation of national incomes and expenditures since these began. But intensive work begins with Abel Smith's intercountry studies for the World Health Organization in the 1960s (Abel Smith 1967), and after a period of neglect health expenditure has become the subject of a considerable literature in the 1980s, directed particularly toward developing countries (see, for example Griffiths and Mills 1982; Cumper 1982).

In this literature two threads are entwined which can usefully be separated. From one point of view we trace the flows of money for a reason familiar to economists; it is the most useful general measure of miscellaneous inputs to the health care sector, though behind the veil of money lurk concrete commodities and services which for a full understanding of the system we need to disentangle. But from another point of view money is a commodity in its own right, without whose availability the physical inputs cannot be procured; full understanding requires that we trace how the finance for health care is mobilized. The two aspects of money are intertwined in practice, but each approach has its own validity.

One reason for separating them is to draw a distinction between the provision of health care and its financing. The difference is not obvious where the client encounters both in a single package, as with fee-for-service payments in cash or under a tax-financed health service system. It becomes more evident where specialized financial institutions for health exist, as with independent social security schemes or private health insurance firms. In the latter case it is obvious that the appropriate expenses of the firm enter into the cost of health care, something often overlooked in the other cases though the expenses of financing (through personal savings or the costs of taxation) are just as real.

It is natural to extend one's questioning about the money side of health care to ask not only 'what is the situation about expenditure and financing today?' (when the two are almost necessarily equal) but also 'what will be their relation in some future planning period?' (when, since they are driven by different forces, they may well diverge unless steps are taken to bring them into equality). This has led to the preparation of a few national 'master plans for health financing' (their preparation so far largely undocumented) which involve the projection into the future of the planned or expected level of health care services, the estimation of their costs, and the designation of future sources of finance (Mills 1987). An early and simple example is described in the following subsection (see Cumper 1982).

Such projections are of special value in understanding the health care system because they direct attention to important economic variables—how the costs of services are determined, how the total cost is likely to vary with changes in their volume and pattern, and how costs are linked with finance at the micro- and macro-economic levels. This last includes the study of how payments are made to providers, and how the consequent incentive effects react on the provision of services. These effects have come very much to the fore in recent years, particularly among North American health economists, and are important to the analysis of any health care system which contains a strong commercial element.

Finally, the estimation of health care expenditure offers the opportunity of comparing the volume of spending on health services with that on other economic variables important to health, particularly when linked to national income calculations. Thus one could in principle compare the importance of medical care with private health measures—for example, the purchase of insecticides—and with the health promotion component in nutrition, water supply, and housing. Unfortunately this can only be done in the vaguest way since no satisfactory method exists of separating this component from the rest. Sometimes an approximation can be made—Sri Lanka's former subsidy to rice consumption, can perhaps be counted as health-oriented. But how to isolate that part of urban water supply expenditure which is directed to purity rather than general convenience? It may nevertheless be useful, and sometimes salutary, to estimate how expenditure specifically on health care compares with that on other, health-related items.

6.2.4   *Money for health care; a Jamaican example*

Jamaica inherited, from its colonial past, a health service system for which money was derived from general tax revenue and spent largely on hospitals and traditional public health measures. This was supplemented by a substantial number of private and semi-private general practitioners. In the postwar period there grew up a network of rural clinics catering mainly for maternal and child health, first under Colonial Development and Welfare (Colonial Office 1944, 1955) and then under a politically independent government. In the late 1970s loan assistance was obtained from the World Bank under the Jamaica Population Project; the nominal purpose, as with other such projects, was to help control fertility, the substantive purpose from the point of view of the borrowers was mainly to improve the health care of mothers and children, but funds were also set aside with the objective of improving health care planning and management. One of the steps taken under this head was to set aside a modest amount of funds for an economic analysis of the Jamaican health sector. This analysis was carried out in 1981 by the writer as consultant, with the support of an enthusiastic Task Force which included representatives of the health and other agencies providing the necessary information.

In some respects the available information was excellent. Like many Commonwealth countries, Jamaica has a good basic statistical system, though now perhaps showing strain at some points. Censuses have been regular and are supplemented now by a twice-yearly household survey, and an effective system of birth and death registration has existed since 1881. The main economic information is synthesized in the annual national accounts. Information about the government health services is acceptable both on the side of service statistics (where the usual hospital returns are supplemented by a massive Monthly Clinic Summary Report) and in terms of expenditure. The government budget could be studied in detail in the Annual Estimates of Expenditure, and at this time estimated and actual expenditures coincided closely, especially for current items. This budget could easily be given an economic interpretation since besides the conventional division into heads and subheads, corresponding in most cases to administrative units and substantive programmes, there existed a cross-cutting division by economic nature ('objects') separating, for example, different kinds of supplies.

The situation was very different for the private health care sector. Here there was no integrated statement of financial flows comparable to that in the public sector, but only a number of separate sources of information on various aspects of private health care; the number of doctors in full and part-time private practice, and of beds in private hospitals; a small survey of the use of doctors' time; the accounts of health insurance companies; and (unexpected, but perhaps the most useful) a sample survey of households recording the main aspects of health care consumption, including the use of private doctors. More recent, and better funded, health expenditure surveys would regard such a sample survey as an essential part of the exercise; in Jamaica in 1981 it had to be attributed to good fortune and the pertinacity of the health planning unit.

There was thus no difficulty in tracing the flow of funds in the government health services; but the size and obscurity of expenditure in the private sector meant that this would be a biased picture of health care on the national scale. What was wanted was an integrated presentation of both public and private sectors, even though their institutional frameworks were very different and the money quantities for the private sector would inevitably rest on sometimes precarious estimates.

The decision was taken to base the integrated presentation on the procedures and categories of the national accounts. This meant that the health care sector, as usually understood, must be broken down into a number of accounts with different economic meanings. On this basis it was decided to break down health care provision into two accounts, one for current production (further divided into private and public) and one for the creation of physical assets, and to create separate accounts for health care financing, health manpower training and medical supplies. The flows between these accounts, and between them and the basic national accounting sectors such as private households and the rest of the world, provided the framework for tracing money flows relating to health. Estimates of aggregate 'health' expenditure could then be constructed on alternative bases, with different approaches giving results whose divergences are not always allowed for in crude comparisons of national expenditures. It matters substantially, for example, whether the total expenditure includes or excludes capital creation, training, and drug supply. This approach enforces an analysis of the structure of the system in a way not required, for example, for an examination of the government health service sector alone. It also draws attention to the need for market equilibrium between the sector providing care and the sectors which provide its inputs on a broader basis than if we simply look at incomes, prices, and shortages in the health services.

These estimates were used as the basis for projections of the cost of health care at current prices allowing for the unavoidable minimum of change in demand conditions—namely, those resulting from policy commitments already made, and from changes in the age and sex composition of the population. A crude estimate was made of cost per service unit by dividing the total cost of providing a service in the base year 1980 by the number of units provided (for example, cost per hospital in-patient day). These units could be given a rough demographic interpretation; thus certain services referred obviously to births and to women in the age range 15–44, while others could be associated mainly with patients aged 60 and over. Recently prepared population projections were used to project demand for different types of service, and so of the cost of future provision of services of the same standard. Some of these results differed markedly from those obtained by an overall demand projection—for example, one could expect a fall in the relative demand for maternal and child health services and an increase in the treatment of conditions characteristic of the adult ages.

These projections of the costs of current provision were further modified to take into account such policy decisions as the transfer of some services from hospital out-patient and casualty departments to health centres, an increase in surgical beds and the extension of maternal health services. In addition, it was assumed that short term salary increases would be necessary, at least politically, to avoid shortages of doctors and nurses. This led to the final projection of the cost of current services at present standards from the base year 1980 up to the year 2000.

The projections of increased current service provision implied an increased demand for the services of health centres and hospitals and thus for additions to the physical stock of health institutions. This could be roughly costed and the required capital expenditure projected in the same way as for current provision, the two together giving an estimate of the required health expenditure up to 2000, for the government sector and in total. Even with a slow-growing population and no change in quality of service, the expansion required would be roughly two-fold. Could this be financed?

The future funds financed were projected on a rather primitive basis. An assumption was made, appearing pessimistic then but less so nowadays, about the likely growth in national income per head of the population. This, with the projected population growth, gave estimates of the future level of the domestic product. For the government sector it was assumed that the health service budget would form a fixed proportion of government current spending, which in turn would be a fixed proportion of domestic product. For the public and private sectors combined, it was assumed that health expenditure would grow slightly faster than domestic product, according to a formula derived from a study of international data. When the projected available funds were compared with those required, it appeared that there should be no difficulty in financing aggregate health expenditure at 1980 levels of service, and that the same would be true in the long run of the government sector, though with some financial stringency in the period to 1990.

Since the government health services have recently been going through just such a period of stringency, while private health expenditure has shown remarkable powers of expansion, it would be pleasant to be able to record that the simple 'financial master plan' prepared in 1981 was accurate. In fact it may have been more or less preserved by two offsetting inaccuracies. On the one hand, it took no account of improvements in the technical and organizational efficiency of the health services (though these, it is true, have been partly offset by the rising level of the demand of the public for health care, in both quantity and quality). But on the other hand, and more important, the projections drew attention to the critical importance of the available economic forecasts for projections of health service financing. In 1981 these forecasts were dutifully optimistic, making no allowance, in particular, for the increasing share of government revenue being eaten up by debt service charges, and the estimates of available health service finance were correspondingly optimistic.

Thus this Jamaican exercise showed how the theme of financing can be used to reach a fuller understanding of the integration of the health service system. It threw up some details which were unexpected, at least to a public view; the large share in health care costs played by the salary levels, not of doctors (the usual villains of health economics) but of nurses, and the increasing reliance by the public on private health insurance even in the presence of a free and moderately efficient public service. But perhaps its most important lesson was the dependence of the health sector, for financing and in other ways, on the rest of the economy, and the need for the health planner to have an appreciation of the overall economic structure and prospects which are preoccupying the (often standoffish) national economic planners.

6.2.5 *Health care and social policy; equity*

One possible system-wide approach to understanding health care is through an examination of its degree of conformity to some aspect of social policy, and the aspect most likely to be used in practice is equity. This was, for example, an important theme in the preparation of a health care plan for the newly independent country of Zimbabwe (Segall 1983). In that case emphasis was placed on equity between racial labels, but in other cases different divisions might be important, such as income and occupation levels and the separation between urban and rural groups. Equity is a goal of social policy in most developing countries, whether explicit or not. It has only been qualified by a few governments like those of Russia and Burma which in their early years assigned explicit priority to those groups (industrial workers and miners) judged most necessary to the eventual success of the revolution.

Equity is a convenient starting point for the evaluator not only because gross departures from it are reprobated in almost all national systems, but also because when considered at anything beyond a superficial level it requires an analysis of almost every aspect of health care and health levels, including the geographical and economic aspects dealt with in more detail above.

The simplest way to approach the subject of equity in health is in terms of equality of geographical access; the governing factor is the distance the client has to travel to reach a health care institution. But even from the brief discussion given above, some things are clear which complicate the concept of equity. One is that we cannot identify equity with equality of *individual* access; for any conceivable population, a situation in which every client lived the same distance from a facility is an impossibility. The most we can ask for is that there is no difference in *average* access for different population groups.

Furthermore, these groups must be defined independently of their need for health care—in terms of income, education, degree of urbanization, or assigned social group. On the other hand, it is desirable, rather than inequitable, that groups with a specific health care need should have better access to the relevant facility than those without it—either because we locate facilities where the need is greatest (malaria clinics in a malarious area) or because clients themselves take steps to achieve preferential access (pregnant women migrating to the city which has the best lying-in arrangements).

It follows that the degree of equality of access must be recalculated for each health condition, or at least each comparable group of conditions. A pregnant woman living under the walls of a mental hospital has good access to health care of a sort, but it is not the sort she requires. There exists a different degree of equality of access for each condition, depending on the pattern of population, institutions, and referral channels; if these are to be combined into a single measure for purposes of equity, we must assign a relative importance to each condition, explicitly or (much more usually) implicitly. It follows that even so apparently simple a concept as geographical access, if considered from the point of view of equity, requires an understanding of many aspects of the working of the health care system.

Access is a comparatively narrow concept, emphasizing the role of one preliminary input to health care rather than the level of health itself. This is affected by both the process of care and the context of health-related variables. At the other extreme one may want to consider equity in relation to health in this more general sense, seen as the result of the process of care and the intersectoral variables. Mortality rates, among infants or for each age group, are the commonest measure of general health, though admittedly an imperfect one, and are usually all that is available in developing countries. We can therefore approach the question of equity in health by asking whether there are unacceptable inequalities in mortality rates between population groups. The answer is of course that for most countries, developed and developing, there are certainly inequalities. Mortality is generally higher among the lower socio-economic classes, as in the United Kingdom; among urban groups (contrary to expectations) as against rural, as in India; among the children of labourers as against those of farmers, as in Bangladesh; and among the uneducated as against others practically everywhere. In developing countries these differences are often so gross that they are taken as *prima facie* evidence of inequity. But in making the transition from inequality to inequity, some of the same caveats apply as for geographical access.

First, we must be clear that we are dealing with an average concept—the proportion who die in a given interval—and not with individuals, whose mortality will be affected by many factors other than group membership. Then we must be sure that the groups concerned are defined independently of health. Otherwise, we have to allow for the fact that ill health may be the factor placing a person in the lowest socio-economic category, or even that a fixed belief in the virtues of six pints of beer a night may account for both poverty and ill health. Lastly, we must be sure (and this is implicit in the use of access for planning purposes) that the inequality is a removable one. It is generally true, and generally ignored because of the political embarrassment involved, that social groups may differ in such physiological variables as blood group, natural stature and others, some of which matter to health (see, for example Beardmore and Karimi-Booshehri 1983). It would be fatuous to aim for the sake of equity at a situation where black and white groups had the same likelihood of a sickle cell crisis. The difficulties are multiplied if we try to relate to equity differences not in mortality but in some more comprehensive measure of health.

Between geographical access at one end, and the output of health at the other, lies the whole field of the distribution of inputs to health care, of the quality of the health care process itself and of the health-related factors which help determine the final result. At the input level, the ratio of doctors to population may be taken as an index of urban-rural equity; in Nepal, for example, it is commonly said that 90 per cent of doctors live in the vale of Kathmandu, and 90 per cent of the population outside. But this, of course, raises the whole question of the hierarchical nature of the health care system and the inevitability of the concentration of certain functions. We would not wish the presence of the pathologist at a tertiary hospital to enter into the calculation of doctor–population ratios as an index of equity in primary health care. A knowledge of the intermediate stages in health care will add to our understanding of the equity question, but it will not produce a simple measure of how far the health care system conforms to the social policy of equity.

Can the distribution of health expenditure, as a general measure of the resources devoted to health care, be used as a guide to equity? This requires the separation of the expenditure associated with different population groups. This is not impossible if the groups are geographically separate, as with urban and rural populations. But it has not generally been attempted in other cases since the attribution of so many expenses between groups of other types—based on income, occupation, or education—would have an arbitrary element. How does one allocate the overhead expenses of a malaria campaign?

But economists have suggested an alternative approach. Equity may be a transcendental goal of social policy, but the health care measures needed to attain it can often be justified on the grounds of overall efficiency (Collison *et al.* 1988). For example, it can be demonstrated that on certain plausible assumptions a shift of health care resources from an urban high-spending area to a rural one will lower average rates of mortality, thus serving the ends of both equity and efficiency. In most developing countries inequalities in health care are so marked that egalitarian changes generate no conflict between the two objectives. Only when we approach much nearer to equality in health care, however measured, do we have to face the twin difficulties of defining equity and deciding whether it should be pursued at the expense of the average national health. Even at the present stage such conflicts are not unheard of; should we, for example, allow the resources of an innoculation campaign to be absorbed in reaching the most remote settlements, even if this reduces the scale of the campaign as a whole? But they are rare enough to suggest as a working rule that in pursuit of equity, health planners and administrators should take measures to achieve equality provided they do not reduce the efficiency of the health care system.

The problem of securing equity may well be one that is of importance in itself to the evaluator and his sponsors. But by its nature it is unlikely to be one he can solve from facts and first principles, as has been shown by the complexity of the British literature on the subject since the publication of Sir Douglas Black's report (DHSS 1980). It is sufficient for the present purpose that the evaluator who pursues the issue in a particular national context will be forced to an understanding of the processes of the health care system—probably a wider understanding than he could attain in any other way.

6.3   The limits of intuition

The results of a national health system evaluation must be objectively justifiable in terms of a comparison of performance with standards. The process of evaluation must, realistically, depend to a considerable extent on intuition for an understanding of the system, an identification of the critical points within it and therefore the fields which must be given priority in the evaluation process. But by sanctioning a partly intuitive approach, are we opening up the field for domination by the prejudices of the evaluator? Will he not impose his own values through the nature of his understanding and the priorities he assigns to different fields for investigation?

It would be idle to pretend that evaluation reports do not fall into sets, each with its own intellectual flavour; and this does not result entirely from the nature of the agency which sponsors the evaluation (as discussed below) but also from the mindset of the evaluator. One person can be relied on to give a neo-Marxist flavour to his conclusions, another will betray a yearning for market solutions to health problems; one will see health care as essentially a medical concern, another will cast the medical profession (excluding himself) as the villain of the piece. Can anything be done to limit the influence of individual mindsets on the results of the evaluation?

At one level, the evaluator has the same obligation as any scientist to examine himself for irrational elements which may affect his scientific judgment and exclude their influence from his conclusions. This is true not only of the emotions individual to him, such as an enjoyment of the catastrophic which biases him toward cometary impacts, ozone depletion, and imminent revolution. It applies also to the biases he may take over from his political and professional education, which are all the more difficult to dismiss because they present themselves with moral authority. To allow for one's own bias as an investigator should be a part of any scientific activity, though it is none the easier for that.

Perhaps a more practical answer to the problem is to take advantage of the fact that an evaluator seldom works alone, and to deliberately share his prejudices and compare his intuitions with those working with him. These may be colleagues on an evaluation team (though in that case they may well share some of his predispositions) or members of a supporting committee or task force. If the latter, the choice of a committee whose members represent a wide range of points of view is likely to increase the objectivity of the planning of the evaluation process and of the final result.

7 The results of evaluation

It is axiomatic that the results of the evaluation of a national health system are to be measured not in terms of the document it produces, but in terms of the favourable changes it generates in health, and particularly in health care. If this is a falsehood, it is one which no one in the field of health planning and administration dares to contradict. Yet experience suggests that this generalization is eminently contradictable. The shelves of health ministries and of international agencies are well provided with evaluation reports which have not led to change (at least directly). Evidently getting implemented the suggestions for change which arise from evaluation is not the easiest part of the evaluator's task. This is the kind of difficulty with which this chapter mainly deals. But it will also be suggested that a national evaluation which leads immediately to no traceable change is not entirely wasted.

The difficulty arises partly from the assumption that the ultimate object of a comprehensive national health care evaluation is an equally comprehensive redesign of the health care system if this is required. For example, this was implicit in the fact that WHO's Country Health Programming called for a stocktaking of the present situation as a preliminary to the development of a national health plan. But there may be other, more limited reasons for evaluation, even on the national scale; and these depend partly on how it fits into the procedures of the initiating organization, a problem dealt with in the next section. It depends also on the inherent difficulty of producing change in any complex organization, and on the extent to which the results call for immediate action as against a long-continuing process of monitoring and adjustment; these problems are dealt with in the following sections. Finally, it depends on the complex of group interests involved in change in the health field and their reconciliation. For this too special provision is needed.

7.1 Who wants evaluation, and for what?

Except in the final section of this chapter, it will be assumed that a national health evaluation is commissioned by some official body which, at least in a general way, intends to act on the results. It excludes cases, not unknown, where evaluation is set in train as a way of postponing decisions; and also cases, which may overlap with the first, where the evaluator has to conclude that his results are inconsistent with the interests of the official agencies concerned. These are dealt with in the final section of this chapter.

This still leaves room for a good deal of variety in the commissioning agency, its objectives and the degree of responsibility it assumes for implementing any recommendations. The simplest situation is one where a national government, acting through its ministry of health, decides on a thorough stocktaking with the full intention of following through on the results, no matter how drastic the changes they suggest. Realistically, this is most likely to happen with a change of government (as in Jamaica in 1972) or a complete change of regime (as with Zimbabwe in 1980). Here at first sight it seems that nothing stands in the way of the implementation of change since commissioning and executing agencies are essentially one. In practice the problem is more complicated.

It must be recognized, first, that while an evaluation is a suitable instrument for identifying the need for change, it is not in itself a good means for translating these changes into implementable form. It is rare to meet a health system which needs only a shopping list of modifications which can be achieved independently of each other and by administrative action. More commonly, the needed changes are interdependent and require some degree of system redesign. Implementation therefore depends on the planning capacity of the health authorities—their ability to produce, not necessarily a classic five-year plan with dated events, but at least a co-ordinated and sequential scheme for future development. This is an ultimate responsibility which no evaluation exercise can remove from them.

In addition, while an evaluation may be initiated by a ministry of health or other body charged with health care, the implementation of any changes required, unless these are unusually limited, necessarily involves other agencies. This is not only because health depends on so many things besides health care, and even health care may be provided through other institutions—for example, school health through the ministry of education. It is also because any substantial changes demand of the health ministry a reallocation of funds, and usually an increase. This may come directly from the budgets of national and state governments, in which case the central agencies of finance—ministry of finance, and perhaps central planning authority and central bank—are clearly involved. Additional funds from international agencies may also be called for; if these are to be obtained on a loan basis it is common for interest and repayment to be handled centrally, again involving the ministry of finance and similar agencies. If the country is presently under the scrutiny of the International Monetary Fund or other international monetary agency, there is no aspect of government health care with which they cannot claim a legitimate concern. It is of course not the affair of the ministry of health's evaluator to prepare submissions to all the agencies which may be involved with change; but it is helpful if he is aware of the criteria by which they will judge his product and as persuasive as possible in their terms. Otherwise, he risks having the changes needed to implement his evaluation dismissed as another medical boondoggle—a highminded scheme whose covert purpose is to enrich the participants.

We must also take account of the fact that even where the changes arising out of an evaluation are limited and lie entirely within the province of the ministry of health, the power of that ministry to implement change is not absolute. Formal constraints may be imposed by the overall administrative system—for example, if ministry staff are integrated into an overall public personnel system. Informal constraints arise from all the factors which limit the flexibility of human service organizations. Hence even where the changes required are limited, account must be taken of the problems discussed in the following sections and the suggested ways of overcoming them.

It is common in developing countries for the effective initiator of evaluation to be not the national government, but an outside agency. This can arise in two ways; in connection with a particular project which involves application for agency funds, or to give the agency the information which will provide the basis for future project or programme aid. Procedurally, the line between these and the purely national evaluation may not be easy to draw, since it is common for ministries of health to be assigned much of the work of assembling the requisite material for an external evaluation, often to the great detriment of the tempers of their senior staff. But the purpose of the agency-directed evaluation is clearly distinctive.

The procedures which govern the decision of a lending agency such as the World Bank about whether a project proposal should be accepted, and if so in what form, are often complex, as is inevitable in a complex organization. Though developed by run of the mill technicians and administrators, the proposals must carry conviction at all levels up to that of the governing body, and must prevent gross errors from arising either because the borrower cannot implement the project successfully, or because he cannot pay. At each level there will be hidden agendas and pressure to avoid reproachable errors. There is the urge to exhaust one's budget allowment (and ask for more next year); there is the need for equity between countries, and a due observance of their lending and voting power. Thus the process by which a health or other project is assessed is not entirely an explicit one. In this situation procedures represent a way of preserving a modicum of rationality and altruism in project selection.

These procedures when applied to a project proposal include a substantial element of evaluation, but one concentrated on the project itself, rather than on the national system of which it forms part. Hence they may provide for cost-benefit and cost-effectiveness analyses and schedules of disbursement and repayment, but with specific reference to the individual project.

But this is not entirely satisfactory. The success of a project will depend to some extent on the quality of the service system of which it forms part, and the prospects for repayment depend on the borrower's general economic and financial situation. It is not prudent to pour new wine into old bottles without at least checking the skin for leaks. Hence the proposer of a health project can fairly be asked to provide at least a background account of the health system concerned.

There are a number of reasons why such an account should include an evaluative element. One is the adoption by international agencies such as the World Bank (e.g. 1980) and WHO of positive policies for the health sector against which it is natural to measure the actual national situation. Another is the pressures exerted by the developing countries' economic problems during the last decade and the need to demonstrate that health care can be improved in spite of the limits on expenditure imposed by policies of 'structural adjustment'. This implies that present national health systems are inefficient and that the inefficiencies are remediable. To demonstrate this is in effect to carry out an evaluation.

Hence there exist evaluations of national health systems designed to serve the purposes of external agencies, official like the health sections of World Bank country reports or private like the reports of Syncrisis (see, for example Syncrisis 1976). In breadth these are likely to be wider than any project report, but since the agency concerned has no direct responsibility for the health of the country's population they are likely to differ in purpose from a national evaluation.

The fact that evaluation exercises originate in different ways and serve different purposes affects both the beginning and the end of the evaluation process. Initially, the purpose will affect the planning of the process, the resources and time required and the fields to be given at least preliminary priority. This is one reason why there has been no attempt here to present a 'how-to' manual prescribing the exact sequence in which the work must be done; instead, the book concentrates on the principles involved and the factors common to all evaluations. In any case, an appraisal carried out for a specific external agency is likely to have its own procedural rules.

Differences in purpose will also produce differences in output. One result of any evaluation is likely to be some kind of report. The shape of this may be determined by procedural rules, if it is undertaken for an outside agency. But if the originator takes some responsibility for introducing the changes required by the evaluation, whether as a national authority or an external agency committed to immediate action, a formal report is not the only output, and should not stand as a document independent of the implementation stage. This stage will involve some of the steps set out in the following sections, and the report should be shaped so as to make these stages easy and to be convincing to the people who will carry the responsibility for implementation. It may well be worthwhile to prepare more than one report, each directed to a different reader, and to release some of them on an interim basis.

All serious evaluation on a national scale can be described as applied research. But some evaluations generate research in a more academic sense, in that they lead to the framing of generalizations which will be of interest to others working in the same field independent of the particular circumstances of the country involved. It is unlikely that a system evaluation, with all the disturbance it entails for the administrator, will be undertaken for purely academic reasons. But it may be entrusted to an academic agency, or arouse in those who carry it out academic ambitions (which, no doubt should be made of sterner stuff, but ambitions are inevitable among workers who are worth having). Results at this level clearly demand a separate form of publication (e.g. as journal articles). These may have to be steered through an administrative mechanism of approval if the writers are public employees, and if in general the writer wishes to maintain his entree for future work. Such mechanisms are not wholly arbitrary. They are meant to prevent the kind of pseudo-research which consists in arranging well known facts into emotionally acceptable patterns, and is all too common on the fringes of the social sciences. Pseudo-research in developing countries is often a way of enlisting academic prestige in the service of political change. Some of the problems this arouses are referred to in the last section below.

7.2 Communicating the results of evaluation

7.2.1 *Evaluation and the policy–planning–budgeting process*

In one branch of the literature on health planning, evaluation is an activity integrated into the policy–planning–budgeting cycle. It belongs at the beginning of a cycle, as the basis on which planning can be undertaken, and possibly some revision of policy. It belongs at the end of the cycle, as an assessment of the extent to which plans have been implemented; but it also forms the starting point for the next cycle. This correctly represents the logic of the process. Further, evaluations with a narrower remit may be undertaken at intermediate points in the cycle, shading off into the monitoring of specific aspects of implementation which is part of the regular business of health care management.

Under such an arrangement, formulating and implementing the changes resulting from his work is not the business of the evaluator. Rather, it falls to the health planners and to health administrators generally. Further, once the evaluation and its implied changes are accepted, implementation is a matter for the administrative machinery of government. This machinery is as susceptible to perfection through evaluation and its results as the rest of the system. If, therefore, implementation does not take place, this is likely to be taken as the result of perversity in high places—in the words of a former Director General of WHO, a lack of political will.

In fact the logical structure of a process is not necessarily a good guide to the required sequence of activities, as any computer programmer knows. The evaluator has to take into account a number of awkward facts. One is, of course, the fact that in many developing countries a formal planning approach is not, or is only newly, established. More fundamentally, the approach is itself subject to certain limitations, as indicated in an earlier chapter. Many planning procedures originated on a project, rather than a programme or system basis; and in a time when planning for expansion was the norm, rather than the kind of structural adjustment which calls for a shift or contraction of resources. It is still far easier to get advice and funds for opening a new hospital, than for closing an old one; but the latter may be as essential to greater efficiency as the former, and one is not simply the obverse of the other. Then, too, a plan or any comprehensive proposal for changes in health care does not include only things which can be changed by immediate administrative fiat from within the health sector. It is likely to include also actions which must be negotiated (with other parts of the government system, like legal change, or with non-government bodies such as professional associations and other trade unions; and factors which can be predicted but not controlled, such as the spread of human immuno-deficiency virus in other countries. The policy–planning–budgeting cycle is therefore a useful mechanism to help translate the results of evaluation into action, and an active planning unit, where one exists, is a natural focus for this translation, especially if, as is likely, it has been responsible for aspects of the evaluation itself. But this will not free the evaluator from the obligation to envisage the implementation of change, so far as he can, in realistic terms and to take into account the need to convince others than the planners of the validity of his conclusions.

7.2.2 *Evaluation and other mechanisms of administrative change*

Reference has been made above, and particularly in Section 5.4, to the administrative framework which controls the government sector of the health services. In spite of its limitations, this is a powerful machinery for implementing the changes suggested by evaluation. These may be pedestrian, requiring only that routine management methods should be applied to bringing what people do closer to what the regulations say they ought to do. Drivers should be prevented from using ambulances as taxis; doctors should be made to do a full four-hours work in a session. On the other hand, evaluation may suggest changes in the regulations themselves and even in the supporting legislation. The evaluator's role in this kind of implementation is limited. But if he bears any degree of responsibility for the final result, there are helpful things he can do in shaping his report and other activities.

One thing he can do is to identify, as well as he can, those factors which may make even a reasonable person break the regulations. Do ambulance drivers cheat out of resentment at having to take the SMO's children to school? Do doctors cheat because the rewards from private practice are disproportionately greater than what they can earn from sessions? The evaluator also has the obligation to draw attention to inconsistencies between different regulations, or between the same regulation as interpreted in different training and operational institutions. Can nurse practitioners be given by fiat the power to prescribe, if pharmacists are told that under their law they must meet no prescriptions other than those of pukka doctors? Generally, the evaluator should do what he can to make it easy for the implementer of change and to ensure that the administrative regulations which emerge are consistent, enforceable, and communicated to those concerned.

The dangers of piecemeal change are in some countries particularly associated with the annual budget. With the absence or increasing difficulty of long-term planning, the budget has taken on the status of an annual plan, with its heads and subheads corresponding to administrative programmes and lines of authority, and the allocation of funds between them reflecting their relative status. In the case of administrative change, the most urgent task for a ministry of health may well be to reflect this change in the organization of the budget documents. But all too often the process of communicating change stops there, and health workers are left to infer the details of their new situation without other guidance. Formal changes not communicated create confusion at the operating level. In this case they also enhance the influence of the financial technicians as the only people willing to take and transmit decisions—an influence which not only medicals currently believe has increased, is increasing and should be diminished.

7.2.3   *Informal communication of the results of evaluation*

The wise administrator, then, in implementing changes arising from an evaluation, will need to follow through fully, in his imagination and in fact, these changes from their formal expression at the central level (whether incorporated in a plan or not) to their expression in detailed instructions to the health workers involved. Beyond this, he and his subordinates will probably need to make use of means of communications which fall outside the system of formal regulations. These may be of many kinds, from the injection of these changes and their rationale into the curriculum of health professionals in training to a ward sister's get-together with her staff to explain a new hospital timetable. With most of these, again, the evaluator is not directly concerned. But there is one respect in which he can be helpful both to himself and to the body of health workers.

In any evaluation which is not simply a desktop exercise, the evaluator will have occasion to meet many health workers and members of the public, taking advantage of their usual garrulity to collect information which helps him to understand the reality behind the annual returns. This is always a two-way process; the evaluator gives information as well as receiving it. It is often economical to do it on a group basis, meeting a number of health workers and clients to discuss a particular problem. When the results of the evaluation begin to take shape, they can be introduced into this process at a point where they can if necessary be officially disavowed, and when they may provoke further information which will confirm or modify them. In so doing, the evaluator is not only doing an essential part of his job. He is also making easier the job of whoever has later to implement change. For he will have shown to a wide range of people (who in turn will show others, particularly if they are forbidden to do so) the logic of the evaluation and the strength of the pressures for change; and he will have done something to turn the evaluation from an external intrusion to a co-operative attempt at self-improvement.

7.3   Strengthening arrangements for further evaluation

Ideally, the evaluation of a health care system should not be a one-off affair. It is true that every major evaluation exercise is unique. But the evaluation function is a continuing part of effective management, and needs resources and some degree of institutionalization. This is a field where the person responsible for a major re-assessment has to function at two levels. On the one hand he is the impartial observer, looking at this as at other aspects of the existing management system from the outside. In this capacity he identifies faults and, by the logic of his work, to some extent suggests the necessary changes. But for the implementation of these changes he bears no direct technical or administrative responsibility. On the other hand, he is also a person specially qualified in the evaluation field—if not when his task begins, then hopefully by its end. He can therefore legitimately be called on to be more positive in this field than elsewhere about the arrangements by which the function is to be carried forward, and to shape his own output so that it forms part of a continuing process. Even though we maintain the assumption of a national health authority committed broadly to accepting the need for evaluation and to implementing the changes to which it points, there is room for a great deal of variation in the specific arrangements for high-level evaluation, and these will depend on the overall shape of the national health care system. This chapter is devoted to the principles and broad problems which must be kept in mind.

It must be remembered, first, that every health authority has some machinery for evaluation of its services, even if this is only the visit of the chief medical officer to a provincial hospital or the briefing of a health minister attacked in the legislature. This machinery is directed mainly toward programme and project evaluation, and just as the health care system is not simply the sum of these, so a system evaluation is more than the sum of the programme and project assessments. But any arrangements for system-wide assessment must be at least consistent with what happens at the lower level.

All evaluation takes place against a constantly changing background, and at the highest level this must be explicitly allowed for. After the last decade, the variability of the economic background needs no demonstration. The technical background may be equally variable. In the last few years, for example, there have been advances in our understanding of the relation between environment and health, and of the place in health care planning of measures to control industrial pollution, nuclear radiation, and atmospheric stability. The importance of these advances should not be discounted because our understanding is not complete. It is manifested presently in the (sometimes undignified) competition for resources between scientists at the research level and for influence in the councils determining health policy in the developed countries and international agencies; it will soon show itself as a need for re-evaluation of health priorities in the developing world. Brazil's re-orientation of its policies towards the erosion of its rain forests may be only the first of many examples.

General social policy, too, is in the long run variable and unpredictable. This is evident, in parliamentary states, if this policy is enunciated by political parties which differ in ideology and succeed each other in power. But underlying the formal political changes, and sometimes cutting across them, are shifts in public feeling about such things as the nature of poverty, the status of nationalism and racism and the obligations of the state.

Certain things follow from the unpredictability of the economic, technical and social background to health care. One is that no day-to-day system of programme and project monitoring can be a substitute for the possibility of high level system evaluation. Another is that such evaluation is not needed continuously, and the occasions for its use are themselves unpredictable. A third implication is that the persons responsible must have some understanding of matters outside the strictly medical field. Poor developing countries cannot afford to keep people with the scarce skills required continuously occupied with evaluation. Put together, these considerations suggest that system evaluation has to be a looser and more flexible affair than evaluation at lower levels, and its initiation and the form it takes remains a responsibility of upper management, not to be taken away by any institutionalized procedures.

This responsibility cannot be fulfilled without generating fear, and perhaps conflict, among the health workers concerned. Evaluating, like planning, is a threatening activity, holding the possibility of criticism and loss of resources for persons unaccustomed to such insecurity. If it is institutionalized in a group within the regular machinery of health service management, the hostility generated by the higher level assessment may spread to the other functions of the group and damage the co-operative relationship with lower level management on which much of their effectiveness depends. Something like this has already happened where specialized planning units are called on both to prepare health sector plans and to monitor project progress. It was not without cause that a wily Regional Director of WHO in South-East Asia added to his management system not a planning or evaluation unit, but a unit for Programme Support and Co-ordination whose functions were often evaluative but whose name arrogated to it nothing that could arose hostility.

These considerations do not dictate a particular form of organization for system level health care evaluation. But they do suggest that we should look more kindly on past practices like the setting up of Royal Commissions which gave temporary form to such evaluation exercises, or on the task forces which under various names are their modern equivalents. The essentials to be secured are the availability of a wide enough range of skills, and support from and access to the highest levels of health care management. Given these, the precise institutional form is less important.

But surely (it may be said) these are precisely the virtues guaranteed to exercises undertaken at the behest of, or as an approach to, international lending agencies? The skills of the agency are at the evaluator's disposal, and the possibility of securing US$10 millions is the best possible guarantee of high level access for his results. It is possible to quibble about the quality of the skills available in untraditional fields to even the most prestigious-sounding agencies. But there is a more fundamental objection to this approach. Essentially, an externally generated evaluation must absorb some unstated premises from the agency responsible, and a developing country trusting entirely to it may find itself faced with a report it cannot in practice accept or implement. It is in a far stronger position in negotiating with other parties, including lending and technical agencies, if its system assessment is a national product. This is not simply a defence of the interests of a national bourgeoisie. It is a recognition of the fact that even though small developing countries have increasingly to recognize that in defence, finance and foreign affairs the locus of power lies outside their borders, a world in which they abandon their remaining functions will rapidly become ungovernable.

7.4   Evaluation and the negotiation of change

An international group of health planners was gathered to drink Bavarian wine in one of those post-conference sessions which all agree are more fruitful than the conference itself. After an exchange of complaints someone asked 'Why do we do this job?' There was only one indecorous answer. One man said thoughtfully 'I do it because I enjoy the intrigue'. His colleagues were not shocked or surprised.

In one sense, intrigue is merely the interpersonal side of the negotiation which must go on if there are to be changes in health care which involve groups more or less autonomous from the public sector. Of course some degree of autonomy is everywhere; a mutinous porter can wreck a new referral scheme without ever breaching hospital regulations. But major changes involve certain organized groups whose agreement must be obtained through mutual discussion and, if necessary, bargaining. The evaluator should bear in mind the need for this agreement and do as little as possible to hinder the processes of negotiation required to reach it. He should not of course commit himself in advance to certain conclusions or certain consequent changes. But he should avoid giving unnecessary offence; as a colleague has said, if you must hit a man over the head with your sandal, you can at least wrap it in clean cloth first. So groups with whom negotiation may later be necessary should be kept fully informed of the evaluation methods used and where possible involved in the investigation. The leaders of such groups should not be deprived unnecessarily of the prerogative of knowing more, sooner than their members, since it is not only needed for purposes of action but also greatly valued. Faced with a rumour of evaluation but no firm knowledge, such groups may be in the position of Kafka's Mole, retreating further and further into his burrow as he agonizes to identify and escape from a harmless but unfamiliar sound.

In the immediate past the groups with whom negotiation might prove necessary were mainly the professional associations—those for doctors, nurses, pharmacists, and an increasing number of others. The range of duties (and how much should be paid for them) has been a principal subject of negotiation. These negotiations have often been acerbic, but there were two things making for a favourable outcome. One thing was that on the whole the pressures for change came from within the professions and had solid technical reasons behind them; another was that in an expansionary period most groups could look to be compensated elsewhere for any ground they lost. Nurses might be forced to accept the legitimacy of the Assistant

Nurse, but could compensate for any curtailment of their function at one end by extending their academic claims at the other. Hence for most professional groups negotiations with the health authorities ended, if not in peace, at least in nothing worse than an armed neutrality.

This state of affairs may not last. Proposals for change are increasingly coming forward from outside the health professions; either from the side of economics and finance, or from that of the health consumer associations which are becoming increasingly active in developed countries (see, for example Which 1987). These associations are only effective in a few of the developing countries such as Malaysia, but they may have to be taken more seriously in the future.

Particularly threatening to the professional associations is the present tendency to question the inevitability of the collocation of roles which today makes up the job of a doctor, or of a nurse, or of another health professional. Could these roles be broken down into tasks, technical and managerial, and these tasks reassembled in different patterns, one appropriate to each country? If so, what would this mean in terms of savings on current costs, and changes in management patterns and in training? Above all, what would it mean to the professional associations (and the corresponding and often subservient councils), and above all what would it mean to Dr. X, who has been president of the Periodontic Society for forty-three years? There is no negotiation so bitter as that whose subject threatens the leadership role of the negotiating body. The evaluator may not intend to intrude into this field at all; but he cannot exclude the possibility that proposals for changes of this kind may result from his evaluation. In the future, therefore, there will be all the more reason for him to avoid gratuitously offending the groups with whom future negotiation may be necessary.

In such negotiation intrigue has an honourable place, as the ensemble of the confidential discussions carried on between the leaders of negotiating groups to reach agreed positions. It can, however, bear another meaning, not necessarily less honourable but certainly more dangerous. Suppose that the evaluator concludes that he must in conscience report in such a way that certain changes in the health care system follow inevitably from his conclusions; but that his evaluative work must run to waste because these changes will not be implemented, for political, group, or personal reasons. Is he justified in trying to muster support for his report and the changes it implies, even if it means striking up an alliance with actors on the political scene whom as a scientist he should keep at arm's length?

There is usually no lack of potential allies. These may be at the highest administrative levels—chief medical officers who have been or hopefully will be. They may be other health professionals, particularly the leaders of the junior doctors, the majors and lieutenant colonels of the clinical world who see themselves as the leaders of profitable revolutions. They may lie outside the administrative establishment, like the leaders of the professional associations; even outside health altogether, like the agents of political parties in search of a cause. If the evaluator is convinced of his rightness— or at least of the wrongness of those who oppose him—is he not justified in enlisting some of these allies to get a fair hearing for his results?

As a matter of conscience, this is a matter for each evaluator operating in his own situation. As a matter of prudence, an economist like the writer tends to come down on the side of caution. If the evaluator is a foreigner, he should remember how many empires were built on honourable alliances later regretted. Romans, Spaniards, British, French—all acquired their empires by supporting the opponents of a host of cruel and corrupt tyrants, and all were embarrassed by the cruelty and corruption their proteges developed in their turn. The ambitious external evaluator should at least stay around, like his imperial predecessors, to answer for the results of his activity.

The evaluator may also want to shape his report—if this is the form his output takes—rather differently from one intended to feed directly into the administrative machinery of government. He may wish to direct it much more explicitly toward the general public, and less toward fellow specialists. In this way he may hope to set up pressure on the government health agencies either through public opinion in general or, in countries where a single political party forms a para-government, through the party elders. But because of the resistances to change to be expected from any complex organization, these are forces which should in any case be enlisted. Provided objectivity is maintained, a report directed to the general public is desirable even where it serves no political end of the evaluator. It is, rather, a recognition that behind one's obligation to government or agency as paymaster, there is a more fundamental obligation to the truth on one side, and to one's fellow humans on the other. Such a report is only devalued if it is perverted to a partisan end.

8 The future of national health system evaluation

A former member of WHO's staff liked to tell how his little son, entertaining an early visitor, had been asked what was his father's job. 'A doctor, eh? If I am sick he will make me better?' 'Oh no, he is a *talking* doctor.' Suppose the young surgeon who was left in Chapter 2 in transition to international consultancy has arrived, a few years later, at the status of the talking doctor, and even conducted a number of evaluations of the national health systems of developing countries. Picture him resting between assignments, perhaps in the Hotel Cornavin ('pas de bruit, jour et nuit'). Outside his windows, if he could only hear it, is the decorous nightlife of Geneva. But he has decided to eat quietly and well in the Buffet Première Classe and retire to his room. Tomorrow he may have to set out again on his missionary rounds, praising rice to the Sikhs, yam to the Bengalis, and vegetarianism to the Masai. But tonight he is among the people of one of the richest and healthiest nations in the world, indistinguishable from them so long as he does not open his mouth to speak. No importunate patient or hospital call can disturb him. In the creak of the opening minibar he seems to hear his bad angel saying 'You see? you've got it made!' But somewhere—in the sough of the air conditioning?—he seems to hear the good angel sighing 'pourvu que ça dure . . .'. He has put both his gradually acquired skills and his heart into his evaluation work, and does not doubt the value of what he has done. But what of its future?

He is aware that the evaluation of health care systems on the national scale has emerged only recently in human history. This is partly because it has only now become common to regard the elements of health care as forming an interrelated system. A long history attaches to clinical medicine, whether Western, Ayurvedic, Chinese, or whatever. An equally long history attaches to some of the basic ideas of public health such as the importance of good food and clean air, even though in the light of the nineteenth century's work on germs and vectors some of the older ideas seem ludicrously misplaced. But until the present century the clinical and public health sides of medicine and their associated facilities were not regarded as forming a single health care system. The exceptions involved certain institutions which were 'total' in the sociological sense, providing their members with all forms of social relationship. Organized armies have always had their health care systems; so have well run monasteries and efficient slave estates.

Perhaps the first modern system evaluation was that of the health care provision for the British army in India, set in train by Florence Nightingale —without, it should be noted, her ever moving far from her valetudinarian couch in England, but with an inspired use of experience, devoted followers, written returns, and the scientific background.

But evaluation at the national level was scarcely meaningful until there existed nation states which provided a substantial part of health care and took responsibility for the results of this provision. The developed countries (leaving aside Russia) did not assume this function until the twentieth century, and at first in a very partial fashion. It was only at the time of the second world war that some of them nerved themselves to attempt system-wide health care planning, and paradoxically often approached the subject more radically in their colonies than at home. When these colonies became politically independent in the postwar period, they found themselves with state health care systems of a sort and, it seemed, the obligation to perfect them. At this point in history, with the convergence of political change with changes in the content and organization of health care—say, from 1960 onward—the widespread use of national health care evaluations became rational, as a preliminary to and as part of national health care planning.

Our consultant will be aware, therefore, that historically health system evaluations can claim only a modest pride of ancestry. This does not worry either his bad or his good angels provided there is a certain hope of posterity —the aspiration of the good angel being that such evaluations will become a permanently useful part of health care management, while the bad angel hopes for them as a source of lucrative consultancies. What prospects do they enjoy?

Some of the situations which since 1960 have generated fundamental evaluations of national health care systems will not recur, at least in the same form. In many cases these evaluations are intended to represent a breakpoint, either between political regimes (as in Zimbabwe) or between health care policies (as with some of WHO's work intended as preliminary to countries' adoption of Health for All by the Year 2000). These exercises are intended to stimulate system redesign; when the new system is in place, further changes will be less necessary, and evaluation can take on a more humdrum character.

We can also look forward, certainly in the long term but perhaps earlier, to changes in the basic elements of national evaluations—the obligations of the nation state (particularly in poor countries) and the nature of health care. The omnicompetent nation state which all ex-colonies aspire to be is coming to be recognized as a mirage, the result of an idealization of the situation of Britain, the United States, and France in the nineteenth century which is itself a mirage, though one consoling to both ex-rulers and ex-subjects. Not even the most developed countries possess, or ever possessed, the unlimited resources and indifference to their relations with others which would constitute absolute independence. The poorest and smallest countries of the world, coming nowhere near this status, are increasingly resigning control of their external relations to whichever of the richer nations will accept them as clients, and of their economic policies, external and, increasingly, internal also, to the international agencies in which the patron nations dominate. The future national health care evaluator will increasingly have to strike from his terms of reference any discussion of the appropriateness of the total resources devoted to health; or, if he tackles this subject, do so in terms convincing to the nation's external paymasters. There is presently no sign in the world of the kind of rapid economic growth which could in principle free developing countries from a high degree of external financial control. Indeed, it is arguable that it is in a strengthening of the world's financial proto-government that there lies the best hope of development.

On the side of the content of the health care system, the future is equally uncertain, and even more difficult to foresee. Some of the ways in which health care is changing are well known and easily extrapolated—the still widening range of drugs and insecticides, the victory over many childhood and other infectious diseases, the increasing prominence (mainly for demographic reasons) of the chronic and degenerative diseases. But other, less noticed forces are at work which may change the tasks of the health care system fundamentally, or create a new Kuhnian paradigm of health care studies. What follows is speculative—the kind of thing the Lancet gives separate but equal treatment under the heading 'Hypothesis' to affirm its scientific liberalism, and the kind of thing a still intellectually curious consultant welcomes to his mind after the second Martell.

McKeown and others (1976, 1988: but see review by Yudkin of Boyd Eaton *et al.* 1988) have accustomed us to the idea that the health state of a society, and its characteristic health problems, are closely related to what a Marxist would call the relations of production, and the material conditions which arise from these. It appears that in the long ages of the hunters and gatherers, scattered groups of humans enjoyed a varied diet, an outdoor life and surprisingly good health (it is not clear why they reproduced so slowly). The agricultural revolution force-fed a more rapidly growing population on the products of its farms, and gathered them into places of permanent and crowded habitation which fostered the spread of the classical contagious diseases—all the more when population eventually outran food supply, as in Malthusian terms it must. The industrial revolution (by which McKeown means mainly the beginnings in eighteenth century England of the massive use of mechanical energy in manufacturing) moved the production and distribution of food once again to a higher level, made the towns into cleaner and more efficient living places and eventually offset many of the threats to health which had arisen in feudal times. Only at the end of this phase, in the twentieth century, does industrial production offer to the health worker a significant improvement in the range of drugs and insecticides he can use; and (to extend McKeown's analysis) the emergence of these drugs marks the transition to a post-industrial phase in which knowledge, finance, and communication generally begin to displace mechanical energy as the sources of increased production. This is the situation of many of the countries now called 'developed', and it is obvious that it has made possible further progress toward the elimination of contagious diseases (at resource costs often so low even poor countries can afford them) and the correction of many of the worst environmental effects of the industrial phase. But we would expect, on the grounds of cosmic pessimism if no other, that new health problems would have emerged from the post-industrial setting. Is there any indication of what these are?

One group seems obvious and non-controversial; keeping alive, and protecting from disability, all those aging people who in a previous age would have died early from measles, cholera, or tuberculosis. The search for solutions to these problems is already under way, and in physiological terms is expanding the boundaries of medical science without changing it fundamentally. But it is also having certain unexpected effects. In different ways, these concern a single subject—the power to control the human mood.

On the one side, the doctor looking for preventive measures against the 'Western' diseases—hypertension, diabetes, cancer, and so on—increasingly finds himself recommending to his patients abstention from the substances which have traditionally been used to stimulate conviviality and control pain and depression—what may be called very broadly the psychotropic substances. On the other hand, doctors increasingly find that for some patients, in extreme old age or the terminal stages of certain diseases, their prime concern must be the control of pain, whether the pain generated by aging nature or that provoked by the medication for specific conditions. Medicine is, perhaps, somewhat less concerned than it was with keeping the machine working, and more with the feelings of the ghost within it, even though these feelings may lead it aside from the path to mechanical efficiency. (Materialists may like to recall that in Capek's play 'R.U.R.', the first generation of robots proved unsatisfactory because, lacking a sense of pain, they took no care to avoid injury.) For such purposes the industrial system has equipped the health worker with a wide range of psychotropic substances. It has not, unfortunately, provided him with a rational basis for their use.

If we look at society at large, we can see that the psychotropics used in medicine are only special cases of a more general class of activities. Their common feature in their present form is that they carry with them a pleasurable or at least mind-bending sensation which can be detached by the consumer from the utilitarian aspects of the activity and intensified to a degree not found in nature. This is the root of many of the current social problems with a health component.

It is obvious that certain drugs are psychotropic in this sense. Some of these are traditional in Western society, and hardly recognized as drugs; the caffeine group (coffee, tea, cocoa), alcohol, nicotine. Generally these are drugs for which means of social control exist, even though these sometimes break down as grossly as the restrictions on drunkenness in British football crowds imply. To these must be added others for which, at least in the West, no social control exists, such as ganja and opium—it is notable that during the wars that were fought in the nineteenth century to force China to permit the importation of Indian opium, the members of the Chinese imperial court did not abstain from this amiable drug. To these again must be added the products of the industrial revolution which have no counterpart in nature. These include most of the standard tranquillizers (which have a valid medical use and can be wheedled out of one's doctor) and drugs such as LSD and the amphetamines, whose medical usefulness is exiguous. And we must take into account also that the enormous increase in the scale of production which has become possible for such drugs as morphine, heroin, and cocaine creates a wholly new scale for their potential clientele.

But reflection will show that other kinds of activity fit the same pattern of the disjunction of pleasure or stimulation from the activity which gives rise to it. One, evidently, is sexual activity; the combination of efficient birth control with an ethos which exalts sexuality as a source of personal pleasure and a necessity for mental health opens the way to something closely analogous to drug taking (as also to the transmission of the human immuno-deficiency virus, cystitis, herpes, and many other quasi-health problems). Another form of psychotropism, again only possible to an industrial or post-industrial society, is an exploitation of the properties of electronic music, which makes available to all a decibel level whose effect is independent of the nominal message of the song. For those whose daily lives seem to them irremediably frustrating, there is no cheaper stupefacient.

'Is there' wonders the consultant, now into his third Martell 'some reason why the human race should desire psychotropics at this time?' One answer is implicit in the work of Trowell and Burkitt (1981), and others who have assumed the role of *laudator societatis actae*; earlier patterns of production forced the ordinary man to take abundant exercise, it is only now we have substituted mechanical for human energy that the ordinary man is well fed and yet uses little physical energy. He misses, therefore, the highs that come from pitching hay or walking six miles to town for the barn dance, and seeks substitutes in strange places. If this point of view is correct, the remedy is clear and morally acceptable; the youngster whose father sweated in the steel mills of Birmingham, and boasted afterward over his beers, must learn to play tennis at the country club and boast in the bar over a less vulgar tipple.

But what if the answer is less simple than this? It is a commonplace that an increasing proportion of workers in both developed and developing countries (though more in the former) are spending their working lives in the manipulation of symbols, not the concrete things they stand for. What (the consultant is now near to dreamland) if symbolic thought necessarily arises from the aborting of action? What if, as a preliminary to *cogito ergo sum*, there stands *frustror ergo cogito*? Will not that indefinable 'stress', that now appears as a risk factor for so many conditions, take on a new meaning? and will not client and health worker be forced to assuage it, if necessary, by the use of psychotropics—under strict social control, understood by both parties, but without shame? And above all what will this mean to the future of health care systems, and those who evaluate them?

Into the mind of the consultant, now thoroughly asleep in his armchair, his good and bad angels send competing visions. The good angel shows him a world in which scientists have developed the perfect psychotropic—perhaps the *soma* of Huxley's 'Brave New World'—and doctors are charged with the duty of administering it in doses which will maximize their clients' happiness without limiting their mental achievements. It is the evaluator's task to see that this happiness is attained—even that of the psychoanalysts who have lost their jobs, and that of the Medellin cartel. The evaluator assures the good angel that he welcomes this broadening of his task, even though he has no idea how he will set about it. Perhaps in his economics minor he should have taken more seriously the discussion of utility, Jeremy Bentham and the greatest good of the greatest number?

Our consultant's drowsy intuition has led him to the heart of a philosophical problem which evaluators will increasingly have to make explicit. Mathematicians may tell us that Benthamites who ask for the greatest good of the greatest number are committing a solecism, since only under special conditions is it possible to maximise a variable in two dimensions at the same time. Nevertheless humanists and ordinary people everywhere would probably accept the phrase as an attempt to state the ultimate guiding principle of secular policy (and for humanists what other policy is there?). For the last two generations it has been possible for an evaluator in the health field to leave aside the difficulties raised by Bentham's formula. In the future of the good angel's vision, these can no longer be ignored.

These difficulties have already begun to emerge from the relatively new field of policy analysis. They are still inchoate, because policy analysis has tended to confine itself to immediate problems—either the consistency of policy statements one with another, or the acceptability of policies when translated into specific activities. Beyond these lies the analysis of health policies in terms of their political, ethical and philosophical basis; and it is here that the evaluator may find that Bentham's formula is no more than an intuitive guide.

The first difficulty with the formula is that it invites us to measure the effects of our policies in two dimensions—the number of persons benefited, and the intensity of the benefit received. In a period of successful curative medicine, the clinical practitioner can decline the invitation by adopting an ethic which bids him maximise the benefit to the patient before him (though he may still face some nasty decisions about the allocation between patients of his personal time and resources). The health policy maker, planner and administrator, dealing with such subjects as family planning and the balance of resources between the care of young and old, does not have this freedom. He cannot look to the modern economist to provide him with a trade-off rate between the numbers benefited and the intensity of the benefit. This is the one thing that cannot be done if, to preserve the purity of our theory, we economists sedulously avoid treating the benefits (in economic language, the utility) of any activity to the persons involved as neither additive between persons nor in the ordinary sense quantitative. Yet without some concept of trade-off we are unlikely to find better than ad hoc solutions to problems of interpersonal and intergenerational equity; and we seem condemned to go on blundering toward a world of 15 billion people who on average are unlikely to be as well off as we are.

A second joker falls out of the Benthamite pack if we ask who is to define the 'good' we aim to maximise. Is physiological health self-evidently good? If so, can it never be in conflict with other forms of well-being? Should the practitioner try to produce a population of what he instinctively recognises as healthy, normal beings fitted to operate successfully within a given society? If so, should he allow his society to define normality, as Russian psychiatrists have been blamed for doing? Or should he leave the definition of the good to the more or less informed choice of the patient? We have Bentham's authority for the idea that pushpenny may make a greater contribution to human good than philosophy; does this imply that amphetamines may be reasonably preferred to exercise?

These are some of the problems to which the future health evaluator will have to pay attention. There is no reason to suppose that his traditional props will entirely fail him. Physiological medicine will continue its advances, even if they increasingly move beyond maternal and child health and the common infectious diseases. Nations will still need periodic health system evaluation, even if the nature of the nation state changes. But we cannot forever trust the good angel to solve the fundamental problems of health policy simply through the moral intuitions bound up in his world-view.

The bad angel presents a rather different future. In this world it is the fathers of Medellin who have developed soma, a little ahead of their Burmese and Pakistani rivals, and have marketed it with all the artifices of market discrimination and no nonsense about health. So cheap is the cheapest grade that not even the poorest person need be unhappy; so expensive the highest grade that it can soak up the most inflated income. The world is full of happy people, but some are too happy to work and some, unfortunately, are cheerfully starving. The evaluator will, as in the good angel's world, be charged with assessing whether an appropriate balance has been struck between health and happiness. He will have the additional problem of deciding how big a bribe he can safely ask for, and what brand of soma to spend it on.

These are, of course, dreams. The consultant wakes to a vague sense that the future is a long way away, and the knowledge that there are still many nations which can profit from his services as an evaluator. Next week, for example, he will face the problem of conveying to the health minister of the Baratarian Republic that an Infant Mortality Rate of more than 100 is neither acceptable nor necessary. He feels, without pleasure but with some reassurance, that the evils of the world will last out his time as an evaluator. He goes to bed.

References

Abel Smith, B. (1967). *An international study of health expenditure and its relevance for health planning.* WHO Public Health Papers, No. 32. World Health Organization, Geneva.

Alleyne, S.I., Morrison, EYStA., and Richards, R.R. (1979). Some factors related to control of diabetes mellitus in adult Jamaican patients. *Diabetes Care*, **2**, 401–8.

Alleyne, S.I., Cruikshank, J.K., Golding, A.L., and Morrison, E.Y.StA. (1979). Mortality from Diabetes Mellitus in Jamaica. *Bulletin of PAHO*, **23**, 306–15.

Ashcroft, M.T. (1979). A review of epidemiological research in a rural Jamaican community 1959–1975. *West Indian Medical Journal*, **28**, 3–16.

Ashley, D. (1983a). *Oral rehydration therapy—the Jamaican experience.* Paper presented at the International Conference on Oral Rehydration Therapy, June 7–10, Washington DC. Ministry of Health Kingston (mimeo).

Ashley, D. (1983b). *Programme for the control of diarrhoeal diseases (CDD: 1983).* Ministry of Health, Kingston.

Ashley, D. (1984) Onslaught on gastroenteritis. *World Health Forum*, **5**, 325–8.

Ashley, D.E.C., Akierman, A., and Elliott, H. (1981). Oral rehydration therapy in the management of acute gastroenteritis in children in Jamaica. In *Acute enteric infections in children* (eds T. Holme, J. Holmgren, J.H. Merson, and R. Mollby). North Holland Biomedical Press, Amsterdam.

Barnum, H. (1987). Evaluating healthy days of life gained from health projects. *Social Science and Medicine*, **24**(10), 833–41.

Beardmore, J.A. and Karimi-Booshehri, F. (1983). ABO genes are differentially distributed in socio-economic groups in England. *Nature*, **303**, 9.

Becker, G.S. (1981). *A treatise on the family.* Harvard University Press.

Borgdorf, M.W. and Walker, G.J.A. (1988). Estimating vaccination coverage: routine information or sample survey. *Journal of Tropical Medicine and Hygiene*, **91**, 35–42.

Bowling, A. (1987). Mortality after bereavement: a review of the literature on survival periods and factors affecting survival. *Social Science and Medicine*, **24**, 117–24.

Boyd Eaton, S., Shostak, M., and Konner, M. (1988). *The palaeolithic prescription: a programme of diet and exercise and a design for living.* Harper and Row. (Reviewed by Yudkin, J. in *Nature*, **336**, 17 December 1988.)

Casley, D.J. and Lury, D.A. (1981). *Data collection in developing countries.* Clarendon Press, Oxford.

Collison, P., Culyer, A.J., Klein, R., and Pinker, R. (1988). *Acceptable inequalities? Essays on the pursuit of equality in health care.* IEA Health Unit Paper 3 (ed. Green, D.G.). Institute of Economic Affairs.

Colonial Office (1944). *Development and Welfare in the West Indies 1943–44.* Colonial Office, Barbados.

Colonial Office (1955). *Development and Welfare in the West Indies 1954*. Colonial Office, Barbados.

Commonwealth Secretariat. (1979*a*). *The use of para-medicals for primary health care in the Commonwealth: a survey of medical-legal alternatives*. Commonwealth Secretariat, London.

Commonwealth Secretariat. (1979*b*). *Report of a combined medical-legal workshop, Barbados 18–22 June 1979*. Commonwealth Secretariat, London.

Commonwealth Secretariat. (1979*b*). *Medical-legal issues: report of a combined medical-legal workshop, Malawi 8–12 October 1979*. Commonwealth Secretariat, London.

Cumper, G.E. (1979). *Costs of alternative patterns of health development: an exploratory study*. In Consultation on Research Programme on Financing of Health Care Delivery July 1979 WHO SEARO (mimeo).

Cumper, G.E. (1982). *Report of consultancy on economic analysis of the health sector in Jamaica*. Jamaica Population Project.

Cumper, G.E. (1983). Jamaica: a case study in health development. *Social Science and Medicine*, **17** (24), 1983–93.

Cumper, G.E. (1984). *Determinants of health levels in developing countries*. Research Studies Press, Letchworth.

Cumper, G.E. (1986). *Health sector financing: a discussion paper*. EPC Publication, No. 9. London School of Hygiene and Tropical Medicine, London.

Cumper, G.E., Robinson, L., Skinner, M., and Vincent, J. (1982). *Building utilization study (second population project) (Jamaica)*. Ministry of Health, Kingston.

Department of Health and Social Security. (1980). *Report of working group on inequalities in health*. HMSO, London.

Department of Health and Social Security. (1982). *Report on confidential enquiries into maternal deaths in England and Wales 1976–1978*. HMSO, London.

Drummond, M.F. (1980). *Principles of economic appraisal in health care*. Oxford University Press, Oxford.

Drummond, M.F., Stoddart, G.L., and Torrance, G.W. (1987). *Methods for the economic evaluation of health care programmes*. Oxford University Press, Oxford.

Economist (1989*a*). *No Stopping Her*. Economist, February 4, 1989*a*.

Economist (1989*b*). *A Time to Die*. Economist, August 5, 1989*b*.

Elzinga, A. (1981). *Evaluating the evaluation game*. SAREC Report R1/1981. SAREC, Stockholm.

Figueroa, J.P., McCaw, A.M., and Wint, B.A. (1983). *Review of primary care in Jamaica 1977–82: PAHO project, consultary report*. PAHO, Kingston.

Finberg, L. (1973). Hypernatremic (hypertonic) dehydration in infants. *New England Journal of Medicine*, **289**, 196–8.

Florey, CduV., McDonald, H., McDonald, J., and Miall, M.E. (1972). *The prevalence of diabetes in a rural population of Jamaican adults. International Journal of Epidemiology*, **1**, 157–66.

Fraser, H.S. (1984). *Health problems in the Caribbean*. Paper presented at PAHO/WHO sponsored Caribbean Workshop on Community Participation in Health Development Antigua June 3–8. PAHO, Barbados.

Ghana Health Assessment Project Team (1981). (report prepared by Morrow, R., Smith, P., and Nimo, K.) *A quantitative method of assessing the health impact of different diseases in less developed countries* (1975). *International Journal of Epidemiology*, **10**, 73–80.

Gish, O. (1975). *Planning the health sector: the Tanzanian experience.* Croom Helm, London.

Gish, O. (1977). *Guidelines for health planners.* Tri-Med Books, London.

Grell, G.A.C. (1978). *Clinical aspects of the management of hypertension in the Caribbean. West Indian Medical Journal,* **29**, 163-74.

Grell, G.A.C. (1982). *Hypertension: a challenge for the providers of health care in the Caribbean. West Indian Medical Journal,* **31**, 105-6.

Grell, G.A.C. (ed.) (1987). The Elderly in the Caribbean: Proceedings at a Continuing Medical Education Symposium Kingston U.W.I.

Griffiths, A. and Mills, M. (1982). *Money for health: a manual for surveys in developing countries.* Sandoz Institute for Health and Socio-economic Studies, Third World Series No. 3.

Gueri, M. (1980). *Management of gastroenteritis in the community. CAJANUS,* **13**, 194-9.

Harland, P.S.E. (1978). *Oral rehydration in gastroenteritis. Caribbean Medical Journal,* **40**, 27-30.

Hirschhorn, N. (1980). *The treatment of acute diarrhoea in children: an historical and physiological perspective. American Journal of Clinical Nutrition,* **33**, 637-63.

HMSO. (1945). *West India royal commission report.* Cmd 6607, London.

Hoffenberg, R. (1987). *Clinical freedom.* Nuffield Providential Hospital Trust, London.

Hulka, B.S. and Cassel, J.C. (1973). The AAFP-UNC study of the organization, utilization, and assessment of primary medical care. *American Journal of Public Health,* **63**, 494-501.

Indian Council for Medical Research (1980). Tuberculosis prevention trial. Madras. *Indian Journal of Medical Research,* **72** (suppl.).

Ironside, A.G., Tuxford, A.F., and Heyworth, B. (1970). A survey of infantile gastroenteritis. *British Medical Journal,* **iii**, 20-4.

Kemball-Cook, D. and Vaughan, P. (1982). *A theoretical model for estimating the coverage achieved by different distributions of staff and facilities.* London School of Hygiene and Tropical Medicine, London.

Kessner, D.M., Kalk, C.E., and Singer, J. (1973). *Assessing health quality—the case for tracers. New England Journal of Medicine,* **288**, 184-9.

King, M. (ed.) (1966). *Medical care in developing countries.* Oxford University Press, Oxford.

Knox, E.G. (ed.) (1987). *Health care information.* Nuffield Provincial Hospital Trust Occasional Papers 8.

McCulloch, W.E. (1955). *Your health in the Caribbean.* Pioneer Press, Kingston.

McGranahan, D.V. and Hong, N. (1979). *International comparability of statistics on income distribution.* Report 79.6 RISD. Geneva.

McKeown, T. (1976). *The modern rise of population.* London.

McKeown, T. (1988). *The origins of human disease.* Blackwell, Oxford.

Medical Research Council (1952). *The treatment of acute dehydration in infants.* Memorandum 26. MRC, London.

Mills, A. and Thomas, M. (1984). *Economic evaluation of health programmes in developing countries.* EPC Publication No. 3. London School of Hygiene and Tropical Medicine, London.

Mills, A. (1987). *Financial planning and the financial master plan.* In London School of Hygiene and Tropical Medicine/London School of Economics/WHO Seminar on Health Economics and Health Financing in Developing Countries: Briefing Notes, Bibliography, Glossary. London.

Ministry of Health Jamaica (1982). *What to do when your baby has diarrhoea.* Ministry of Health Kingston.

Ministry of Health Jamaica/London School of Hygiene and Tropical Medicine (1986). *Report on evaluation of health care in Jamaica.* Kingston.

Ministry of Health Jamaica/PAHO (1984). *Workshop: mental health legislation issues: October 19–20 1984,* Kingston.

Morrison, EYStA. (1982). *An approach to the diagnosis and management of diabetes mellitus in Jamaica.* University of West Indies, Kingston.

Musgrove, P. (1987). *The economic crisis and its impact on health and health care in Latin America and the Caribbean. International Journal of Health Services,* **17** (3), 411–41.

Nalin, D.R., Harland, E., Romlal, A. *et al.* (1980). *Comparison of low and high sodium and potassium content in oral rehydration solutions. Journal of Paediatrics,* **97**, 848–53.

Nalin, D.R. (1985). *Effect on clinical outcome of breast feeding during acute diarrhoea. British Medical Journal,* **i,** 1217.

PAHO (1983). *Report and proceedings of the meeting and papers of expert committee on chronic diseases in the English-speaking Caribbean.* PAHO, Barbados.

Picou, D. *et al.* (1978). *Malnutrition and gastroenteritis in children: a manual for hospital treatment and management.* CFNI and PAHO, Kingston.

Ross, D.A. and Vaughan, J.P. (1984). *Health interview surveys in developing countries.* EPC Publication, 4. London School of Hygiene and Tropical Medicine, London.

Samadi, A.R., Wahed, M.A., Islam, M.R., and Ahmed, S.M. (1983). *Consequences of hyponatraemia and hypernatraemia in children with acute diarrhoea in Bangladesh. British Medical Journal,* **286**, 671–3.

Samadi, A.R., Chowdhury, A.I., Huq, M.I., and Shahid, N.S. (1985). *Risk factors and death in complicated diarrhoea. British Medical Journal,* **i,** 1615–17.

Schofield, F. (1984). *Health planning in developing countries.* In Ghosh, P.K. *Health, food and nutrition in Third World Development.* Greenwood Press, Westport, Conn.

Segall, M. (1983). *Planning and politics of resource allocation for primary health care: promotion of meaningful national policy. Social Science and Medicine,* **17** (24), 1947–60.

Simeonov, L.A. (1976). *Better health for Sri Lanka.* WHO SEARO, New Delhi.

Smith, M.G. (1963). *Dark Puritan.* Department of Extra Mural Studies, University of West Indies, Jamaica.

Swaby-Ellis, E. (1984). *Natural history of rotavirus infection and its relationship to nutritional status in urban Jamaican children.* Working Paper 7 at Third Scientific Working Group on Viral Diarrhoeas. WHO, Geneva.

Syncrisis (USAID). (1976). *Syncrisis, the dynamics of health: 20 Jamaica.* Washington.

Teeling Smith, G. (ed.) (1988). *Measuring health: a practical approach.* Wiley, Chichester.

Trowell, H.C. and Burkitt, D.P. (1981). *Western diseases: their emergence and prevention.* London.

UNICEF (1987). *Adjustment with a human face: protecting the vulnerable and promoting growth* (ed. G.A. Cornia, R. Jolly, and F. Stewart). Clarendon Press, Oxford.

Wagner, E.M., Williams, D.A., Greenberg, R. *et al.* (1978). *A method for selecting criteria to evaluate medical care. American Journal of Public Health*, **68**, 464–70.

Walker, G.J.A. (1983). *Medical care in developing countries: assessment and assurance of quality. Evaluation and the Health Professions*, **6**, 439–52.

Walker, G.J.A., Ashley, D.E.C., McCaw, A., and Bernard, G.W. (1986). Maternal Mortality in Jamaica. *Lancet*, **i**, 486–8.

Walker, G.J.A., Ashley, D.E.C., and Hayes, R. (1988). The quality of care is related to death rates: hospital inpatient management of infants with acute gastroenteritis in Jamaica. *American Journal of Public Health*, **78**, 149–52.

Walker, G.J.A. and Wint, B. (1988). Quality assessment of medical care in Jamaica. *World Health Forum*, **8**, 520–4.

Waterlow, J.C. (1988). *Post-neonatal mortality in the Third World. Lancet*, **3**, December.

Waterston, A. (1965). *Development planning.* Johns Hopkins University Press.

Waterston, A. (1971). *An operational approach to development planning. International Journal of Health Services*, **1**(3).

Wheeler, M. and Volpatti, J.B. (1980). *Health service finance.* Departemen Keuangan Djakarta.

Which (1987). *Making your doctor better. Which*, May 1987.

WHO (1979). *Formulating strategies for health for all by the Year 2000.* WHO, Geneva.

WHO (1980). *Sixth report on the world health situation.* WHO, Geneva.

WHO (1981*a*). *Global strategy for health for all by the Year 2000.* WHO, Geneva.

WHO (1981*b*). *Development of indicators for monitoring progress towards health for all by the Year 2000.* WHO, Geneva.

WHO (1983). *Tuberculosis and leprosy control. Weekly Epidemiological Review*, **15**, 109–10. 15 Apr 1983.

WHO (1988). *Second report on monitoring progress in implementing strategies for health for all.* EB83/PC/WP6 Geneva (internal document).

WHO/Ministry of Health Dacca (1977). *Country health programming Bangladesh: programme proposal.* WHO, Dacca.

Winckler, H. (1987). *The Lunatic.* Kingston Publishers, Kingston, Jamaica.

Williams, A. (1985). *Medical ethics: health service efficiency and clinical freedom.* Nuffield/York Portfolios 2.

World Bank (1988). *World Tables.* World Bank, Washington.

Appendix Evaluating a health care system: the Jamaica health services evaluation project

1 Introduction

Over the period 1983–85 an evaluation of the Jamaican health care system was carried out by the Planning and Evaluation Unit, Ministry of Health, Jamaica and the Evaluation and Planning Centre, London School of Hygiene and Tropical Medicine (EPC). A detailed report on the project has been presented to the Ministry of Health, and to the UK Overseas Development Administration, the principal funding agency. This appendix draws attention to the results, particularly those which have important implications for international work on the evaluation of health care systems. A list is attached of papers associated with the project published up to April 1986.

There appear to be few examples of research projects which have attempted a comprehensive evaluation of health care on a national scale, for either developed or developing countries. Research projects have usually concentrated on single issues or sectors of the health services. Administrative evaluations have been carried out by national authorities, and also by international agencies (e.g. the health sector reviews of the World Bank, and the evaluative component in WHO's Country Health Programming). But these have lacked a research element, and have therefore been limited by the pre-existing information. The attempt of the Jamaica project to transcend such limitations raised issues of methodology and technique which should be of interest to others planning to work in this field.

In addition, the substantive results of the project appear to have international applicability. Some of the conclusions reached are specific to Jamaica, but a surprising proportion refer to problems which, when fully analysed, turn out to be common to health care systems over a wide spectrum of degrees of national development. The relatively small scale of the Jamaican system permits one to identify issues and trace the connections between them more clearly than in the developed or the larger developing countries.

On many of the issues identified, only tentative conclusions could be formulated because further research was needed which could not be accommodated within the resource limits of the project. Hence one outcome of the project is a menu for further research on which many of the items not only have international implications, but could most effectively be conducted on a comparative international basis.

The following section gives a summary picture of the Jamaican health care system, with particular attention to its representativeness in relation to other developing countries. Further sections deal with the methodological and technical basis of the Jamaica project, the international implications of the substantive results and some promising fields for further research.

2 The Jamaican health care system

Jamaica has a population of 2.4 million, of whom 40 per cent live in Kingston, the capital. The land area is 10 000 km^2; the terrain is hilly, but with a good road system. National income per capita in 1974 was over US$ 1000, placing it in the upper part of the income range for developing countries; it fell by about 20 per cent by 1980, and foreign indebtedness increased substantially. Since 1980 national income has grown slowly but there has been no increase in government funds available for purposes other than debt servicing.

Health indicators also place Jamaica's health level in the upper part of the developing country range (e.g. infant mortality rate about 25 per thousand, life expectancy at birth about 70 years). The same is true for the main infrastructure factors related to health (water supply, literacy, nutrition).

Health care provision takes place through both the governmental and private sectors. Secondary and tertiary care is mainly a government responsibility, the exceptions being the University Hospital of the West Indies (which, however, is ultimately funded by West Indian governments) and a small number of private hospitals accounting for about 10 per cent of total beds. Bed/population ratios in Jamaica have traditionally been moderate; the present ratio is about 2 beds per thousand population, and in the short term is declining because of financial limitations.

In terms of policy, the intended agency for the delivery of formal primary care is the system of 400 health centres, widely dispersed in both rural and urban areas. However, about 40 per cent of primary contacts in practice are with private doctors, and there is a substantial provision of primary care by the so-called 'out-patient' and 'casualty' departments of hospitals.

The importance of informal health care is certainly great though hard to measure. Traditional agencies such as 'nanas' (birth attendants) and healers are of diminishing importance. Most informal care is provided through the family and household, with medicines largely supplied by private pharmacists who act as unofficial prescribers.

Government spending on health care takes place through the Ministry of Health, whose budget, financed from general revenue, covers the costs of government hospitals and health centres (with a nominal contribution from user fees), non-personal preventive services such as vector control, technical support services, training, administration, and subventions to autonomous bodies such as the National Family Planning Board. Private medical care is paid for on a fee-for-service basis, with rapidly increasing use of private health insurance among middle income groups. Total spending on health care amounts to about 5 per cent of national income, with private spending (including that on self-care) substantially exceeding that of government.

In its levels of health, of health-related infrastructure and of economic development Jamaica clearly resembles the 'newly industrialized countries' such as Singapore or Hong Kong, or other countries at a relatively high level of health development such as Mauritius, Sri Lanka, or Cuba, rather than the larger and, usually, poorer countries in which the greater part of the Third World population lives. *Prima facie* this would suggest that Jamaican experience has limited international applicability. There are further considerations, however, which even in the absence of pre-existing links between the sponsoring institutions, would have made it a logical venue for an experimental evaluation project:

(1) Jamaica's present health situation is a relatively recent development (Cumper 1983), reached by paths which poorer countries can be expected to follow in the next years or (pessimistically) decades;

(2) poorer countries generally lack the information infrastructure which makes such an experimental evaluation possible;

(3) the proportion of the world's population which has reached an intermediate level of economic and health development is larger than appears at first sight since it includes not only large areas of Latin America, but also important components within large poor countries (e.g. Kerala in India, Shanghai in China);

(4) most importantly, the management system, the locus of many of the Third World's health problems, is similar to that in many of the poorer developing countries, particularly those which at some time have been British colonies.

There is, in addition, the fact that health care systems in all countries exhibit a high degree of consistency in the relation between health inputs and the resulting health levels, regardless of cultural and political differences (Cumper 1984). It is argued, therefore, that it is legitimate to search the conclusions of the Jamaica project for generalizations likely to be useful in the international evaluation of health care systems.

3   The methodological basis of the project

The nature of the project inevitably raised methodological problems. On the one hand, it involved a commitment to data collection and analysis over a very wide range of topics; on the other hand, being directed toward applied rather than basic research, it also carried a commitment to producing a usable synthesis of the results within a limited period (field work actually began in April 1983 and a draft report was submitted in October 1985). This had to be done within a limited budget (£150 000 of which about a half was salary costs); however, it should be said that while there were many occasions when additional resources would have been welcome for particular purposes, any massive increase in the scale of the project would probably have been self-defeating since it would have compounded the organizational difficulties inherent in this type of project.

The wide range of topics covered meant that the project had to be inter-disciplinary; from the EPC side the team included a community physician/epidemiologist, an anthropologist, and an economist, while the Ministry of Health, Jamaica, provided a health planner and made available the services of a number of medical specialists and other staff. The difficulties are well known of bringing collaborative projects, particularly interdisciplinary ones, to an integrated and timely conclusion.

The approach adopted in an attempt to deal with these problems had the following features:

(1) agreement on a logical framework for the evaluation process;

(2) co-ordinated use of data from different sources;

(3) frequent review of progress and results in representative committees;

(4) use of the 'tracer' approach to clinical and other issues.

These features are discussed below.

3.1   Framework for the evaluation process

A proposal for an agreed framework was prepared in 1983 and placed before the Jamaican Steering Committee and other colleagues. It was based on the concept of evaluation as the comparison of actual performance with appropriate standards and norms, and concentrated on the choice of standards for the wide range of health sector activities.

It was accepted that in principle health impact is the most fundamental variable in evaluating health care. But there are well-known difficulties in assessing the impact even of limited measures with well-defined goals, and these are compounded when we are dealing with broad policies and system changes. We could expect very few cases where we could observe directly the impact of a particular operation. There would be more situations where we could observe an outcome (e.g. of an immunization program) and translate this into impact terms through the use of technical information and professional judgment. But in most cases the practical work of evaluation has to be concerned with standards of an intermediate kind.

Three such types of standard were identified:

(1) standards arising from the policy–planning–budgeting–implementation cycle;

(2) standards formulated independently of this cycle (mainly concerned with the management of the implementation phase), based upon considerations of general social policy, technical (medical) norms, administrative efficiency, and cost;

(3) standards based directly on public preferences and attitudes.

Each of these types of standard is valid for certain purposes, and all must be taken into account in a comprehensive evaluation.

The policy–planning–budgeting–implementation cycle can in principle be used as a powerful instrument of evaluation since each stage in the cycle can be regarded as an attempt to make more concrete and specific what has been developed in the preceding stage, and can therefore be tested against that stage for consistency and probable effectiveness. Each stage can be looked on both as an aspect of performance (e.g. a health plan seen as an achievement to be tested against national health policy) and a standard of evaluation (e.g. a plan used as a standard to evaluate a particular year's health budget). How effective evaluation on this basis can be depends on the precision with which policies, plans, and budgets are stated. In Jamaica we certainly did not find the ideal situation in which each level of the policy–planning–budgeting process is embodied in a document appropriate to that level and enjoying full official support. This process could not therefore be the sole basis of our evaluation.

A second way of evaluating performance is through comparison with management standards formulated independently of the planning cycle. In the literature on health service management in the 70s these standards were perhaps neglected since if one takes planning as one's point of departure they appear as constraints or background influences rather than positive factors in their own right. But they are of great practical importance in situations where planning is inadequate, or formal plans are rendered inoperative by rapid economic or social change. In such circumstances, it is management standards which maintain the cohesion and impetus of health care systems. It is obvious that standards formulated on professional and technical grounds play a crucial role in the field of health care, where inputs and processes can be controlled for management purposes more effectively than outcomes or, especially, impact. It is largely on the basis of such standards that we are justified in assuming that planned changes in inputs will result in the desired impact on health. But administrative and financial standards (as incorporated, for example, in civil service and finance regulations) are also of great importance. Standards based on cost and efficiency are also potentially important, though in Jamaica these are just beginning to be developed.

A third form of evaluation is by comparison of performance with public need and demand. These terms have been defined differently by different authors; need is used here to mean the gap between present health status and that technically attainable, as professionally defined by providers of health care or epidemiologists, while demand is used to mean the actual or potential expression by the public of their desires in relation to health and to the activities of health care providers. Need appears at first sight to be a promising basis for evaluation because it is in principle objective, and in relation to individual conditions the identification of unmet needs is an important part of epidemiological evaluation. At the system level, however, needs must in practice be discussed in relation to the available resources, and their use as standards becomes absorbed into the planning process. Demand, as expressed, for example, in interviews with consumers or by user pressure groups, is a less congenial standard to medical planners since it may include subjective or frankly irrational elements, but it cannot be neglected in a comprehensive evaluation.

The approach set out above was intended to base the evaluation of the health care system on standards generated within Jamaica, or derived from external sources whose authority was acknowledged there (e.g. PAHO). It was intended to minimize the role of the values of the research team. It was hoped that it would have the advantage that where performance differed from the specified standards, the nature of the required corrective action would in many cases emerge from the evaluation process—whether it related to the planning cycle (stage by stage), to management standards (and if so what type of standard), or to conflicts with public demand; and whether it was correctible by direct management action, or implied the need for a system change. It was recognized that the approach could be applied fully only to the government sector, but it was envisaged that some evaluation of the private sector would be possible in terms of costs, professional standards, and public demand, as well as of the degree of success of the government planning and policy machinery in influencing the private sector.

This approach was not intended as a fixed blueprint controlling the work of all members of the research team. But it is believed that it was of value in providing a common framework for discussion, reducing the need for *post hoc* reconciliation of divergent approaches and keeping in view the multiple standards to which health care providers are expected to conform.

3.2   Co-ordinated use of data

The project drew data on the performance of the Jamaican health care system from a number of sources:

(1) standard public and administrative statistics;

(2) investigations undertaken *de novo* as part of the project;

(3) further processing of the results of investigations undertaken independently;

(4) published results of other independent investigations.

The third category (which included processing data from a sample survey of health care consumers initiated by the Ministry's Planning and Evaluation Unit in 1981) proved an especially profitable use of limited funds.

There are obvious difficulties in incorporating, in a single overall evaluation, data drawn from diverse sources, and therefore possibly differing in concepts and terminology. The first and last of the above categories were obviously outside project control. The first was crucial since it provided the framework into which the results of individual project elements were to be fitted. It was therefore logical to try to co-ordinate the data collection and processing of individual team members on a basis consistent with the overall statistical framework, so far as possible and necessary. This was attempted through direct discussion between the research team members early in the project on a minimum of common concepts and procedures, and the circulation of interim results of individual project investigations. It should be noted that Jamaica has a sophisticated official statistical system, co-ordinated by the Statistical Institute of Jamaica, of which one of the research team had formerly been a staff member, and which continues to promote interministerial unity in statistical approach.

3.3   Committee review of progress

Reviews of the progress of the project were prepared at approximately three-monthly intervals. These were intended to serve not only the sponsoring agencies, but more particularly the Jamaican project Steering Committee, which received and discussed the reports and whenever possible the verbal presentations of the research team members. (A smaller number of workshops were also held at the Evaluation and Planning Centre in London, with Jamaican representatives present.)

The Steering Committee included, besides members of the research team, those members of the Ministry staff most closely involved in the project, and representatives of agencies which had research or action projects operating in related fields (UWI, PAHO, USAID). Its function was to co-ordinate the activities of the project, keep the research team in touch with the concerns of the Ministry and other agencies and act as a forum for interdisciplinary comment on the interim results.

3.4   Studies of 'tracer' problems

From the beginning of the project it was planned to carry out studies of the quality of care in the Jamaican hospital system using the concept of 'tracer' conditions already well established in this field. As the project developed it became clear that the essence of this concept was applicable in other fields of evaluation—namely, the choice and conduct of specific investigations in such a way that they were representative of the problems in a wider field, and could be located within this field by using a framework of aggregative statistics and general information.

Examples of 'tracer' problems used in the project were the attitudes of women toward antenatal care and child diarrhoea; hospital costs; the legal basis of the work of nurse practitioners and community health workers, and the level and composition of maternal mortality. Each of these substudies, while valuable in itself, carried implications for broad areas of health care practice and management. Without this approach it would have been difficult to carry out a comprehensive evaluation while keeping the project within a manageable compass.

4   Some generalization of the project results

Many of the issues discussed in specifically Jamaican terms in the report already submitted to the project sponsors can be seen, on further analysis, to involve considerations of very wide applicability. These are dealt with in the following subsections using the framework set out in Section 3.1 above.

4.1   The effectiveness of planning

For a decade the Ministry of Health in Jamaica has been nominally committed to a strategic policy–planning–budgeting cycle ('planning') but the results are generally admitted to be unsatisfactory. Many other countries have in practice had similar experiences. Why should this be so?

Planning necessarily involves a restriction on the decision-making power of managers at all levels, and for some managers it involves acceptance of decisions contrary to their own interests. It can only work, therefore, if there is some motivation for plan acceptance. How can this be provided? There are essentially four possibilities; the exercise of power or authority, the offer of inducements, and the acceptance of a common ethical framework.

Authority—manifested as formal instructions from higher to lower levels of an organization—is not in itself a satisfactory basis for planning in the health sector, even for government health services. Without support from other forms of motivation, instructions either remain too general to be effective or proliferate in a way which generates all the defects of bureaucracy.

Power is accessible to planners in two main ways. One is through alliances with powerful individuals within and outside the health ministry; there is no doubt that sometimes planners have taken this path, but it is an unstable basis for a planning system. The other is through access to meaningful information generated within the planning system. Jamaica has put far too little resources into the kind of data collection and analysis needed for this purpose. But, as elsewhere, the power of the planners has been narrowly limited by the economic uncertainties of the last decade, which have meant that plans could not be treated by their participants as a reliable source of information about the future shape of the health care system.

Inducements are not, generally speaking, a powerful weapon in the health planner's armoury. Rewards and punishments for individuals are not usually at his disposal, except that there may be personal implications in the up- or downgrading of particular programs in the plan (and even here the penalties are limited by the high degree of security of tenure enjoyed by senior staff in most health ministries). Accretions of power and authority to a particular group or program may emerge from a plan in a period of expansion, but this is a much less potent factor in a period of stability or contraction like the last decade.

It follows that at a time like the present the remaining form of motivation, through the value systems of health care providers, is of crucial importance for planning (as indeed for the general management of the health services). But in Jamaica, as elsewhere (Williams 1985), medical ethics do not form a single consistent set of values. At one extreme is the clinical ethic relating the health care provider to the individual patient, at the other the 'public health' ethic relating the provider to a collective clientele. The latter is easily reconcilable with health economics and resource-limited planning. The former offers no bridge to planning concepts, and may be used as a weapon against planning when it appears to limit professional autonomy.

Jamaica remains committed in principle to effective health care planning, and is therefore faced with very high level decisions about the way in which this commitment can be implemented. It appears most likely that the path chosen will involve a strengthening of the authority component, a reinforcement of the planning unit's capacity for generating information and a strengthening of the 'public health' ethic through basic and in-service training. It has to be recognized that, in Jamaica as elsewhere, this path has important implications for change in a management system which has hitherto depended heavily on the exercise by individuals of their professional authority, and that the problems will be particularly severe in the fields where the clinical ethic is strongest—the hospitals and the private medical sector. (These management issues are taken up again below.)

The project experience showed that Jamaica is well endowed with one of the infrastructural elements of planning—a good data base of service statistics.

To a large extent these are of a conventional type—for example, data on hospital admissions—but these have been supplemented since 1980 by an elaborate computer-based system of health centre reporting, the Monthly Clinic Summary Report. Input data are less satisfactory; budget and accounting records are of standard British ex-colonial type, and personnel records are uneven though improving. The main limitation on using such data for planning and management purposes has been a lack of analytical capability, either in the Ministry of Health's information unit or its planning unit. The project tried out various ways of exploiting this data system which required a modest resource input, and it seems likely that some of these would be generally applicable in developing countries.

One elementary step was the use of sampling to ease the burden of data processing. Walker used a 5 per cent sample (with higher sampling fractions for smaller institutions) to analyse hospital admissions for 1982 by place of residence, condition and other variables. A similar approach can no doubt be used elsewhere to break the log-jam often caused by the accumulation of data at a central institution which lacks the resources for timely processing of the whole body of data.

Another simple technique was the use of mapping for the co-ordinated presentation of data from different sources. This was used to link together data on hospital admissions, health centre utilization and (so far as available) use of private practitioners to give an overview of coverage. This technique should be useful wherever there is a minimum basis of reasonably reliable maps and basic population statistics.

Jamaica provides a number of examples of large stores of data which are not being effectively used for planning or indeed any management purpose, such as the health centre output data collected under the MCSR and the issues data of the Island Medical Stores. The common factors in such cases appear to be a concentration of information systems development on isolated areas of management (perhaps because external funds are available for the purpose), an assumption that all data collected must be aggregated to the level of census-type national totals, and the misuse of the enormous mechanical capabilities of large computers. In developing countries, and perhaps in all countries, information system development needs to be integrated, selective, and based on a realistic assessment of the absorptive capacity of the management system it is intended to serve.

In spite of a shortage of resources, some weaknesses in planning and information techniques and the pressures of external economic factors, the Jamaican health sector has produced since 1974 two five-year plan documents, and a number of policy statements at the national level and partial statements for particular sectors. The content of these points to problems at the levels of policy, planning, and budgeting which probably have international applicability.

At the policy level, one weakness is the failure to give precision to certain key terms, particularly perhaps 'community'. Thus Jamaica faces the same problem in the mental health field as the UK—the displacement of patients from hospital care into a nominal 'community' care for which there is no clearly assigned and accepted responsibility. Another weakness is the underestimation of the role of non-government care by private practitioners or as household or self-care.

The latter weakness carries over to the planning level, where little provision is made for influencing the standard of non-government care. However, perhaps the most important weakness at this level is the virtual absence of contingency planning in a period of increasingly unpredictable availability of resources not merely for expansion, but for maintaining present levels of activity. It seems evident in principle that plans should provide for alternative levels of future resources, and shape programs so as to minimize the ill-effects of variations in resource availability. This seems to be a neglected subject in the health planning literature. At an earlier period the resource variability applied mainly to external funds, and many countries found a pragmatic solution by basing their core service program on a relatively firm estimate of national revenues and using external funding for relatively dispensible 'plug-in' developments. External agencies are increasingly turning away from this type of development and placing more emphasis, in principle quite correctly, on improvements to the core system and its management. The failure to implement a project of this type, perhaps because of the unavailability of national counterpart funds, has much more serious effects than the non-completion of an additional hospital or health centre. Hence there is a need for more comprehensive and sophisticated contingency planning than has been common in the health field.

Contingency planning implies contingency budgeting. The British colonial system provided various *ad hoc* mechanisms for dealing with shortfalls in funding, including the keeping of a clear distinction between permanent and temporary staff, with strict controls over the numbers of the former, and the squeezing, in bad years, of non-personnel expenditures, particularly maintenance. In Jamaica these are proving inadequate to deal with a prolonged period of economic uncertainty, resulting in massive cumulative over-spending. This situation is not wholly within the control of an individual ministry, but a minimum step towards securing more prompt recognition of the problems would seem to be the maintenance of alternative budget projections linked to contingency planning.

A final point may be made about policy and planning which emerges from the relatively long historical perspective over which the modern Jamaican health services have developed. The substantial progress made between 1920 and 1970 took place without formal planning machinery, but on the basis of a different concept of planning under which long periods of stability or slow expansion were punctuated by reassessments which resulted in system changes incorporated, more often than not, in legal provisions. Whatever its shortcomings, this pattern meant that at any period the legal basis for the work of health care providers was clear. Current trends have led to more rapid innovation which has sometimes left its legal foundations far behind, leading to confusion about the roles of providers and the relative rights of themselves and the public. This is a neglected aspect of policy and planning.

4.2   *The application of technical standards*

The technical evaluation of a health care system may be carried out at two levels; in 'clinical' terms, focusing on the quality of care received by the individual patient, or in 'public health' terms, taking into consideration the overall success of the system in terms of access, utilization, and coverage as well as the quality of care provided. At the clinical level, the Jamaica project concentrated on the quality of care of hospital patients. Walker collaborated with members of the staff of the health services and the University of the West Indies in studies which compared the treatment received by a sample of hospital patients with standards derived from local consensus, for a number of tracer conditions; and in a study of maternal deaths in the period 1981–3. The latter, in particular, involved some evaluation of the quality of the primary care received before hospital admission.

The specific results of these studies are fully reported elsewhere. Some general implications of the results are relevant to the present purpose. It is encouraging that such an investigation, based on standard hospital records and on a consensus of physicians in Jamaica, proved feasible and economical to carry out, particularly as the physicians involved had been trained not only at the University of the West Indies, but also in developed countries (US, UK) and other developing countries (e.g. India). It is expected that the consensus reached on the various conditions will form a basis for standard protocols for secondary treatment analogous to those already used in

Jamaica at the primary level. Such protocols may prove an important instrument for future health service management.

It is less encouraging that the studies tended to confirm that the weaknesses of the health care system lay less in the area of clinical knowledge than in the area of health service organization—liaison between primary and secondary care, and functioning of support services such as laboratories and blood bank. We are thus brought back to basic managerial problems, common to many countries and discussed further in Section 5 below.

The project undertook no independent investigation of the technical performance of the primary care system, which had been extensively studied by other groups (e.g. Figueroa *et al.* 1983), though some assistance was given with the consolidation of treatment protocols for use by nurse practitioners and other health centre staff. Nevertheless some relevant conclusions emerged from MacCormack's interviews with users of the primary services. In Jamaica a large part of the work of these services is preventive and promotive, especially in the field of maternal and child health, and therefore depends on effective communication between users and providers. MacCormack's results confirm that even in a country where language differences between provider and user are relatively small, formal statements by providers, even when conscientious and correct, often do not achieve effective communication. This is likely to be *a fortiori* true in countries with greater linguistic and cultural barriers than in Jamaica between the users and providers of health care.

MacCormack's results also permit some assessment of the extent to which household and self-care conform to the technical standards of Western medicine. They produced a number of examples of ignorance of anatomy and physiology, though not apparently much more so than would be found in developed countries, and of ineffective treatments, but few of dangerous practices, or of folk beliefs which would offer obstacles to well-conceived health education. Knowledge of health matters was clearly drawn from many sources, including media and word-of-mouth as well as formal education. These results can probably be generalized to those populations in developing countries whose social and economic mobility is comparable to that of Jamaica.

The project attempted to build up a comprehensive picture of health care coverage by linking data on hospital in- and out-patients, health centre attendances and utilization of the private sector as shown in a PEU sample household survey carried out in 1981 (see internal project reports on Health Consumer Survey 81). The latter survey also yielded data on the distribution of dwellings by distance from various types of health facility, which was checked against mappings of population distribution and location of facilities. The HCS provided vital information on private sector use and (through its link with the Jamaican Labour Force Survey) on the socio-economic status of health care consumers. Although conceived as a pilot operation, its results were consistent with those from administrative statistics. The project helped prepare a more sophisticated survey proposal for the future (implemented 1989). The use of such surveys in developing countries is becoming more widespread and should be encouraged.

The HCS also provided an indirect estimate of the contribution of the household to health care. A wholly unexpected finding was that large households had lower levels of reported morbidity and use of health services than small ones. It proved impossible to resolve this difference in terms of the obvious explanatory variables (household age structure, socio-economic status, educational levels, etc.) and it has been provisionally accepted as a reflection of the health care provided by mutual support between household members. It is estimated that without such support, the demand on health care facilities would increase by about 50 per cent. If confirmed this would have wide implications; for example, it would call for qualification of some arguments used by family planners in favour of small families.

Perhaps the most significant fact about the Jamaican health care system is simply that in spite of all qualifications, it represents a successful working system created pragmatically over a long period, much of it before Alma Ata and some of it before the availability of modern drugs and insecticides, at modest levels of national income per capita. To those who distrust current international health policies which appear to identify Health for All with an act of ecstatic conversion to the spirit of Alma Ata, it may be an encouraging indication that substantial progress toward better health in developing countries can be achieved by the consistent and realistic application of limited resources.

4.3 Management issues

The report made to the government of Jamaica included references to administrative and financial issues which were specific to Jamaica's current situation and are not pursued here. On the other hand, some issues can be identified in Jamaica which are essentially the same as those exercising health sector managers in a very wide range of countries, developed and developing. Their universality suggests that they arise from the very nature of Western health care at its present technological level. They concern the relation between technical and administrative authority, the suitability of the standard civil service framework to government health services and the relative roles of government and private health care institutions.

The first of these issues is sometimes envisaged in terms of the choice between doctor and administrator as manager of a particular facility, but it is much wider than that. Since the 19th century, the training of the medical professions has involved not merely the acquisition of technical knowledge, but the absorption of rules and attitudes which allocated authority between the professions and within them. This allocation provided the management framework for the health services. It may be conjectured that it worked with reasonable success because the state of medical knowledge and practice allowed a high degree of autonomy for each program and institution and because the relatively low level of technology moderated the demand for non-professional inputs and hence the competition for external resources. Recent technological advances on the curative side have meant that an almost indefinite increase in inputs could be justified in terms of the clinical ethos. The less spectacular advances in preventive medicine have also increased the demand for resources for public health. Further, the nature of the development of medical knowledge has been such that it enforced specialization on individuals, at the same time that its full potential could only be realized by close collaboration between specializations, professional groups, and institutions. Hence there has been an increase in the frequency of situations in which more than one professional could claim technical authority. These changes may explain why the traditional technically based authority system has more and more come to be regarded as inadequate for health service management. The difficulties have been exacerbated by tensions arising from the changing relative status of the clinically and public health oriented groups within the medical and, to some extent, the nursing professions.

An extreme response to current management problems would be to insist that all participants in the health care process should be under the control of managers at various levels who would enjoy administrative authority independently of any professional qualifications they may possess. This may be appropriate to highly developed health systems like that of the UK, but it is hard to see how it could be applied as a general solution in countries like Jamaica. The supply of potential managers who have enough knowledge of health matters to control a health care institution without having gone through a conventional professional training is simply not adequate for this purpose. A more practical approach at present may be to build on the traditional system (symbolized at the hospital level by the triumvirate of doctor, nurse, and administrator) but stressing the public health, rather than the clinical elements in the medical ethos, and improving the non-medical professionalism of administrative staff so that they can introduce into the public health approach an economic element. If such a 'health team' approach is to work consistently, however, it must rest not merely on a common ethos, but on concrete prescriptions about professional practice which reconcile this ethos with the needs and pressures of different groups in their working situation, particularly where this is one where the clinical ethos has previously been dominant. Essential drugs programmes may be seen as one example of this (e.g. Jamaica's VEN (vital–essential–necessary) drug listing). But practice protocols may offer a way of introducing economic elements into other aspects of the health services in a clinically acceptable form.

In Jamaica, as in many developing countries, the government health services operate largely within a standard civil service framework which, while nominally mainly concerned with uniformity in personnel and financial matters, in practice constrains all management decisions. These constraints are particularly irksome when the market situation for health personnel diverges widely from that for other government staff, or when it is desired to decentralize decision-making—for example, in the hospital system. It is possible to evade such constraints—for example, on the market side, through factitious 'allowances', through officially permitting or unofficially winking at private practice, or more fundamentally by employing key professionals on a contract-for-services basis. But it may be that many countries would benefit from a general discussion of the question to what extent uniformity of conditions is necessary over both service and regulatory ministries, and to what extent it can be relaxed while still preserving the essentials of public accountability.

The above two issues are linked with a third which was addressed by the Jamaica project—that of the balance between government and private provision of health care. It is a topical issue in many developing countries because the transfer of activities to the private sector promises to relieve the resource problems of health ministries, because it removes from them some of the responsibility for the issues cited, and because it is being promoted by some external agencies such as the World Bank and USAID. It is linked with the promotion of the insurance approach to health sector financing (Abel Smith 1985). In the project report it is argued that in the specific circumstances of Jamaica, social policy is best served by maintaining something like the present distribution between the government and private sectors. This is an issue which probably needs to be argued afresh in terms of the social and economic conditions of each country. But the Jamaica analysis does suggest one general point not often mentioned; our experience of wholly or mainly private health care systems relates to cases where private care has always been dominant, and therefore offers only limited guidance on the problems of privatizing an ongoing public system such as is found in many developing countries.

4.4 Evaluation of efficiency

The Jamaica project did not attempt to apply sophisticated techniques of efficiency evaluation such as cost/benefit or cost/effectiveness analysis. It did include some investigation of cost distribution and unit cost levels in a

selection of hospitals, the results of which were combined with administrative and budget data and information from independent studies of
primary care to give a broad picture of unit costs over the whole range of
formal health services. The hospital cost study pointed out some weaknesses
in management control (e.g. uncertainties about the number of 'subordinate'
staff employed) and shows that meaningful cost estimates can be derived
from standard accounting data if the analytical capacity is available. The
overall cost estimates have a broader implication. They show that many of
the unit cost differences found between types of institution (e.g. between
units of ambulatory care in hospitals as against health centres) can be
resolved into differences in the content of the service provided; and they
therefore suggest caution in assuming that economies can be achieved
simply by promoting 'cheap' institutions at the expense of 'dear' ones, if the
nature of the service is to remain the same.

Another note of caution regarding cost containment measures came out
of a study associated with the project of the evolution of the role of community health workers in Jamaica (Community Health Aides). Since these
were experimentally introduced in 1968 they have moved from a voluntary
basis to an increasingly secure location within the personnel hierarchy of the
Ministry of Health, with their associated costs rising until they are now little
less than those of an Assistant Nurse. A parallel progression seems to have
taken place in other developing countries, and clearly has to be kept in mind
in assessing the long term cost implications of Primary Health Care.

4.5   Public attitudes toward the health services

It is not possible to make sense of the results of the Jamaica project if one
thinks of the members of the public as passive applicants for health care,
naively presenting themselves at the nearest health facility at the first
symptom of ill-health. Rather, they must be thought of as actively assessing
their own needs and the alternative ways of meeting them. These alternatives
include self- and household care, public and private institutions, and in the
public sector a choice between health centres and hospitals, with a good deal
of assessment of the appropriateness of a particular institution to a client's
self-diagnosed condition and general situation. The degree of public choice
in Jamaica may be exceptionally high; richer countries with a mainly public
health care system, like the UK, limit the client's freedom of access to the
system, while in some poorer countries the wide dispersal of the population
and of facilities imposes a physical constraint on choice. But the widespread
complaints by health administrators about 'leapfrogging' of peripheral
institutions suggest that the general situation is not uncommon.

Compulsory limitation of channels of access seems an unlikely development in Jamaica, though in some countries its organizational neatness may

be held to outweigh its strengthening of the bureaucratic tendencies inherent in public service industries. But certain measures suggested in the project report seem to have wide and non-controversial applicability. These are, first, measures to make it easier for the clients to follow the intended flow of the public system, such as the opening of government facilities outside civil service hours and the granting of queuing preferences to patients referred from one facility to another; and secondly, the education of the public to improve the efficiency of the spontaneous triage operating at the lower levels of the system (with recognition of the role that commercial pharmacists can play in influencing consumer choice at this level).

5   Implications of the project results for further research

The results of the Jamaica project suggest a number of areas for useful further research. They can be summarized under three headings:

(1) studies already initiated but left incomplete for lack of time and resources;
(2) new studies arising directly out of the project and its associated activities;
(3) broad topics on which research programs need to be developed, perhaps on a comparative inter-country basis.

5.1   Completion of studies already initiated

In two cases data already collected and partly analysed would repay further development. These are the studies of hospital costs and of the catchment areas of health facilities. It would also be desirable to complete the work on development of a modern Mental Health Act for Jamaica.

5.2   New project-related studies

The study of maternal mortality by Walker and others leads naturally to an investigation of the effects of a mother's death on the health and welfare of her family. This could usefully be carried out in co-ordination with the study of perinatal mortality in Jamaica undertaken by Ashley, McCaw and others and now being processed.

The project was able to collect only limited information on the drug supply system in Jamaica. This is an important cost component with a high foreign exchange content. A study in this field might usefully be focused on the implementation of the essential drugs program in Jamaica.

A substantial part of the future need for health care in Jamaica will come from the population aged 65 and over. Some basic data on this age group were collected during the project, and a fuller statistical survey is likely soon under PAHO auspices. Analytical studies in this field might be focused on the implied requirements for reorientation of services, and particularly the possibilities for preventive care among the middle age groups (Grell 1982).

5.3   Areas for program development

The Jamaica project was originally put forward as one component of an inter-country comparative study. A logical extension of the project would be a review of the project procedure in order to design a condensed evaluation scheme which could be applied to a limited number of countries with different historical and socio-economic backgrounds. It should be noted that evaluation 'from the inside' of the kind practised in Jamaica would require full country participation, a factor which may limit the countries available for study.

The Jamaica results provide evidence of the importance of the household and family as providers of health care. A comprehensive view of this relationship, and of the converse relation between health experiences and household composition, formation, and dissolution, seems to be missing from agenda for health research. Such a view could integrate existing knowledge on specific topics in a number of fields (e.g. family planning and MCH studies of women as child-bearers; studies of family support for the old; studies of differential mortality in married persons as against isolates), and generate new topics for investigation and new perspectives on existing data. It can be seen as a means of making more specific the concept of community care which is of great practical importance currently in both developed and developing countries. Research proposals in this field might concentrate on the role of the household and family in developing countries in providing care for medically identifiable vulnerable groups (children and the old with specific conditions) and the reaction of the household to health-generated crises (e.g. the effects of maternal mortality, referred to above), against the background of contrasting cultures.

A number of project participants were impressed by the increased understanding of current health service problems which could be obtained from a knowledge of the history of health service development in the Commonwealth Caribbean. There are already publications on specialized topics—demographic (Roberts 1957), health care under slavery (Higman 1978), histories of health in Grenada and Dominica (Clyde 1980, 1985); the results need to be supplemented from the abundant and accessible documentation in London and the Caribbean and focused toward analytical topics such as the impact of changes in medical technology and health service policy and organization.

The final program area suggested is the study of the legal basis of the provision of health care in Commonwealth countries, with emphasis on topics such as the powers of health authorities over the public and over private practitioners, the enforcement of professional obligations, and the provision made for guardianship of children and the mentally ill.

6 Conclusion

The Jamaica project attempted an evaluation of the health care system which would be comprehensive, interdisciplinary, and co-ordinated with other on-going studies in Jamaica. It was successful to the extent that it has been well received in Jamaica (and action has been initiated on the basis of some of its findings); and that all the investigators made their planned contribution to the country report and are still talking to each other and to their co-workers in Jamaica. It may have useful implications for evaluation in other settings in respect of the methodology used, the generalizations suggested on the basis of Jamaican health service experience, and the areas it suggests for further research.

References

Clyde, F. (1980). *Two centuries of health care in Dominica*, New Delhi.
Clyde, F. (1985). *Health in Grenada: a social & historical account*, London.
Cumper, G.E. (1983). Jamaica: a case study in health development. *Soc. Sci. Med.*, **17** (24), 1983–93.
Cumper, G.E. (1984). *Determinants of health levels in developing countries.* Research Studies Press, Letchworth.
Figueroa, J.P., McCaw, A.M., and Wint, B.A. (1983). *Review of primary care in Jamaica 1977–82 PAHO Project Consultancy Report.* PAHO, Kingston, Jamaica.
Grell, G.A.C. (1982). Hypertension: a challenge for the providers of health care in the Caribbean. *West Indian Medical Journal*, **31**, 105–6.
Higman, B.W. (1978). *Slave Population and Economy in Jamaica 1807–1834*, Cambridge University Press, Cambridge.
Roberts, G.W. (1957). The population of Jamaica. Cambridge University Press, Cambridge.
Williams, A. (1985). *Medical ethics: health service efficiency and clinical freedom.* Nuffield/York Portfolios no. 2.

Publications from Jamaica health service evaluation project

Cumper, G.C. (1986). Neglecting legal status in health planning: nurse practitioners in Jamaica. *Health Policy and Planning*, 1(1), 30–6.

Cumper, G.C. and Vaughan, J.P. (1985). Community health aides at the crossroads. *World Health Forum*, 6(4), 365–7.

Cumper, G.E. and Wint, B. *The role of the hospital in primary health care.* World Health Organization, Geneva.

MacCormack, C.P. (1985). Lay concepts affecting utilisation of family planning services in Jamaica. *J. Trop. Med. Hyg.*, 88(4), 281–5.

MacCormack, C.P. and Draper, A. (1985). The concept of salts in the lay treatment of diarrhoea. *Diarrhoea Dialogue*, 23, 5.

Matadial, L., Grell, G., Walker, G., and Forrester, T. (1985). Hypertensive diseases of pregnancy. *West Indian Medical Journal*, 34, 225–33.

Walker, G.J.A. and Wint, B. (1985). Quality of medical care assessment and assurance with particular emphasis on the first line referral hospital GHS/EC/85/WP1D2. World Health Organization, Geneva.

Walker, G.J.A. and Wint, B. (1986). Quality assessment of medical care in Jamaica. *World Health Forum*, 8, 520–4.

Walker, G.J.A., Ashley, D.E.C., McCaw, A., and Bernard, G.W. (1985). Maternal mortality in Third World countries. *Lancet*, ii, 215–16.

Walker, G.J.A., Ashley, D.E.C., McCaw, A., and Bernard, G.W. (1985). A confidential enquiry into all maternal deaths in Jamaica 1981–3. Paper given at Interregional Meeting on Prevention of Maternal Mortality 10–15 Nov. FHE/PMM/85.9.10. World Health Organization, Geneva.

Walker, G.J.A., Ashley, D.E.C., McCaw, A., and Bernard, G.W. (1986). Maternal mortality in Jamaica. *Lancet*, i, 486–8.

Walker, G.J.A., Ashley, D.E.C., McCaw, A., and Bernard, G.W. (1986). Confidential enquiry into maternal deaths in Jamaica. *World Health Forum*, 8, 75–9.

Internal project reports

1981 Health Consumer Survey, Jamaica: Informal Report for Use of Ross/PEU Health Services Evaluation Project

Health Consumer Survey 1981: Determinants of the Level and Pattern of Health Service Utilisation

Health Consumer Survey 1981: Nature and Cost of Episodes of Illness

Health Consumer Survey 1981: Socio-Economic Background to Health Problems

Health Situation of the Population Aged 60 and Over in Jamaica: Preliminary Indications from Health Consumer Survey 1981

Costs in a Selection of Jamaican Hospitals 1984

Use of Financial Resources in the Government Health Service

Group presentations, Jamaica, 20–30 November 1985

Minister of Health, Permanent Secretary, Director of Finance

Senior Management Committee, Ministry of Health

Hospital SMOs, Matrons, Administrators

Obstetricians

Departments of Government, Sociology, Social and Preventive Medicine, University of the West Indies

Persons involved in the project and in the main project report

Principal responsibility for this report lay with the following:

Chapter	1	Socio-economic background	G.E. Cumper
	2	Issues in the evaluation of the health services	G.E. Cumper
	3	Primary care	G.E. Cumper
	4	Secondary and tertiary care	G.J.A. Walker
	5	The health services from the user's perspective	C. McCormack
	6	Integration of the health care system	G.E. Cumper
	7	Conclusions and recommendations	G.E. Cumper C. McCormack G.J.A. Walker
Appendix	1	Development of health policy and planning in Jamaica	E. Tulloch
	2	Health service administration in Jamaica	X. Ellington
	3	Legislative framework of the health services in Jamaica	G.C. Cumper
	4	Epidemiological background	A.M. McCaw

G.E. Cumper acted as editor-in-chief for the main report. A. McCaw acted as editor and co-ordinator in Jamaica and provided research management services for the project.

Preliminary results have been discussed in the Project Steering Committee in Jamaica, and in workshops organized by the Evaluation and Planning Centre in London with Jamaican participation. The Steering Committee included, in addition to those named above:

Dr D. Ashley (PMO(P), Ministry of Health)
Mrs P. Desai (Department of Social and Preventive Medicine, UWI)
Mr O. Gordon (Health Information Unit, MoH)
Dr G. Grell (Department of Medicine, UWI)
Dr A. Jackson (Tropical Metabolism Research Unit, UWI)
Mr L. Lyons (Medical Records, MoH)
Dr J. McHardy (CMO, MoH)
Mrs H. McKenzie (Department of Sociology, UWI)
Professor G. Mills (Department of Government, UWI)
Dr C. Moodie (Health Management Improvement Project, USAID)
Mrs C. Parker (Director of Finance, MoH)
Dr A. Samuels (Department of Social and Preventive Medicine, UWI)
Mr S. Singh (PAHO)
Mr D. Taylor (PAHO)
Miss J. Vincent (Deputy Director, Planning and Evaluation Unit, MoH)
Dr B. Wint (PMO(S), MoH)

The EPC workshops were attended by Professor P. Hamilton, Dr J.P. Vaughan (Director, EPC), Miss E. Tulloch, Dr D. Ashley, Dr B. Wint, and staff of the EPC. Anthropological field assistance was provided by Dr A. Draper, and assistance in data collection by Grace Magnus and Densie Davis.

The project investigations of the quantity and quality of secondary care reflect the contributions of many people in the Ministry of Health and the study hospitals. Particular mention should be made of Mr L. Lyons, whose untimely death was deeply regretted by all those involved in the project, and the hospital records staff (Mr Anglin, Mrs Wynter, Miss Garvie, Mrs Andrade, and others); Mr O. Gordon and Miss C. Gayle (HIU); Drs W. Bernard, G. Grell, and R. Francis; Mrs Davis (St. Anns Bay), Mr Brown (Black River) and Mr Frater (Alexandria). Special data collection for the study was carried out by Miss Ellis and by Philip Ireland, Randolph Thomas, and Marie Ireland. An important role was played by all those doctors who completed the 'quality of care' questionnaires (at the initial request of Dr A. Samuels) and the obstetricians who helped with maternal mortality assessments. In London, C. Hutson (Tropical Epidemiology Unit) organized the statistical processing of the 1982 hospital discharge data.

The investigation of hospital costs was based on contributions from the Finance division of the Ministry under Mrs Parker, and of a number of hospital administrators and their staffs (Mrs Miller, Kingston Public Hospital; Mr C. Davis, University Hospital of the West Indies; Mrs Hamilton, St. Anns Bay and Mr Robinson, Savanna la Mar). The results were discussed at length with Mr D. Taylor (PAHO). Information on drug expenditure was made available by Mr Wollery and the staff of Island Medical Stores.

Administrative support, and practical help of all kinds, was received from the staff of the Planning and Evaluation Unit. Miss X. Ellington also provided administrative guidance and valuable discussion of the management issues raised by the Project report. Dr J. McHardy took an invaluable interest in both technical and management issues.

The organization, decrypting, typing, and production of the main report was carried out by Liz Inman, Lucy Paul, and Kate Jennings.

Index